Gypsies in Madrid

Mediterranea Series

GENERAL EDITOR: Jackie Waldren, *Lecturer at Oxford Brookes University; Research Associate CCCRW, Queen Elizabeth House, Oxford; and Field Co-ordinator, Deya Archaeological Museum and Research Centre, Spain.*

This series features ethnographic monographs and collected works on theoretical approaches to aspects of life and culture in the areas bordering the Mediterranean. Rather than presenting a unified concept of 'the Mediterranean', the aim of the series is to reveal the background and differences in the cultural constructions of social space and its part in patterning social relations among the peoples of this fascinating geographical area.

ISSN: 1354-358X

Other titles in the series:

Marjo Buitelaar
Fasting and Feasting in Morocco: Women's Participation in Ramadan

William Kavanagh
Villagers of the Sierra de Gredos: Transhumant Cattle-raisers in Central Spain

Aref Abu-Rabia
The Negev Bedouin and Livestock Rearing: Social, Economic and Political Aspects

V. A. Goddard
Gender, Family and Work in Naples

Sarah Pink
Women and Bullfighting: Gender, Sex and the Consumption of Tradition

David E. Sutton
Memories Cast in Stone: The Relevance of the Past in Everyday Life

Gypsies in Madrid

Sex, Gender and the Performance of Identity

P A L O M A G A Y Y B L A S C O

Oxford • New York

First published in 1999 by
Berg
Editorial offices:
150 Cowley Road, Oxford OX4 1JJ, UK
70 Washington Square South, New York NY 10012, USA

Berg is the imprint of Oxford International Publishers Ltd.

Library of Congress Cataloging-in-Publication Data

A catalogue record for this book is available from the Library of
Congress.

British Library Cataloguing-in-Publication Data

A catalogue record for this book is available from the British Library.

ISBN   1 85973 253 4 (Cloth)
          1 85973 256 5 (Paper)

Typeset by JS Typesetting, Wellingborough, Northants.
Printed in the United Kingdom by Biddles Ltd, Guildford and
King's Lynn.

For Liria and Carmen, who wanted to learn about my world as much as I wanted to learn about theirs

Contents

Acknowledgements

It is impossible to thank all the people who, in one way or another, have contributed to the writing of this book. I am grateful to them all but I feel indebted to some in particular.

In Spain, my deepest gratitude goes to the Gitanos of Jarana: they endured the constant presence of a non-Gypsy outsider and were extremely patient with me. Some spent much time and energy teaching me to become a 'proper woman' and I cannot repay their kindness and their concern. Throughout the book I have disguised their names and personalities, and I have also changed to the fictional 'Jarana' the name of the neighbourhood in Madrid where they live. I am particularly grateful to Liria de la Cruz, Ramón Jiménez, Neni Jiménez, Angel Jiménez, Francisco Hernández Jiménez, María Hernández Jiménez, Carmen de la Cruz, Francisco Hernández Hernández, Elisabeth Hernández and Emilia Ramírez. They became my family among the Gitanos. I also wish to thank Consuelo Borjas, Carmen Gabarre, Antonia Gabarre, Carmen Hernández, Carmen Ramírez, Luis Ramírez and his wife Paloma, Aquilino Ramírez, his wife Luz Divina and their children, Eugenia de la Cruz, María Hernández de la Cruz, Rocío Hernández, Antonio Hernández and his wife Isabel, Emilio Hernández and his wife Dolores, Angel de la Cruz, his wife Tunda and their daughters Neni, Azucena and María, Arturo de la Cruz and his wife Remedios, Isabel Borjas, Fifo de la Cruz and his wife Consuelo, and Carlos Hernández and his wife Noemí.

Teresa San Román helped me find a fieldwork location and provided me with constant advice and emotional support during and after fieldwork. My debt to her and her work is immense. The Missionaries of María Mediadora in Villaverde Alto gave me a home, fed me, and helped me in every possible way. I literally could not have completed my fieldwork without their assistance. I am particularly grateful to Sister Ana Riera, who was the head of the small community in which I lived for seven months. The staff of the Consortium for the

Resettlement of Madrid's Marginal Population were also helpful. Mari Paz Arriaza in particular became a good friend and contributed with the collection of numerical data. The staff of the El Rocío kindergarten in Jarana gave me much encouragement as well as their friendship. My family, who lived in Madrid at the time of my fieldwork, helped me in every way they could. In particular I wish to thank my mother, María Jesús Blasco, for her love and encouragement throughout the years, and my sister Carolina Gay y Blasco who drove me to and from Jarana countless times.

In the UK, I wish to thank Henrietta Moore and Stephen Hugh-Jones for their constant support and constructive critiques before, during and after fieldwork. Huon Wardle has helped enormously with his intuition, imagination and patience during the whole of the writing-up process. He understands the Gitano material better than I do and I find it difficult not to call this book a collaborative exercise. Deema Kaneff has contributed greatly to the structuring of the argument. Sharing an office has meant much more than working side-by-side: she has questioned every one of my assumptions and pushed me into sharpening my ideas. Our friendship has grown with this book. Paola Filippucci, Frances Pine and Mario Pajares have read some chapters and their suggestions have no doubt improved the overall presentation and analysis. Marilyn Strathern examined my thesis and her advice has proven invaluable, as has that of Michael Stewart, who was both my thesis examiner and the anonymous reviewer for Berg. Sue Benson has read the final manuscript from cover to cover, carefully correcting my English and pointing out areas for improvement. I am sure that I have not done justice to her insights. In particular, Chapter 1 owes much of its form and content to her. Jonathan Skinner has also read the complete manuscript, combed it carefully for typographical mistakes, and made many useful suggestions. Finally, I want to thank Peter Abrahams for his exceptionally useful help in coming to understand Gitano ideas about female virginity.

The project was financed by New Hall, Cambridge, who gave me a Doctoral Studentship, and by Girton College, Cambridge, where I was a Junior Research Fellow from 1995 until 1998. Living and working at Girton was a privilege, and I wish to thank the Mistress, Juliet d'A. Campbell, Fellows and non-academic staff of the College for their support during the writing of this book. I also wish to thank the Department of Social Anthropology at Cambridge for giving me an office and thus providing the physical space where this book could develop. I am particularly grateful to Sally Reynolds, Margaret Story and Jo Gilliard for their help with photocopiers and other pieces of unruly office equipment. Parts of the book were written in St Andrews, and I am indebted to the staff at the Department of Social Anthropology there for their friendship and encouragement.

Part I

Gypsies in Contemporary Spain

one

Introduction

My aim in this book is to explore some of the key processes through which the Spanish Gypsies or Gitanos construct their distinctive way of life and their understanding of themselves as a group different from the non-Gypsies – whom they call *Payos*.[1] In other words, this book represents an attempt to elucidate the way in which people who see themselves as living 'under siege', who have been oppressed and marginalized throughout five centuries, go on creating a lifestyle and a shared identity clearly separate from those of the dominant population among which they live.[2] My starting point is the fact that the Gitanos appear to reproduce their singularity *without recourse to the usual anthropological prompts* of attachment to land or territory, appeals to a shared past or a communal memory, or internal unity or cohesiveness in the present. A look at Gitano life thus immediately presents the observer with an apparent paradox: although the Gitanos have an extremely strong sense of themselves as a people, set apart from the non-Gypsies, they are not preoccupied with constructing a harmonious or united community. Rather, the opposite is closer to the truth: they seem intent on objectifying fragmentation and differences between themselves. The obvious conclusion is that, in the Gitano case, common identity is the main support of community – and the word 'community' in this context has to be carefully nuanced, as I explain below. In this book I ask where the Gitanos' sense of themselves as such is located, and how they construct it – that is, what the sources of Gitano distinctiveness are. One of my main premises is the awareness that analysing how the Gitanos conceptualize themselves as a group – and what kind of group they imagine themselves to be – necessitates analysing their constructions of the person. The basis of the book is fifteen months of fieldwork carried out among the Gitanos of Jarana, a 'special Gitano neighbourhood' built by the State in the district of Villaverde Alto, on the southern periphery of Madrid.

Gitanos and Other 'Damned Peoples'

Anthropologists and historians writing on the Gitanos portray them as descendants of the so called 'bands of Egyptians' that, according to written records, crossed the Pyrenees and arrived on the Peninsula in the early fifteenth century (Sánchez Ortega 1986: 18; San Román 1994). The general assumption is that groups as diverse as the Manouches, the Kalderash, the English Travellers and the Gitanos are in fact 'one people',[3] the overall consensus being that they originally came from India. Okely (1983) is practically alone in having disputed this theory. More recently, Stewart has argued that what needs explanation is the 'persistence of cultural difference' between Gypsies and non-Gypsies, rather than the 'mere existence of foreign origins' (1997: 263).

In fact, there are wide variations among Gypsy groups – including the ways in which they construct their difference from the dominant populations and express their identity as Gypsies. While some have remained nomadic up to the present, others became sedentary decades or even centuries ago. Many speak one of the many Romany dialects but there are others – for example the Gitanos – who speak the language of the non-Gypsy peoples among whom they live.[4] Some earn their living through 'typically' Gypsy activities – such as telling fortunes or collecting scrap – whereas others work in factories along non-Gypsies. Many uphold intricate pollution taboos, but some – including the Gitanos – do not.[5] Other important features, such as kinship and political organization, marriage forms, or religion, also vary significantly from one Gypsy group to the next. All Gypsies, however, elaborate on the contrast between themselves and the non-Gypsies and also share a) a peripheral or marginal status in relation to the non-Gypsies among whom they live; b) a preference to engage in economic activities over which they themselves exert control; and c) a lack of an elaborate social memory and of permanent, physical markers of Gypsy identity (see for example Sutherland 1975a; Stewart 1997; Okely 1983; Williams 1993a; Kaprow 1991). The chapters that follow have to be read with this combination of difference and similarity among Gypsy groups in mind.

Two main groups of Gypsies live in Spain: Kalderash Gypsies, known by the Gitanos as *Húngaros* (Hungarian) and by the Payos as *Cíngaros*, who came to Spain from Eastern Europe in several migration waves during the nineteenth century (Mulcahy 1988), and Gitanos, who are themselves divided into various sub-units. San Román (1976: 60) and Ardevol (1986: 64) gather together Castilian Gitanos and Gitanos from

Extremadura into a single category, and distinguish them from those from Andalucía, Catalonia, and from non-Catalan Gitanos who have migrated to that region during the second half of the twentieth century – known as *Cafeletes*. Their argument is that these groups differ in some aspects of their social and cultural organisations. In Jarana, the Gitanos uphold a somewhat different classification. They distinguish between *Húngaros*, Gitanos *Castellanos* (from Castile) – who are the majority of those in the neighbourhood – and Gitanos *Extremeños* (from Extremadura) – who are a very small minority in Jarana but live in other areas of Madrid in great numbers. At the same time they are aware of other Gitanos in other areas of Spain and believe that there are Gitanos in 'all the countries of the world' (*en todos los paises del mundo*). Although they consider the *Húngaros* to be the 'truest Gitanos' (*los Gitanos más de verdad*) because they are nomadic and speak Romany, they see all of the different Gitano and non-Gitano Gypsy groups as being equally Gitano – equally part of the 'Gitano people' (*el pueblo Gitano*) – in spite of the fact that they may have different 'customs' (*costumbres*). This book deals only with the Castilian Gitanos of Jarana – more specifically, with the ways in which they construct 'the Gitano people' as an imagined community and come to see themselves as part of it.

It is important to stress that the Gitanos are not the only minority of local origin in Spain – by 'of local origin' I mean historically established in the country, in contrast with recent Latin American, Caribbean, North African and Filipino immigrants. In fact, the Gitanos are considered by historians and anthropologists alike to be just one of several *pueblos malditos* ('damned peoples') – 'marginal populations considered by their neighbours with aversion' (Cátedra Tomás 1991: 662). These are the Maragatos of León (muleteers and cloth traders), the Vaqueiros de Alzada from Asturias and the Pasiegos from Santander (both transhumant cattle herders), and the Chuetas from Mallorca (descendants of Jewish *conversos*, converts to Christianity) (Tax Freeman 1979: 223–45; Cátedra Tomás 1989 and 1991; Laub 1991). As in the case of the Gitanos, the Spanishness of these minorities is questioned by other Spaniards: Maragatos, Pasiegos and Vaqueiros are frequently said to be of Moorish descent, and Chuetas are thought and think themselves to be descendants of *conversos*. What all these minorities share, apart from specialized and – except for the Chuetas – marginal occupations, is a perceived inability to prove their *pureza de sangre* (purity of blood), their undisputed descent from old Christian stock (*cristiano viejo*). Maragatos, Pasiegos, Vaqueiros and Chuetas, however,

e different from the Gitanos in that they are found only in highly
localized areas, in that there are very few of them, and in that many
Spanish people are not even aware of their existence. They only play
the role of 'the Other' for small groups of Spaniards, and their position
vis-à-vis those Spaniards is tied up with the geography and particular
history of the areas where they live.

On the other hand the Gitanos, who live throughout Spain, both
in the cities and in the countryside, have come to epitomise Spanishness outside Spain. Take the flamenco, or the image of the black-eyed
Gitana that appears in the wrapping of hotel soap, wearing carnations
in her hair and red flouncy skirts, and playing the castanets. To many
foreigners, *this* is Spain. Or take the following statement, from John
Hooper's popular book, *The New Spaniards*: discussing the strength of
Spanish coffee, he attributes it to the Spaniards' 'seemingly instinctive
enthusiasm for whatever is bold, strong and decisive', which 'has
bedevilled their history, turning it into a succession of abrupt changes
in direction' (1995: 197). The Spaniards, according to Hooper, practice
the 'cult of excess' (1995: 196). Spanishness and Gypsyness – irration-
ality, passion, mystery, honour – definitely overlap in popular, non-
Spanish representations of Spain. And the Spaniards are well aware of
this fact. One of the best film directors of the Francoist period, Luis
García Berlanga, produced a satire of Spanish–American relations in
the post-war era, *Bienvenido Mr Marshall*, telling the story of a Castilian
village that disguises itself as an Andalusian village – full of Gypsy
dancers and flamenco singers – in the hope of pleasing the American
representatives of the Marshall Plan and obtaining in return something
for each of the villagers – a trumpet for one, a pair of oxen for another
and so on.

At the same time, non-Gypsy Spaniards are careful to differentiate
between themselves and the Gitanos. The Castilian villagers who
dressed up as Gypsies in *Bienvenido Mr Marshall* were acting a role,
catering for American preconceptions. In his analysis of school children's
attitudes towards the Gitanos, Calvo Buezas (1990) makes clear that
the Gitanos play an undisputed star role in the Spanish communal
imagination as the embodiment of all that is evil and wrong. Payos
are keen to state that the Gitanos are a group apart, clearly different
from, worse than, and even inferior to the rest of the Spaniards. To
start with, Payos portray the Gitanos as having a different physique –
'dark skin and black and greasy hair' (Calvo Buezas: 247) – or of
belonging to a different race. Secondly, the Gitanos are said to have
different customs, values, language, attitudes and lifestyle – more often

than not the 'wrong' customs, values, language, attitudes and lifestyle. They are dancers and singers by nature, and they put great stress on family ties – positive features – but they are also poor, lazy and dirty, and many are thieves or – worse – drug dealers. In current use, the word *Gitano* works as an insult. In the words of a schoolchild from Andalusia, 'the Gitanos who live in this village, I don't mean to imply that they are the same as us . . . most people say that if they are Gitanos, then they are not like us' (Calvo Buezas: 291).

Gypsies in Madrid: A 'Special Gitano Neighbourhood'

In March 1992 I began fieldwork in Villaverde Alto, a district in the south of Madrid with a large Gypsy population. Social workers from the *Consorcio* – the Consortium for the Resettlement of Madrid's Marginal Population – had suggested that I base myself in Jarana, a housing estate built by the local authorities in 1989, designed to fulfil the 'special needs' of particularly 'marginalized' or 'backward' Gitanos (*los Gitanos más marginales, más atrasados*). Physically demarcated and isolated from the rest of Villaverde Alto, Jarana was a ghetto even in name: when it was first built a huge placard was placed at the entrance to the estate which read 'Colony for Marginal Population' (*Colonia Para Población Marginal*). At the beginning of 1992, while the 'problem' of Gitano drug dealing was receiving peak attention in the national media, my contacts in the *Consorcio* considered Jarana the safest Gypsy settlement in Madrid: the Gitanos who lived there had themselves made it a 'law' that no drugs were to be sold inside the neighbourhood. I was told that there would be no Payo addicts coming for their daily doses, less need for secrecy in the part of the Gitanos, and overall a more secure environment for a Payo woman and a more friendly disposition towards an inquisitive anthropologist.

Gitanos have been living in Villaverde Alto since the 1950s when they came to Madrid from villages in Castile and Extremadura as part of the massive rural-urban exodus that swept across Spain in the late post-war period. The original shanty-town was replaced in the early 1960s by what was then called an UVA or *Unidad Vecinal de Absorción* (Neighbourhood Absorption Unit): a 'colony' of one-floor houses inhabited by 3000 rural migrants, Payos and Gitanos. Villaverde Alto expanded from this first nucleus, partly through government initiatives and partly through private investments. By the late 1980s the UVA had deteriorated so much that the *Consorcio* and the local authorities pulled it down and built two new housing estates. One of them is Jarana. The other is located in Villaverde Alto itself: it consists of standard blocks of flats occupied mainly by Payos.[6]

Today Villaverde Alto is very similar to some of the other working-class areas of the south of Madrid – Orcasitas, Villaverde Bajo, Leganés, Vallecas and so on. Much of the housing in these districts is provided by the State, and standard of living is low by comparison to that of the rest of the population of the city. It is there that the huge increase in drug addiction and spread of AIDS that has taken place over the last ten to fifteen years have had their greatest impact. Levels of unemployment and conflict are also very high – at the time of my fieldwork, Villaverde Alto had one of the highest numbers of inhabitants with criminal records of the city.[7] Lastly, these zones have received the bulk of the influx of poor Latin American and North African migrants that have arrived in Madrid over the last ten years.[8] Intense social work, commissioned by the State and by the Catholic Church, is carried out in all these areas.

By building Jarana the *Consorcio* wanted to resettle part of what it considered to be a particularly problematic 'marginal population'. This referred mainly to Gitano families who did not wish to live in flats, who were considered by the *Consorcio* social workers too 'ignorant' (*ignorantes*) and 'uncivilized' (*incivilizados*) to do so, or who were thought to require specific kinds of housing because of their economic activities – some of them are scrap collectors or fruit and vegetable vendors who, it was argued, needed space to keep their produce. Like most Gitanos in Madrid, the inhabitants of Jarana – Payos and Gitanos – had lived in shantytowns or low-quality temporary council housing in various areas of the city, and had already gone through several government-directed resettlements.

Writing in 1986, Juan Montes, the architect who designed Jarana, could foresee some of the negative features that would eventually come to characterize the neighbourhood. He explained how the wish to provide for the needs of those Gitano groups that, in the eyes of the social services, 'displayed evident signs of mis-adaptation to normal urban areas' would mean that

> the neighbourhood will be specifically planned for Gitanos . . . Secondly, the people who already live in areas likely to be chosen will oppose radically the building of this neighbourhood in their vicinity. This increases the risk of creating a ghetto far away from the nearest populated zones. Lastly, it often happens that this kind of neighbourhood is programmed with a minimum of resources . . . the results are often disastrous: the deficient construction, together with the Gitanos' misuse

of facilities and the lack of social services and of adequate conservation soon turn these neighbourhoods into *de facto* shanty towns (1986: 162).[9]

He thus recommended a location where the Gitanos would have easy access to public services, and suggested the construction of a social assistance centre and a kindergarten. The opposition of the population of Villaverde Alto to the proposed settlement was not strong in comparison with the reception that plans for similar neighbourhoods were given in other areas of the city, such as the nearby Villaverde Bajo where there were massive public demonstrations in 1991. However, many of Montes' predictions have come true. At the time of my fieldwork Jarana was very well demarcated spatially and architecturally. It was clearly separated from the main body of Villaverde Alto, where the nearest shops and public facilities are located: on foot it could only be reached through an open and often muddy field or by walking along a road that links Villaverde to the motorways that surround Madrid. Sixty-five of the eighty houses in the neighbourhood were occupied by Gitanos, nine by Payos, and six by mixed families: out of the four hundred inhabitants of Jarana approximately three hundred and fifty were Gitano.[10] Although in 1992 they had been living there for three years, a public telephone had been installed only a few weeks before I began my research, and it was only after I had been there for some months that one of the municipal bus lines began to stop near the neighbourhood.

Jarana consists of four rows of two-storey terraced houses along three streets. From a distance all that is visible is a line of feeble trees and a handful of cream-coloured buildings sticking out of the skyline in the middle of the suburban no-man's-land. The neighbourhood is encircled by hard-soiled, dusty, empty fields and, on one side, by the Villaverde cemetery. Because it stands isolated on a hill-top it receives the worst of the scorching Madrid summers and of the freezing, windy winters. On a not-too-close inspection the cheapness of the materials used to build Jarana becomes clear: there are huge cracks threatening to bring down the walls of the houses, the street lamps are broken, and potholes and missing slabs dot almost every square metre of pavement. During the cold months most families complain of the leaks that develop with the slightest shower of rain and threaten to inundate their bedrooms. Many also resent the apathy of the local authorities who, they insist, have 'dumped' (*tirado*) the Gitanos in a neighbourhood not fit for human habitation. Jarana, many Gitanos say, 'is not a place intended for civilized people' (*no es un sitio pensado para gente civilizada*). By contrast, the local social workers insist that

Jarana is a Gitano-friendly neighbourhood, built with the needs and wishes of the Gitanos in mind. The houses have large covered yards – 'because the Gitanos need space for scrap metal' – open ground floor plans – 'because the Gitanos are very sociable people' – and coal stoves – 'because the Gitanos are too poor to afford any other kind of heating'. The inhabitants of Jarana, for their part, complain of the cooking smells that, in the absence of separating walls, permeate every single piece of furniture, of the huge smoke stains on the ceilings and walls, and of the uselessness of having a yard when what they 'really need is an extra room for the son who has just married and has brought his wife to live in'.[11] Most importantly, they find it difficult to understand why they are forced to live in a housing estate that is patently 'different' and 'special'.

One of the most revealing examples of the lack of communication between the Gitanos who live in Jarana and the Payo local authorities who orchestrated their resettlement regards the naming of the estate's three streets. All the street names are drawn from the works of Federico García Lorca, the writer who is most closely associated with the Gitanos in the Payo popular imagination: one of the streets has the title of a famous anthology, the other is named after one of his best known poems, and the third after the protagonist of one of his plays. The Gitanos, who have never heard of Lorca, complain that they have been granted housing in a backwater neighbourhood with ludicrous street-names. Tío Juan, the elderly head of the most powerful kinship group in the area, put it rather succinctly: 'Where have you heard of a street called *Verde Viento* [Green Wind]! They should have given us proper names, of famous people, just like they have done in Villaverde. But we are Gitanos so they take the piss.' In fact, only the social workers persist in using the streets' official names. Everybody else calls them *La Calle de Arriba* (Upper Street), *La Calle de Enmedio* (Middle Street) and *La Calle de Abajo* (Lower Street).

Upper and Lower Streets face large, barren stretches of land, and their inhabitants have planted a tree or a bush here and there. Some use the empty space in front of their houses – rather than their yards – to park their scrap metal, others to burn cables and recycle the inside copper, and yet others to hang lines for drying clothes. Little children build themselves huts out of discarded bits of cardboard, plastic and corrugated iron and 'play at shantytowns' (*jugar a las chabolas*). Their fathers and older brothers spend the balmy spring and autumn afternoons taking the sun by their doorsteps, or playing cards or dominoes under the shade of one of the mangy trees. The women stay indoors with their female relatives, watching the daily Venezuelan soap-opera over a cup of sweet Gitano coffee. People keep to themselves, interacting only with kin and not even bothering to nod their heads in greeting when an unrelated Gitano passes by, the only exception being the Evangelical converts, who go out of their way to shake hands 'the way Payos do' (*como hacen los Payos*).

In Middle Street the houses face each other closely and what little space there is between them is used to park cars and store scrap metal. The sun does not enter easily, and the atmosphere is dark and almost claustrophobic. For some reason unknown to me the social workers in charge of the resettlement allotted the houses in Middle Street to Gitano families who have more precarious occupations, a lower standard of living, and larger numbers of drug-addict members than most other Gitano families in Jarana. And indeed, Middle Street appears to be much poorer and more dilapidated: the houses are in a worse state of disrepair, the walls are covered in graffiti, and the people who live there look much more dishevelled than their Upper and Lower Streets neighbours. There are no trees in Middle Street and when it rains the pavement becomes a small river carrying bits of half-eaten food and other cast aside rubbish. Because the Gitanos of Jarana dislike socializing with non-relatives and consider that the space in front of a house belongs to its inhabitants, the children of Middle Street are rarely allowed to play in the open fields that surround the estate. Instead, they spend much of their time in the dim, murky alley. During my last weeks in the neighbourhood their greatest source of entertainment was a child-sized car with pedals that somebody had found on a skip in Madrid. Five or six tiny children aged three and four would pile themselves on the car and whiz by at full speed until 'an accident' made them lose their course and crash against the wall of a house or an absent-minded passer-by. Then the *peluditos* ('little hairy-ones') would have to pick themselves up and board their vehicle again, rubbing their bruised heads and knees.

During the long summers, when Lower and Upper Streets simmer quietly under the strong Madrid sun, Middle Street is the only area of coolness. On those days the Gitanos open the water hydrant and drench their houses and themselves, openly contravening state regulations that forbid the use of public water in July and August, and thoroughly enjoying themselves. In a similar vein, many Gitanos of Jarana 'steal the light' (*roban la luz*), diverting the electricity supply from the street lamps to their houses, criss-crossing the skyline of the neighbourhood with cables. They know well that the chances of the

Figure 1.1 Middle Street

police turning up to check why their electricity bills are so low are slim. In fact, the police tend to leave Jarana well alone and when they come – two or three times every year – it is to raid the neighbourhood on the look-out for drugs or firearms, or in the aftermath of a robbery when somebody identifies the plate of a vehicle that belongs to a Gitano from the neighbourhood. They arrive in large groups, finding comfort in numbers and facing the open outrage of the inhabitants of Jarana who yell at them and place curses on them and their ancestors.

Two of the most important landmarks in Jarana are the kindergarten, staffed by Payo teachers but attended almost solely by Gitano children from Jarana and Villaverde, and the UTS (*Unidad de Trabajo Social*) or social assistance centre where the Gitanos of the neighbourhood take part in a series of compulsory re-education schemes that I discuss in Chapter 2. The third is the Evangelical church that the Gitano converts of Jarana and of Villaverde Alto built soon after they were resettled in the area. It is a small pre-fabricated structure with metal walls that allow the sound of singing to be carried away into the evening air. Services – which the Gitanos call *cultos* or 'cults' – last well over two hours and are for many Gitanos the main and most exciting sociable activity of the day. Men, women and children dress in their finest clothes and turn up in advance to have a coffee, a soft drink or a hot-dog in the church's bar while they catch up with gossip from relatives and convert friends. During the service some people listen attentively to the minister, others chat distractedly with their neighbours. If the day is warm, a deacon walks up and down the aisles, spraying people with eau de cologne from a big plastic container in an attempt to reduce the smell of enclosed humanity. At other times somebody shouts, *¡una rata!* (a rat!), and the Gitanos lift their feet from the floor while going on listening, or not listening, to the preacher. Meanwhile older children run around asking for money for *cositas* (little things), sweeties from the nearby shop, and babies are openly breast-fed, handed around, and generally admired by men and women alike.

After the service the converts go back home to have dinner and watch TV with their non-convert relatives. If 'there is nothing on' and they have not hired a video they may build a fire on the pavement and sit around it until the early hours of the morning, in large groups of kin. Then the Gitanos make small talk, perhaps do a little bit of singing and flamenco dancing, or celebrate the *gracias* (gestures) of a little boy who attempts to light a cigarette single-handed or of a young girl who demands money in exchange for sitting on her grandfather's knee. Again large quantities of coffee are drunk, this time passed around with biscuits or fruit. If it is a hot summer night many Gitanos will sleep outdoors, laying their mattresses in their yards or in the street outside. The fragmentation that divides the neighbourhood by day dissolves, and one can hear laughing, quarrelling and even snoring from two or three houses away.

The Sources of Gitano Distinctiveness

Like so many other pieces of anthropological research, this book is the result of my growing realization of the distance between my initial concerns and those of the Gitanos amongst whom I lived during fieldwork. Before leaving for the field I had planned my research around a theoretical issue: to investigate the social memory of an illiterate minority encapsulated within a dominant literate society. The Gitanos came into the project because they seemed to provide the necessary conditions to make it viable. However, once in Jarana I found that they displayed very little interest in the past, talked about it only rarely and became patently bored whenever I tried to introduce the subject. They found my preoccupation with the past rather puzzling, and even suggested that I changed the subject of my 'study'. Grand-mother Ana put it succinctly: 'you are rather stupid. You could have been a lawyer or a doctor and here you are, asking about things no one cares about.' I soon realized that, unlike many other minorities, the Gitanos do not look to a historical or mythical past for explana-tions of their way of life or of their difference from the dominant majority.

Instead, the Gitanos of Jarana focus on their 'way of being' (*manera de ser*) in the 'now' (*ahora*) as the foundation of their singularity. This 'way of being' can best be described as a stance in relation to a series of moral rules that the Gitanos see as given and unquestionable. It is their different 'ways of being' that separate Gitanos from Payos: the Gitanos link Gypsyness to actions or performances rather than stress-ing essences or substances.[12] At the core of their ideas about who they are is their firm belief that, of all Spaniards, they alone are truly honourable and righteous. Throughout my time in Jarana I was con-stantly reminded of the Payos' endless deficiencies: according to the Gitanos, Payos neglect their children, despise their elders and kill each other through terrorism and war; their women are all whores on the lookout for sex, and their men are all weaklings. But this is a two way process because, on their part, the Payos condense in their portrayals of the Gitanos a multiplicity of stereotypes of negative and anti-social communal relations. Gitanos are said to be *incultos*, people 'without culture',[13] who live surrounded by dirt, refuse to work, and earn their living by sponging off the State, stealing, and selling drugs to young non-Gypsies. In the representations of the Gitanos widely current among Payos, Gitanos damage the fabric of non-Gitano life. The Gitanos of Jarana reject these images and premise their identity as Gitanos on the assertion that it is themselves and not the Payos who conform to the highest ideal of morality. To the Gitanos, it is the Payos who lack the knowledge and the ability to behave as proper human beings.

The Gitano distinction between themselves and the Payos, which is the single most important principle through which they organize their world-views and daily life, is therefore constructed in moral terms. Secondly, this Gitano moral divide between themselves and the Payos is gendered: it is built around particular understandings about what persons, as men and as women, are and particularly should be like. These Gitano understandings about men and women, in turn, are widely different from those of other Spaniards and demand a careful investigation into the processes through which Gitano femininity and masculinity are created – a task that I undertake in Parts II and III of this book. According to the inhabitants of Jarana, the perpetuation of 'the Gitanos' as 'a kind of people' (*clase de gente*) depends on the ongoing enactment of the Gitano morality by each Gitano man and woman: ideas about the group and ideas about the person are therefore inextricably intertwined. The gendered person is metonymically – rather than metaphorically – tied to the ideal of the group and effectively, through its moral performances, brings it about: it is Gitano persons that are seen by the Gitanos as the repositories of Gypsyness.

Various ethnographers (Stewart 1997; Sutherland 1975a; Okely 1983; Salo 1977 and 1979; San Román 1976; Pasqualino 1995; Williams 1993a) reveal how Gypsy groups consistently stress their own superior moralities as the quality that distinguishes them from the non-Gypsies. The better known authors, however, endorse paradigms that emphasize the expression of difference rather than its generation: in their analysis of gender relations and of the symbolism of the body, Okely (1983) and Sutherland (1975, 1977) take as their starting point Mary Douglas' view that 'the human body is always treated as an image of society' (1970: 98). They put forward structuralist approaches in which the body is portrayed as being 'good to think with' and in which society acts upon individuals in a Durkhemian manner. This results on models that take social relations as given and focus on imagery. The Gitanos of Jarana do not so much express – metaphorically – their relationship with the Payos through body symbolism; instead they effectively create a multiplicity of localized differences through personal performances that are both age- and gender-specific.

Harmony or unity among Gitanos are not conceived in Jarana as paths to shared identity. Instead, the inhabitants of the neighbourhood actively avoid interaction with unrelated Gitanos for a host of reasons that I discuss in Chapter 3, and make tangible their 'internal' fragmentation in multiple ways – from their use of communal space to their marriage strategies. Instead of grounding Gypsyness on social cohesiveness, the Gitanos see themselves as a group of people who are similarly positioned vis-à-vis the rest of the world – a community in the sense of 'commonness', not of 'communion'.

The Gitano emphasis on the personal enactment of a gendered morality means that, although the Gitanos recognize patrilineal descent and have a rudimentary social memory, they focus on the present rather than on the past as source of shared identity. Gitano commonality is more performative than reproductive or, as Stewart explains for the Hungarian Rom, it is 'something that is constructed and constantly remade in the present in relations with significant others, not something inherited from the past' (1997: 28). In fact, as I have just pointed out, and as I explain at length in Chapter 3, the Gitanos of Jarana actively downplay the 'before' (*antes*) in accounts of themselves. By the same token, their shared sense of self, their shared identity, does not depend on current or former links with a particular territory: they have no land of origin and no promised land. The Gitanos are seen by the Payos and, most importantly, see themselves as unwelcome guests in somebody else's house. Even in the late twentieth century, when they are fully sedentary, they are settled and resettled according to the wishes of the Administration and themselves show little interest in establishing practical or symbolic holds over the places where they are made to live. As Luis, a young man from Jarana, explained: 'being a Gitano is an eternal passing without going anywhere' (*ser Gitano es un eterno pasar sin ir a ninguna parte*). In this sense the Gitanos are clearly different from other Spanish peoples who elaborate on concepts of time and space in their constructions of local, regional and national 'imagined communities': among non-Gitano Spaniards, it is through traditions that territories are rendered meaningful, and through the interplay of both factors that particular kinds of group identity emerge.[14] By contrast, the Gitanos focus on realizing Gypsyness in the here and now – wherever and whenever that may be.

This book, then, is a study of a particular way of constructing a shared identity. It explores the links between a specific sense of personhood and a specific sense of 'community'[15] – and I use inverted commas to emphasize the distance between anthropological/Euro-American understandings of what makes people a community or a society, and the Gitanos' understandings of what makes them a 'kind of people' (*una clase de gente*). These Gitano philosophies of personhood and 'community', however, are also Western: the Gitanos have been part of European history for at least the last five centuries. In this sense, as Stewart explains in relation to the Rom, this book is also a 'story about the sources of cultural diversity in modern industrial society' (1997: 2). Lastly, to a very large extent, this is a book on gender both because the Gitanos themselves stress the gendered dimension of their shared identity at the expense of any others and because I draw on feminist insights throughout my analysis. In my approach to the issue of Gitano singularity I build on the feminist awareness that in many societies personhood is gendered, and that the relationship between the gendered person and the group cannot be regarded as straightforward or unproblematic.[16] Rather than taking Gitano masculinity and femininity as 'givens', I ask what are the processes through which they are constructed, and I question as much the production of sex and sexed bodies as the production of the less bodily aspects of gender.[17]

The Plan of the Book

The main body of this book – that is, Parts II and III – explore the relationship between the Gitano construction of the person and the Gitano construction of a communal identity as it plays itself out in Jarana. The starting point here is the awareness that, among the Gitanos, personhood is always gendered: it is through the performance of particular Gitano gendered moralities by Gitano men and women that the ideal of 'the Gitanos' as a group is achieved. Whereas Part II (Chapters 4, 5 and 6) focuses mainly on Gitano ideas and practices to do with women and femininity, Part III (Chapters 7 and 8) examines the role of men and masculinity in bringing about the Gitanos' distinctiveness. These chapters assemble a layered picture of Gitano masculinity and femininity, exploring how they are created across multiple spheres of everyday life – from wedding rituals to relations between husbands and wives to confrontations among kinship groups.

Part I introduces and sets the scene for the rest of the book, both ethnographically and theoretically. Chapter 2 discusses the different developments that have affected the Spanish Gypsies over the last fifty years, and the complexities of their current situation. By exploring the ways in which the Gitanos are viewed and dealt with by the Payos, Chapter 2 also offers an insight into contemporary Spanish society. In Chapter 3 I describe the pattern of sociable relations in Jarana. In doing so, I examine at length the main theoretical question that this book addresses: given the extreme centrifugal forces that govern Gitano sociality, and in the absence of a social memory and of links with a territory, how is it that the Gitanos manage to see themselves as a group and to reproduce their shared identity?

Notes

1. The Gitanos of Jarana use the word 'Payo' – which means non-Gypsy – as an insult, as well as to refer to the non-Gypsies. For their part, Payos also use the word 'Gitano' as an insult. During my fieldwork, whenever the Gitanos

of Jarana referred to somebody – a doctor, a social worker – as a Payo in my presence they apologized profusely. They usually attempted to avoid the embarrassment by describing Payos as *señores* (gentlemen), *chicos* (boys) or *paisanos* (locals). Only the Gitanos who became very good friends realised that I was not offended by the word 'Payo' and used it freely in front of me.

2. For historical accounts of the Gitanos since their first appearance in the Iberian Peninsula in the fifteenth century see San Román 1976, Sánchez Ortega 1986, Gómez Alfaro 1992.

3. See for example Leblon 1985, San Román 1994, Fraser 1993.

4. The Gitanos speak Spanish both among themselves and when addressing Payos – the one exception being Catalan Gitanos who also speak Catalan. In this the Gitanos differ from other Gypsy groups who have Romany dialects as their mother tongues, and use the local languages only in their interaction with the host populations. The Caló, traditionally considered the Romany dialect of the Gitanos, consists only of a few hundred non-Spanish words, many of which have been said by scholars to have Romany roots. The plurals and verbal conjugation are Spanish, like the vast majority of the Gitanos' vocabulary, and in fact many of the Caló words are Spanish words to which Caló-like endings have been added (San Román 1976: 66). In Jarana only a few of the older Gitanos know more than a handful of Caló words, and they remember using them in their youth in order to communicate information in front of Payos, and not for daily life conversations among Gitanos. The Spanish that the Gitanos of Madrid speak, however, is easily distinguishable from that of the surrounding Payos and can be considered a Spanish dialect: the Gitanos have a particular accent and intonation, and deviate from rules of syntax and grammar in consistent ways; they employ many Spanish words that are out of use among the Payos, and give a particular non-Payo meaning to other words.

5. The Gitanos of Jarana sometimes explain that objects and part of the body have to be cleaned according to specific rules. These rules specify that food and utensils that go inside the body have to be kept separated from objects or substances that are in contact with its surface. However, these rules are much less articulated than in the case of the Rom (Sutherland 1975a; Stewart 1997) or of the English Travellers (Okely 1993), and play only a minor role in the Gitanos' views of themselves and of the non-Gypsies.

6. The most usual kind of housing in Madrid is blocks of flats. Houses are usually associated with either high or low economic status.

7. *Centro de Asistencia Social de Villaverde Alto*, personal communication.

8. Many engage in economic activities within the informal sector as do the Gitanos.

9. This text was originally in Spanish and the translation is mine. All the translations in this book (from Spanish, Catalan or French) are mine and I do not mention this fact again in order to avoid repetition.

10. The majority of the Payos who live in Jarana are Quinquilleros, members of a social group with a nomadic or semi-nomadic tradition who – before the

urban expansion of the 1960s – specialized in door-to-door selling and have an argot and some social organisation of their own. Although the Gitanos of Jarana consider the Quinquilleros to be Payos, they also see them as being somehow different from other Payos. The Quinquilleros' modes of earning their livelihood are similar to the Gitanos': some collect and resell cardboard and cloth; others search for scrap metal. The etymology of the word 'Quinquillero' suggests strong parallels with the word 'Tinker': *quincalla* means ironmongery, and in common Spanish the word *quinquillero* means both ironmonger and villain or rogue. There is almost no literature at all on the Quinquilleros. De las Heras and Villarín (1974: 271) state that the Quinquis '"appear" in our society, with a strength unknown up to then, towards the middle of this century', and there seems to be little mention of them in the historical record before 1900 (1974: 271; see also León-Ignacio 1976). The only two published works on the Quinquilleros that I know portray them very differently. León-Ignacio sees them as 'another society, with no relationship at all with our own, even if apparently there may seem to be links and even if both are found in the same country' (1976: 29). By contrast, de las Heras and Villarín stress their links with Spanish society: 'what characterises the Quinquis is the social level to which they belong, their traditions and their lifestyle . . . the Quinquis are a mini-society formed by the movements of a population that has been subject, at different times, to particular social pressures for alienation' (1974: 266–7).

11. In fact, many Gitanos have turned their yards into extra rooms or tiny houses where newly married couples live until they are granted council housing of their own. More often than not the process takes years and couples have two or three children before they all can move out and their 'house' can be taken over by a younger brother and his wife.

12. See Devereux who talks about ethnic and gendered difference in Zinacantan and explains how distinctions between men and women are established 'without emphasising essence or substance as the source of difference so much as stressing action and appearance as appropriately displaying difference' (1990: 89). The same can be said about the distinction between Payos and Gitanos as seen by the Gitanos of Jarana.

13. Similarly, Stewart writing of the Hungarian Rom describes them as a 'people deemed by its social superiors too stupid and uncivilized to have a culture at all' (1997: 2).

14. See Behar 1986, Díaz Viana 1988, Velasco 1988, Devillard 1988, Caro Baroja 1970, and the papers in Prat et al. 1991.

15. 'An understanding of community identity must take into account cultural philosophies of personhood' (Linnekin and Poyer 1990: 7).

16. 'What becomes remarkable, then, is . . . the ease with which it is argued that people represent "society" to themselves. This assumption on behalf of others is, of course, an assumption on behalf of the observers who "know" they belong to a society' (Strathern 1988: 9).

17. 'It is not enough to argue that there is no prediscursive "sex" that acts

as the stable point of reference on which, or in relation to which, the cultural construction of gender proceeds. To say that sex is already gendered, already constructed, is not yet to explain in which way the "materiality" of gender is forcibly produced . . . Which bodies come to matter – and why?' (Butler 1993: xi–xii).

Those Awkward Spaniards

I don't like the Gitanos, because they are filthy and bandits. The Gitanos are different from the Payos because they are not civilised and they are given places where they can live, all together and without stealing, and they don't want to live there, they destroy those places, kill the animals and then leave. The Gitanos can be told apart from decent people because of all these things, and also because they steal and kill.

This statement, taken from a school composition written by a twelve-year old boy from Madrid (in Calvo Buezas 1990:188), embodies some of the key stereotypes through which many Spaniards portray those other awkward Spaniards, the Gitanos.[1] To many Payos, the Gitanos break all the rules of proper human behaviour and, in so doing, place themselves outside the bounds of 'society' (*la sociedad*): they are dirty, lazy, deceptive and dishonest, and they kill and steal. Moreover, in the 1980s and 1990s the Gitanos more often than not have been portrayed as drug dealers: as such they are said to corrupt and destroy Payo youths and, with them, the hopes for a better life of a large sector of the Payo community.

However, there is more than one Payo standpoint on the Gitanos and their place within Spain. Analyses of representations of the Gitanos in the press, for example, show that besides this dominant 'discriminatory' discourse there stand other subordinate ones, with a more benevolent and 'paternalistic' content (López Varas and Fresnillo Pato 1995).[2] The fragmentation that characterizes Payo representations of the Gitanos reflects the varying relationships of different Payo social groups to the Gitanos and, significantly, to each other as well. The roots of this fragmentation are to be found in the processes of change that Spain has undergone since the beginning of the twentieth century – processes that also have led to the current diversification of the Gitanos.

In the early 1900s most Gitanos lived in the countryside, dispersed among the Payos in small groups of patrilineally related kin. Most

were semi-nomadic and, in a manner reminiscent of Gypsy populations elsewhere (Mayall 1988), provided services to the non-Gypsies
in a symbiotic system of relations that revolved around the Gitanos'
high mobility. In the 1950s and 1960s, and along with the Payos,
many Gitanos moved to the urban areas and became completely
sedentary. Since then they have experienced an increasing encroach-
ment on their lifestyle by the non-Gypsies. They have been subjected
to growing control from local authorities, to forced resettlements, and
to the demise of the most lucrative and flexible of their ways of earning
a living. When the 'benefits' of the welfare state were extended to the
Gitanos, the perpetuation of their distinctiveness came under greatest
threat. Some Gitanos have sought a solution to these crises by partici-
pating in the massive Gypsy movement of conversion to Evangelism
that began to grow in the late 1960s and has gained increasing momen-
tum during the 1990s. Others have consciously chosen to abandon
the 'Gitano way of doing things' (Anta Félez 1994). In Villaverde, many
Gitanos are attempting to remain Gitano in a rapidly changing world
– a world in which they find it increasingly difficult to persist at the
margins or in the interstices of Payo economy and social life, that is,
to sustain their singularity and their lifestyle as Gypsies.

These developments are taking place against a complex framework
of radical social, economic and cultural change in the country as a
whole. In 1976 the Francoist dictatorship ended and Spain began the
process of democratization. Then came the incorporation into the
European Community, the economic crisis of the mid-1980s, and the
recovery of the 1990s. During the last decade, Spain has become a
target for migration from Latin America, the Spanish-speaking Caribbean, the Philippines and North Africa. Social relations are in a process
of profound change, and mores and ways of perceiving the nation,
the local community and the self are similarly being transformed (cf.
Thurén 1988). The Gitanos, as a distinct group competing for space
and resources in the crowded peripheries of the large cities – a group
that rejects the dominant work ethic and signs of communal identity
– have come under growing pressures to conform. Firstly, Gitanos have
been the object of large numbers of violent protests. Secondly, the
1990s have witnessed unparalleled attempts towards the institutionalization of the Gitanos: through an ever-growing expansion of the social
services the Gitanos have been brought, more than ever before, under
the control of the State. This represents the culmination of a trend
that started at the end of the dictatorship, when local authorities
throughout the country begun to reassess their policies towards the

Gitanos. Since then, thousands of Gitanos have been resettled from shacks into blocks of flats or into houses. Some are now living among the non-Gitanos, but others wait their turn in state-planned 'provisional Gitano colonies' or still in the shantytowns that grew in the peripheries of the main cities in the 1950s and 1960s. Most often, these resettlement programmes are accompanied by lengthy compulsory re-education schemes aimed at encouraging the Gitanos to adopt the lifestyle of the non-Gitanos or Payos.

Gitanos at the Start of the Twentieth Century

In the communal memory of the Gitanos – which is transmitted orally and is highly schematic – the *antes* (before) is clearly separated from the *ahora* (now). The phrase 'the life of before' (*la vida de antes*) is used to refer to the Gitano lifestyle roughly up to the 1940s and 1950s. When I asked Tío (Uncle)[3] Juan, an elderly and highly respected man from Jarana, to describe for me the 'life of before' he explained:

> Before, that is thirty or forty or fifty years ago, the Gitanos went from village to village. They stayed in a village for a while until the *Guardia Civil*[4] came to throw them out. Some *guardias* were polite, others were evil, but very evil. A Gitano woman would be cooking some food over the fire and the *guardias* would kick the pot and break it and spill all the food. Some Gitanos used to make baskets with wicker from the sides of the river. When the Gitanos arrived into a village the Payos would shout: 'the Gitanos, the Gitanos are coming!' They said they stole everything. It is true that the Gitanos would take a hen, or a cabbage, or vegetables from the fields.

Accounts of 'the life of before' revolve around four basic themes: the Gitanos were poor; they often stole from the non-Gypsies; they were mistreated by the Civil Guard; and they were nomadic.[5] However, when describing their own lives rather than the 'life of the Gitanos', the older men and women of Jarana add layers of complexity to this picture. To start with, only a few of them were strictly nomadic in their youth: most were semi-sedentary and some were completely sedentary. Before and in the years immediately following the Spanish Civil War (1936–9) the majority lived in groups of kin dispersed among the Payo rural population. Their semi-nomadism enabled and was enabled by their occupational versatility: Gitanos tended to earn their livelihood from two or more sources at a time. Many worked as hired labourers in periods of intense agricultural activity, supplementing their income through flexible trades such as sheep shearing, muleteering or fortune telling (Sánchez Ortega 1986: 59). Some had occupations that in Spain are seen as being typically Gypsy: they were horse dealers, blacksmiths, musicians, peddlers or basket makers. Payo records reveal that horse dealing was one of the Gitanos' most prominent occupations: 'horse dealer' and 'Gitano' appear as synonyms in late nineteenth-century documents (EEPG 1991: 24).

Tío Juan and his wife Tía Tula provide a good example of the flexibility that characterized the Gitano lifestyle in the first half of the century. Before her marriage to Tío Juan at the age of twenty-two, Tía Tula lived with her parents, her married brothers, and their wives and children. They earned their living as basket makers and peddlers, moving from village to village throughout the north and north-east of the Peninsula, often in a group with some other related Gitanos. Tía Tula married Tío Juan at the end of the Civil War, which he had spent in Madrid. He was keen to move to the countryside where food would be more readily available and where he would be better able to develop his skills as a horse dealer. Thus, in the early period of their marriage they lived in several villages in Castile, twice buying houses that they occupied for years at a time, but also spending considerable periods 'on the roads' (*por los caminos*), moving from one horse fair to the next. They supplemented Tío Juan's income as horse dealer by peddling and selling baskets that Tía Tula made.

Other elderly Gitanos who now live in Jarana engaged in less 'typic-ally Gitano' trades in their youth, working in mines, in brick-making factories or as domestic servants. Grandmother María, for instance, was born in 1918 in a village in the mountains of León, where her father, mother and brothers worked in the coalmines. Her family were the only Gitanos in the village, and she attended the local school and experienced good friendships with Payo girls. She married a Gitano at eighteen and, with her husband and her new in-laws, moved first to Palencia, a northerly town, and then to Madrid, where they eventually settled for good. Once there, they rented a small house and she had four children before her husband was killed in a fight with other Gitanos. With her mother-in-law, Abuela María worked in the streets of the city, collecting and reselling cloth and scrap metal. She also washed clothes for Payo families and, in the harvest season, moved to the countryside to work as a day labourer gathering grapes and olives.

Urbanization and Sedentarization[6]

The year 1939, which saw the end of the Civil War and the beginning of the Francoist dictatorship, also heralded a new era for the Gitanos. Two main factors were to transform their way of life radically: the abandonment of the countryside and a series of new repressive policies. In Spain the economic recovery following the post-war years led to a huge exodus from the rural to the urban areas. As a response to the country's growing industrial development at least 7.5% of the Spanish population moved from villages to the large cities during the 1950s, and two million people were displaced over the five years between 1961 and 1965 (Cebrián Abellán 1992: 40). It was then that the Gitanos' rural modes of livelihood became obsolete, mainly because of the replacement of the horse with motor machinery in agricultural work, and through the depopulation of the countryside, which left many Gitanos without customers for their services and goods. As in the case of the Payos, large numbers of Gitanos migrated to the cities. The majority of the older Gitanos of Jarana arrived in Madrid at this time. Once there, many were to earn their living by begging, scavenging at rubbish dumps, and reselling scrap metal, cloth and paper.[7] Tío Juan, who had moved to Madrid with Tía Tula and their children in the early 1950s, continued trading horses for a few years, but the demand declined and he begun to work at a rubbish dump, as street vendor and as bricklayer. His wife sold flowers and textiles in the streets of the city.

In the 1950s and early 1960s the Gitanos came to share the most marginal urban areas with other rural migrants, creating 'cardboard neighbourhoods' (barrios de chabolas) in many large cities. With the economic expansion of the 1960s and 1970s, the Gitanos and other shack dwellers were repeatedly pushed to the receding urban periphery in order to make ground available for industrial or building expansions. The 1960s Plan de Erradicación del Chabolismo (Plan for the Eradication of Shack-Dwelling) actively – often through physical violence – forced the urban poor to concentrate in ever more isolated and deprived zones. Tía Tula described to me one such forcible resettlement. In the mid-1960s, while her husband was in jail, she spent some months living with her children in a small shanty town in the Puente de Vallecas area of Madrid – then close to the periphery. One night, armed policemen obliged her and her neighbours to climb onto big rubbish trucks, leaving their few possessions behind. They were 'dropped off like garbage' (nos bascularon como basura) much further away in an empty field and told that they were to live there from then on. There was no source of water nearby, no drains and no electricity, and it was years before these poor Gitanos and Payos received charity help to exchange their cardboard and plastic shacks for small cement houses with corrugated metal roofs.

Of the inhabitants of these deprived areas, the Payos were the first to get access to State housing and so slowly moved into the city and up the social scale (San Román 1986a, 1994). Although some Gitanos were resettled, the vast majority were deemed too 'uncivilized' to receive standard council accommodation. The shanty-towns and some other zones of very low quality housing thus became virtual ghettos of overwhelmingly Gitano population – and have remained so to the present day. Throughout these processes, the Gitanos' favoured forms of political and economic organization – in small dispersed patrigroups, careful not to impinge on each other's territory – came under increasing strain (San Román 1986a; Anta Félez 1994). Forced contact between Gitano patrigroups who had not known each other or which had a history of mutual hostility led to greatly increased levels of intra-community conflict. As my friend Clara explained to me: 'in those neighbourhoods the Gitanos used to kill each other, they were not like they are now, they didn't understand, everything was different, they didn't live with Payos, there were only Gitanos, living in shacks with each other, and they quarrelled all the time.'

In these ghettos – such as El Pozo del Tío Raimundo in Madrid or La Perona in Barcelona – the Gitanos were 'alone, isolated and uncared for, dependent on charity institutions, marginalised; and, to the eyes of the Payos, dangerous' (San Román 1986a: 222). During this period, at the point when the dictatorship's hold over the nation begun to weaken, paradoxically the control over the Gitanos by the State grew stronger. With their poverty, their relative independence from the State, and their 'irregular' ways of earning a living, the Gitanos were easily turned into key targets of a government eager to demonstrate its strength in the face of growing public dissent (EEPG 1991: 25). Regular and massive raids of Gitano settlements followed events in which Gitanos had not participated – such as anti-Francoist demonstrations and terrorist attacks (San Román 1986a: 211). Local authorities made ample use of a vagrancy law (*Ley de Vagos y Maleantes*) which had been passed in 1933 and that made it legal to prosecute individuals who were considered to be potential offenders.[8] San Román, who carried out her fieldwork during this period, has provided a vivid description:

> During Francoism the Gitanos were very harshly repressed, both to keep them in the settlements where they were forced to live and to use them as examples of public control. Raids were extremely frequent, particularly towards the end of the period. They happened often while I was in the field, and had no justification whatsoever. We feared the nights, partic-

ularly the small hours, and used to leave the doors of the shacks open
so that (the police) would not kick them down. The men, taking even
the younger boys, would sleep in the house of a wealthier relative, or of
a priest, a social worker, or a Payo friend. And those who knew none of
these would take a blanket . . . and sleep in an open field . . . Mornings
brought the return of the fugitives (1994: 125).

The Impact of Economic Regularization

Although since the advent of democracy in 1976 punitive assaults no
longer take place, the State has attempted, more than ever before, to
incorporate the Gitanos into its formal structures. Particularly since
the mid-1980s, local authorities throughout the country have endeav-
oured to assimilate the Gitanos into the dominant population, both
at an economic and at a cultural level. A good example is the *Consorcio*
(Consortium for the Resettlement of Madrid's Marginal Population),
which was founded in 1986 as an agreement between the central,
regional and local governments to deal with the problem of shack
dwelling in the city and which, during my fieldwork, worked intensively among the Gitanos of Jarana. Its 'main objective' was to 'incorporate this (marginal) population into the structures of the dominant
society, attempting to give them . . . all the mechanisms that would
favour such integration without the loss of their idiosyncrasy as ethnic
minority' (Consorcio Para el Realojamiento de la Población Marginada
de Madrid 1986: 4). The aim was to encourage the Gitanos to develop
an unobtrusive and almost decorative Gitano identity, the kind of
identity that San Román has described in the following terms:

> One option is to reduce the Gitano identity to the minimum necessary
> cultural support, to the cultural support that is indispensable in order
> to symbolise an ethnic identity. Put simply, this means not to practice
> the Gitano culture, the Gitano social organisation, the Gitano strategies
> and moral codes, whilst retaining the odd Gitano trait as a symbolic
> support of identity. In this way, Gypsyness becomes militancy, while
> the cultural content, the cast-aside and forgotten culture, is enthroned
> as myth (1986a: 203).

In their attempts to transform the basis and meaning of Gypsyness,
these local authorities have used two key tools. Firstly, they have
developed a series of social policies aimed at improving the living
conditions of the Gitanos – mainly through resettlement programmes
that have come hand-in-hand with compulsory re-education schemes.
In this context the Gitanos are being treated as 'the children of an
adult society' (Anta Félez 1994: 90). Secondly, local authorities have

pushed the Gitanos into the formal economy. Given most Gitanos' reluctance or inability to take up 'normalized employment', the trend has been towards the regularization of their 'traditional activities' – mainly scrap collecting and street vending.

Vending and scavenging at rubbish dumps now require official permits that are very difficult to obtain. Those Gitanos who, for example, sell melons or underwear in the streets of Madrid without a license risk having their merchandise confiscated by the urban police: for them vending has become an extremely precarious and rather unprofitable undertaking. The family of Tía Lola, a distant relative of Tía Tula who also lives in Jarana, have been very badly hit by the regularization movement. Tía Lola, a woman in her fifties, buys synthetic lace that she cuts to make napkins, tablecloths and bed covers. She sells them without a permit in different zones of the city – her husband, who suffers from asthma and is said to be unable to work, drives her around. When she goes selling, Tía Lola places her merchandise on a large square piece of cloth, which she can fold and hide rapidly if the police approach. Nonetheless, she is fined regularly and has her wares requisitioned. Once in the summer of 1992 the police even confiscated her new slippers, which she had taken off because of the heat. Making a profit under these circumstances, no matter how small, is difficult. At the same time, Tía Lola's monthly expenses are high: she has been resettled in a house and has to pay rent and bills, and she supports her husband, her elderly mother-in-law, her widowed youngest daughter – who takes care of the housework – and her daughter's two small children. Tía Lola often describes how 'lately' *(en estos últimos tiempos)* making ends meet has become particularly difficult. Before her family was resettled in Jarana they lived in a semi-derelict house, which Tía Lola's husband kept in shape with regular repairs. The house 'belonged to nobody', had no running water and officially no electricity – Tía Lola's husband had in fact diverted the electricity supply – so they paid no bills. Under a relatively tolerant state policy towards street vending Tía Lola's income was enough to keep everybody going. Once they were resettled in Jarana and vending became more regularized, things changed, according to Tía Lola, 'for the worse'. Tía Lola's case is not unusual in that large numbers of Gitanos have seen their incomes plummet as the movement towards regularization has grown: like her, many Gitanos have become trapped between the formal and the informal socio-economic spheres. Moreover, since the economic crisis of the 1980s they have had to face the re-entry of many low-skilled Payos into the informal sector.

Throughout the 1990s, they have also been competing for marginal resources against growing numbers of illegal Latin American and particularly North African migrants.

Regulatory policies have worked to the advantage of those Gitanos who, unlike Tía Lola, were skilled enough to deal with local authorities and who wanted to or were able to, keep up monthly payments for vending or scavenging permits. Many Gitanos found a stable niche in the weekly open markets that are set up in neighbourhoods and villages throughout Spain, and the few who were lucky enough to obtain licences for searching at rubbish dumps similarly benefited from a very significant decrease in competition. Although they remain some of the poorest Spaniards, Gitanos belonging to these two groups have fared better than those who have been left out of the process of regularization.

Estela and Esteban, a couple in their mid-forties who were resettled in a flat in Villaverde in 1989, have done particularly well. Esteban's father Tío Sebas, who died a few months before I arrived in the field, was a widely known 'man of respect' *(hombre de respeto)* or conflict mediator. He had good contacts among the Payo authorities and was able to use his influence to help his son obtain selling permits in five weekly open markets in the periphery of Madrid. Esteban and Estela have five daughters: at the time of my fieldwork only three lived with them, Carmen and Loli, who were still unmarried, and Marga, who had brought her husband Pedro to live with her parents – Pedro is also Esteban's sister's son. Every day, Carmen and Loli stay at home to do the housework while Esteban, Estela, Marga and Pedro drive to one or other of their various markets. They sell bed linen and are extremely successful: they shout their wares and 'work' their customers in pairs, skilfully mixing flattery and intimidation to persuade them to buy.

Even these privileged Gitanos are attempting to subsist in a hostile economic environment. Local authorities are more susceptible of being influenced by the demands of small Payo businessmen than of Gitano street vendors for the simple reason that Payos use their right to vote whereas on the whole Gitanos rarely do so. Payo shop-owners fear the competition posed by open air markets and as a result many licensed vendors have seen the monthly instalments of their permits rise, sometimes so dramatically as to make the setting up of licensed stalls a liability rather than a profit. In the Christmas of 1997/1998 the local council in Villaverde Alto put up the fees for setting up temporary stalls by 50% from previous years. They also moved the location of the open Christmas market from the main promenade to a peripheral street. Faced with having to pay up to 150,000 pesetas for a five-day license, most Gitanos choose to set up illegal stalls, either in Villaverde or in other areas of the city. Sara, a daughter of Esteban and Estela, explained it to me: 'that amount of money, if you have to pay that you don't make any profit, it's not worthwhile. Every year we rely on the Christmas vending, you know well that it keeps us going for a long time afterwards. They want us to give up, to turn to selling drugs, I don't know.'

With the spread of environmentalism, recycling has become a concern for many local authorities, which have been eager to take it away from the hands of the Gitanos. In 1997 licenses for scavenging at the Valdemingómez dump in Madrid were cancelled and the Gitanos from Jarana who worked there – among them three of Tío Juan's sons and several of his grandsons – were offered jobs in a recycling plant instead. They were to work at the very bottom of the Payo socio-economic hierarchy, opening rubbish bags and sorting through the different kinds of refuse, earning less than they did before and under much stricter schedules. Although some Gitanos accepted, most turned to scrap collecting or illegal street vending – rather more hazardous ways of earning a living.

In the face of these difficulties, some Gitanos have turned to drug dealing as a source of income. This has been the case in particularly deprived areas, among individuals or kinship groups with little or no skills or no wish to find a niche for themselves in this increasingly regularized economic world, or else among those Gitanos who, before the 1980s, had earned their livelihoods through criminal activities. In some Gitano neighbourhoods and shantytowns, such as Los Asperones in Málaga, trafficking in hard and soft drugs has become one of the main sources of income: drug dealing 'generates high earnings, does not need a specialised labour force, and has a very easy exit into the (black) market . . . so that between 50% and 80% of the money generated is gross profit' (Anta Félez 1994: 77). Some Gitanos – particularly where whole kinship groups engage in trafficking on a medium to high scale – have seen their standard of living rise enormously. For others – isolated and impoverished individuals selling small quantities – the benefits are much lower and the risks of being convicted considerably higher. The latter rather than the former is the case for most of the dealers who live in Villaverde. At the same time, growing numbers of Gitano men have become addicts, and often relatives find themselves selling drugs to non-Gypsies in order to be able to supply them to their sons, brothers or husbands (San Román 1994: 95). The spread of drug-dealing and drug-addiction – *la droga* as it is called in Spain – has had enormous consequences, and has been seen by some authors as a key factor leading to the Gitanos' absorbtion into the urban underclass:

> *La droga* has changed the relationship between the Gitanos and the wider society . . . *la droga* has changed the traditional relationships of status, leadership and power . . . *la droga* has introduced among drug-users and within the community at large a new dimension of instability and violence, which threatens to destroy the traditional world-view. It is also leading the Gitanos to their disappearance as a distinct ethnic group, accelerating their transformation into a social group completely marginalised and impoverished (Anta Félez 1994: 90; see also San Román 1994: 94–101).

The Gitanos themselves are well aware of the negative impact that involvement in drug dealing is having upon their way of life. The ones who live in Jarana often discuss the possibility that the Gitano lifestyle may become extinct because addicts and dealers no longer uphold the moral norms that, ideally, should regulate relationships among Gitanos. *La droga*, they say, 'will be the end of us' *(va a terminar con nosotros)*.

Social Assistance: A New Economic Strategy

As a result of State pressures and through increasing competition with impoverished Payos, the Gitanos' favoured ways of earning a livelihood – those that allow them to control their own labour and time – are becoming less and less profitable. Drug dealing appears to be a strategy that may permit the economic success of some kinship groups or individuals but that ultimately undermines the basis of the Gitano way of life. Under these circumstances, many Gitanos are relying on a relatively new and apparently innocuous source of income: the numerous types of economic incentives that local authorities throughout Spain have devised as 'bribes' to get the Gitanos to participate in equally numerous re-education schemes. Moreover, as a genuinely impoverished and disadvantaged population, the Gitanos also collect large amounts of State subsidies in the form of compensatory benefits. The social services, which have been expanding since the end of the dictatorship, have become the providers of an economic resource that requires little input of effort on the part of the Gitanos and that is 'there', ready to be exploited. It is also a resource that perpetuates itself the more erratic the Gitanos' response to it is.[9]

During my fieldwork in 1992 and 1993 there was approximately one Payo full-time social worker per thirty inhabitants of Jarana. These social workers set up several workshops: driving lessons for the illiterate, hairdressing for young unmarried women, plumbing for young men and so on. They also organized talks on family planning, health and education. The overt purpose of these lessons and workshops was to teach the Gitanos skills that would help them to gain their livelihood in the formal rather than the informal sector and improve their position vis-à-vis the Payos. In fact, one of the primary objectives of the activities that used to take place at the social assistance centre was to provide a space for discussion, a place where the social workers could talk to the Gitanos, and provoke them into questioning their lifestyle. One of the key tools that helped the social workers to get the Gitanos to attend these lessons and workshops during my fieldwork was the *Ingreso Madrileño de Integración* (Madrid Income for Integration) or IMI. This was a system set up in 1990 by the *Comunidad Autónoma* (Regional Government) of Madrid whereby an individual, as representative of a family, signed a contract agreeing to a series of demands and in return received a significant monthly financial package from the State. During 1991 forty-two Gitano families of Jarana received this income, and at one time or another most of the Gitanos of the neighbourhood had access to it. The recipients committed themselves to keep the children clean, send them to school daily, attend particular lessons at the social assistance centre and pay the house bills regularly. In return they received from 7,000 to 57,000 pesetas every month, depending on the number of dependants and their declared income. If they failed to fulfil any of these conditions they lost their IMI. One of the main tasks of the social workers was to monitor the Gitanos' response to the IMI and report it to the relevant authorities.[10]

In many cases, however, the 'system' turns against the Gitanos. Take again an example from Villaverde. In 1996 a large number of Gitano families were resettled in newly built blocks of flats among the non-Gypsy population. The flats belonged to the Ministry of Housing, and the Gitanos signed contracts agreeing to pay 20,000 pesetas (approximately £100) per month as rent. From previous experience, the Gitanos expected that it would be acceptable if they neglected to pay. Two years later, in the Christmas of 1997–8, they were served with eviction papers. Many had to borrow in order to be able to face the huge debts that they had accumulated. Some were among the licensed vendors mentioned above, who had just seen the price for their Christmas selling permits double as a result of a change in policy on the part of the local authorities.

Civil Protests and *La Droga*

How are the Gitanos perceived or represented by other Spaniards? A glance at the newspapers and at the sociological and anthropological literature quickly reveals the multiple confrontations between Gitanos and Payos that take place every year in Spain. Since the end of the dictatorship inhabitants of Spanish towns and villages have regularly shown their refusal to have Gitanos as neighbours, sometimes violently.[11] They have burnt Gitano shacks and houses, and have blocked roads and railways. Repeatedly, they have demonstrated against the admission of Gitano children into local schools. During the last few years, these non-Gypsy protestors have increasingly avoided phrasing their complaints in overtly racist terms, and have focused on the Gitanos' supposed involvement in drug-dealing.

Take the example of Villaverde Bajo, just down the highway from Villaverde Alto, where in September 1991, just a few months before I began my fieldwork, a group of local Payo men burned the showhouse of a housing estate that was being built for the resettlement of shack-dwelling Gitanos. The conflict escalated rapidly: the number of protestors grew and they organized rallies against the resettlement and demonstrations at the City Hall. They also blocked access to the district from the highway and the railway and organized a general strike in the area. After a violent confrontation between locals and the police, a group of neighbours squatted in the construction zone and camped around it, wanting to delay the works as long as possible. During October and November, demonstrations and meetings between the Administration and local representatives continued on a daily basis. Finally, the Neighbours' Association succeeded: the Administration began by accepting a reduction in the number of Gitano families to be resettled; later, they agreed to stop the building works completely (López Varas and Fresnillo Pato 1995: 23–4).

In their analysis of the 1991 conflict of Villaverde Bajo, López Varas and Fresnillo Pato (1995) make it clear that Payos do not constitute a monolithic block, a united front acting vis-à-vis the Gypsies. Their argument is worth following in some detail. They explain how clashes like the one in Villaverde, where 'the Payo neighbours' and 'the Gitanos' appear at first sight to be the main actors, have to be seen predominantly as an example of antagonism and dissent among

different Payo interest groups – the 'neighbours' and the Administration, for example. Thus, in the various journalistic accounts of the
conflict 'we find the glance that the Payos cast over their own selves,
rather than their image of the Gitanos' (1995: 108).

López Varas and Fresnillo Pato argue convincingly that protests
against Gitanos like the one in Villaverde Bajo constitute 'an openly
defensive reaction in the part of the lowest echelons of the middle or
lower middle classes . . . in the face of the processes of social decline
in which they are immersed' (1995: 109).[12] The representations of the
Gitanos put forward for example by the Villaverde protestors make of
the minority a master-symbol of the marginality and social decay that
they fear threatens them. *La droga* – drug dealing and drug addiction
– which appears in these characterizations as the epitome of Gypsyness, works as a metaphor that transcends the actuality of Payo/Gitano
relations, 'condensing with great intensity the representation of the
negativity of life, of death, and of social degradation' (1995: 110).
The fight against *la droga* – and hence against the Gitanos that are
pictured above all as dealers and addicts – feeds on the social fears of
those social groups who live in violent and conflictive neighbourhoods, or else who are currently experiencing losses of status and
processes of social exclusion (1995: 110).

There is also a broader economic dimension to these developments.
Not only those Payos who live in deprived areas, but important sectors
of the middle classes, view *la droga* as an extremely irregular economic
activity that nonetheless yields very high profits. *La droga* facilitates
what is perceived as an undeserved upward mobility that challenges
normalized models of labour relations – and it also makes high consumption levels possible. Thus,

> The two dimensions of *'la droga'*, as symbolic condensation and as
> economic structure, intertwine and reinforce each other within the
> context of a moral discourse. In this discourse the processes of loss of
> status of the medium classes or the paralysis of the mechanisms of
> economic and social integration of the lower classes are set up against
> the economic promotion – through drug-dealing – of (the Gitanos) . . .
> Together, these different processes are interpreted as a phenomenon of
> inversion of the basic categories of the social hierarchy: what is negative
> and corrupt comes to occupy the higher echelons of the social order,
> and what is positive and honourable is progressively displaced to the
> inferior places (López Varas and Fresnillo Pato 1995: 112)

This moral discourse, within which 'the people' *(el pueblo)* is set
up as 'the victim' of *la droga*, and in which *los Gitanos* appear as 'the

executioner' of 'the people', masks and attempts to legitimize the processes of social exclusion that affect the Gitanos (López Varas and Fresnillo Pato 1995: 118). By identifying the Gitanos at large with *la droga* this discourse constructs a stereotype of social deviation rather than of racist segregation: the Gitanos are rejected, it is claimed, not as Gitanos, but as dealers and addicts (López Varas and Fresnillo Pato 1995: 118). The poverty and marginality of the Gitanos are presented as misleading appearances, and the distinction between 'the poor' and 'the offender' is collapsed.[13] Moreover, the Gitanos are portrayed through stereotypes that 'condense the negative archetype of the values that currently dominate the economy and the broad social organisation', such as 'savage competition and unrestrained individualism . . . complete lack of respect for the values of solidarity and for the collective needs' (López Varas and Fresnillo Pato 1995: 119). Middle- or upper-class Payos and Gitanos are put forward together as epitomes of the same amoral behaviour. Within this framework, the programmes of resettlement of Gitanos from shantytowns into houses or flats among the non-Gypsies are seen as instances of the preferential treatment that Gitanos unreservedly receive at the hands of the Administration. Whereas Payos face great difficulties in obtaining council housing or compensatory subsidies, these are given 'freely' to Gitanos – who neither work nor contribute to 'the society' at large (López Varas and Fresnillo Pato 1995: 76–7).

This dominant or hegemonic discriminatory discourse coexists with others that López Varas and Fresnillo Pato call the subordinate discourses of 'integration' or 'difference' (1995: 121). These are highly atomized, and are restricted to the professional middle classes – mainly those working in education, medicine or social work. They encompass strong criticisms towards 'the masses', which are seen as the protagonists of the racist movements that are currently sweeping through Europe (1995: 92). *La droga* is here portrayed as a cover up for the 'ancestral' hatred that the uneducated sectors of the dominant society feel towards the Gitanos. In fact, these discourses strive to establish a difference between the *Quinquilleros* or marginal Payos and the true Gitanos. Gypsyness is separated from the actual marginality in which the Gitanos live and phrased in terms of a Gitano system of values – the Gitano 'culture'.

At some points the Gitanos are portrayed as 'bohemians, lovers of freedom and of nomadism, careless of ties to work or housing' (López Varas and Fresnillo Pato 1995: 96). More frequently, the cultural difference between Payos and Gitanos is described as a result of the

Gitanos' backwardness vis-à-vis the standards of the dominant society (López Varas and Fresnillo Pato 1995: 94). The role of the Administration is to correct the racist attitudes of the lower social groups as well as to offer the Gitanos the possibility of entering fully the structures of the Spanish State. This is the 'educational stance' which views marginalization as 'a stage of social underdevelopment' (López Varas and Fresnillo Pato 1995: 98) and which, from a paternalistic and moralistic standpoint, turns the Gitanos into 'children' or 'objects of education' (López Varas and Fresnillo Pato 1995: 123). The social services – the main tool that the State uses for dealing with the Gitanos – take this 'educational' standpoint more often than not. For instance, manuals for social workers and teachers often stress the 'childishness' of the Gitanos. De Pablo Velasco, taking a typical stance, explains how among the Gitanos 'the sentimental prevails over the rational' (1994: 10). García et al. describe the Gitanos' lack of social memory in similar terms: 'without memory there is no consciousness, without consciousness there is no imagination, without imagination there is no development' – no possibility of moving from a state of 'enslavement' to a state of 'freedom' (1996: 24). From this point of view, integration is seen as a concession, an opportunity for improvement that is given by the majority to those groups 'who live immersed in backwardness and misery' (López Varas and Fresnillo Pato 1995: 123).

Conclusions

The Spanish Gypsies live at the bottom of the dominant economic and social scales. They earn their livelihood in the most precarious ways. The State puts them under constant pressures to change their lifestyle – from the occupations they pursue to where they live or how they bring up their children. Moreover, they are also placed by other Spaniards in the lowest rungs of the Payo moral hierarchy: either they are seen as threats to the rest of 'the society' (la sociedad) or they are deemed 'children' who need to be taught how to behave. My main concern in this book is with the mechanisms through which, against the kind of context that I have just described, the Gitanos of Jarana reproduce their singularity. This means studying their sense of themselves: uncovering where their pride in being a Gitano is located and how it is sustained day after day. Elucidating how Gitanos resist assimilation requires a clear understanding of how Gitanos create relations among themselves. In the next chapter I set out a problem: how to reconcile the Gitanos' very strong sense of themselves as a 'people' with the fact that their lifestyle militates strongly against their construction of enduring ties among themselves – ties that transcend the immediacy of the kinship group.

Notes

1. The Gitanos of Jarana are adamant that they are Spanish and should be entitled to the same benefits as other Spaniards.

2. See Calvo Buezas (1990) for a detailed analysis of attitudes towards the Gitanos of Payo schoolchildren and their teachers.

3. The Gitanos of Jarana call Gitano men and women over roughly fifty years of age 'tío' (uncle) or 'tía' (aunt). They explain that they do so as a mark of respect.

4. 'The two main forces are the Guardia Civil, which has traditionally patrolled the countryside, the highways and frontiers of Spain, and the Cuerpo Nacional de Policía which is responsible for provincial capitals and other large towns' (Hooper 1995: 211). 'Although often thought of, and even referred to, as a creation of Franco, the Civil Guard actually traces its history back to 1844 when it was set up to combat banditry' (ibid. 213).

5. These accounts replicate current Payo stereotypes of the 'true' Gitano life. See for example two statements produced by two social workers from Jarana:

> a) It cannot be said that there are Gitanos in Madrid because the true Gitanos are nomads. The characteristics that differentiate these people who call themselves Gitanos are integral to urban marginality and poverty: they have little culture – for instance they don't know how to manage in a flat – and they cannot deal with the bureaucracy on their own and so on. Particularly the younger ones cannot be considered to be true Gitanos, because they have never known the nomadic situation that produced the authentic characteristics of the Gitano culture.

> b) The Gitanos are bohemians, in the sense that they act following their impulses. They are also immature: this is transmitted from parents to children, because they marry very early, so that the parents pass onto their children the adolescent immaturities that guide their behaviour. Instead of decreasing, these traits become even more ingrained once they become adults.

6. For a fuller description of these processes see San Román 1986a, 1994, and GIEMS 1976.

7. It was the Gitanos' own ability to 'adapt to scarcity that made them bypass less marginal occupations and remain peripheral to the new economic system just as they had been peripheral to the old' (San Román 1994: 38).

8. In 1943 the new regulations of the *Guardia Civil* had stipulated that one of its key roles would be to exert a 'conscientious vigilance' over the Gitanos: throughout the next thirty years the *Guardias* were to fulfil their role thoroughly.

9. Sutherland (1975a, 1975b) has provided detailed descriptions of Californian Rom use of the social services as economic resources. For example:

> Travelling family groups have several schemes for making a living, but the one they most used in Barvale is what the welfare department calls the 'pending transfer system'. They establish a residence for a few weeks, receive their first cheque, and then transfer to a new place before a social worker can visit them. It takes two months to transfer their cheque, and meanwhile they can receive their cheques for these months. Before the two months are up, they transfer to another place . . . In this way, they not only avoided the questions and interference of a social worker, but they were able to keep on their income from welfare cheques while working on the move. Alternatively, they may come to town, hide their cars and/or trailers, stay with friends or relatives in order to have an address long enough to get their first cheque, and then move to the next place (1975b: 16).

10. Another example is provided by Rodriguez Martín's description of social assistance to shack-dwelling Gitanos in the extremely deprived neighbourhood of Montemolín, in Zaragoza (1995). Social workers set up a 'Self-Employment Programme', a series of 'Formation Courses', and a 'Workshop for Personal Development'. Their general aim was to 'promote (cultural) development and social change' among the Gitanos (1995: 150). Women were taught such things as 'Hygiene', 'Health and Sexuality', 'Literacy' or 'how to read and pay electricity and water bills'. Men were taught house-painting and masonry. In exchange for their attendance to these courses the Gitanos received the minimum legal wage. Those who were prepared to attempt to become street vendors and who needed to buy cars or vans were given economic assistance covering 50% of their expenses – even though eventually they refused to provide the remaining 50% themselves and the experiment failed.

11. See Calvo Buezas (1990: 15–19) for a detailed description of the conflicts between Payos and Gitanos which took place in different areas of Spain between 1979 and 1989.

12. A similar argument is put forward by San Román (1986a, 1994).

13. The Gitanos are very often portrayed as reluctant to adopt the lifestyle of the Payos, and thus to be the true agents of their precarious situation. Their characterization resembles the one that, according to Howe, Northern Ireland benefit officers make of 'undeserving' unemployed claimants who are 'considered to deviate in some way or another from a set of "traditional" moral values . . . endorsed by benefit officers, (and who) should not really be eligible for benefit in the first place' (1990: 108).

three

A Divided Neighbourhood: the Problem of Gitano Shared Identity

> We Gitanos are the only people who don't know their descent. We have always roamed the roads and we had no neighbours who could tell us who we were.

In this statement Colombo, a man from Jarana in his thirties, proposes a specific model of Gitano identity. He denies that Gypsyness may be fixed in memory – 'we don't know our descent' – in links to others – 'we had no neighbours' – or in space – 'we have always roamed the roads'. Not knowing where they came from and caring little where they were going, 'the Gitanos of before' (*los Gitanos de antes*) roamed the roads. Whether or not their parents or grandparents were in fact nomadic, today the Gitanos think of their ancestors as such: transient, passing through other people's lands and subject to other people's whims. In this sense 'the Gitanos of before' are not very different from the Gitanos of today who are settled and resettled according to the wishes of the Administration, the object of constant protests and demonstrations, and subjected to what they see as the arbitrary control of the social services and the police.

The model of identity that the Gitanos of Jarana hold denies that a shared memory may play a role in the constitution of Gypsyness. The Gitanos, they say, are a group of people who 'don't know' (*no saben*). They ignore their 'descent', as Colombo explained: what their origins are or where they came from. They cannot read or write, they are a people 'without schooling' (*sin escuela*). They also do not know the important things that the non-Gypsies know, such as medicine, science or law. However, unlike the Payos, they are a people with knowledge (*conocimiento*) of what is right and wrong: in this sense they are a people 'who know' (*saben*). They know how to live their lives according to the set of universal norms that define propriety and decency and that the non-Gypsies disregard.

It is this moral knowledge – of the norms and of how to follow the norms – that makes the Gitanos who they are: distinct from the Payos and also superior to them, a 'better kind of people' (*una clase de gente mejor*). The Gitano view of their distinctiveness is rooted in an ideal of personal righteousness. Memory, links to place, accumulation of material culture and even ties between non-kin are all downplayed: they are said to be 'Payo things' (*cosas Payas*), which do not contribute to the Gypsyness (*gitaneidad, lo Gitano*) of the Gitanos.

In fact, Gitano sociability is governed by strong centrifugal forces, and the characteristics of the Gitanos' image of themselves as a group correspond to the dispersed nature of their everyday life. All sorts of factors contribute to divide Gitanos from each other: religious and kinship affiliation, economic differentiation and region of origin within Spain among others. However, their sense of commonness, their awareness that they share with each other *who they are* – their identity – is extremely strong. The Gitanos believe that they are different from the non-Gypsies and are proud of this fact.

Unlike many other acephalous minorities whose singularity and lifestyle survive under the pressure of dominant majorities, and indeed unlike some other Gypsies, the Gitanos do not premise their image of themselves as a group on an ideal of unity. The Hungarian Rom, for example, strive to transcend inequalities and achieve uniformity among themselves throughout multiple contexts – singing and drinking celebrations, exchanges of horses, dress, house decoration and so on. Their ideal is one of 'unity among brothers', and is threatened not only by the non-Gypsy world, but by the links of men to women and to their kinship groups (Stewart 1997). The Buid, shifting cultivators from the Philippines whose livelihood is jeopardized by settled Christian agriculturalists, similarly emphasize the subordination of the individual to the group. The Buid believe that 'life depends on the maintenance of solidarity' (Gibson 1986: 220) so that among them 'the idioms that dominate social life are those of community, companionship and sharing' (Gibson 1986: 218). Even among the Australian Pintupi who lack a concept of an overarching 'society' or 'community' (Myers 1986: 257) it is the 'smoothly running, co-operative relations of mutual help that recognize shared identity' (Myers 1986: 256).

The Gitanos of Jarana do not link Gypsyness to communal unity or to solidarity. Instead, it is the scarcity of ties linking unrelated Gitanos that strikes the outside observer. In Jarana, the Gitanos live with their backs to each other, purposefully restricting daily sociability to their own kin. A particular kind of imagined community emerges, one that does not depend on connections with a shared territory, on cohesiveness or even harmony among its members, or on the exaltation of a shared past, but rather on the belief that each Gitano man and woman upholds the Gitano morality in the present. The ideal of the group thus revolves around the ideal of the person, and the two are tied by a metonymic link. The very use of the word 'community' in relation to the Gitanos needs to be nuanced: it refers not to a cohesive or harmonious whole, but to the Gitanos' *awareness of each other as moral beings*.

Fragmentations in Everyday Sociability

Two months after I began my fieldwork in Jarana, I heard Tía Tula say that she did not know who lived in Middle Street, literally 50 m away from her house. A young girl had knocked on our door selling nappies from the rubbish dump and Tía Tula, after remarking on her dishevelled appearance, had distractedly wondered whose daughter she was. In an isolated neighbourhood of less than four hundred inhabitants, where people spend much of the day in the streets, I was surprised that Tía Tula would not know who was who. She was proud, she told me, to have nothing to do with the 'hairy Gitanos' (*Gitanos peludos*) – for 'hairy' read 'poor' – who lived in Middle Street: *she* did not want to know *them*. Shortly afterwards I noticed that Gitanos attended the literacy classes at the Social Assistance Centre in groups with their same-sex close kin. One of the social workers explained to me how difficult it was to organize schedules and lessons when people had to be taught alongside their aunts, sisters and mothers-in-law, and not alongside others with a comparable ability. The Gitanos, it seemed, had flatly rejected any other system: either they came with their relatives, or they would not come at all.

As I came to know the Gitanos of the neighbourhood, and came to be known by them, I began to feel constrained by their preference to restrict sociable interaction to their own kin. When I moved in with Tío Juan and Tía Tula, they warned me not to talk to the Gitanos of Middle Street. What was wrong with them remained vague. Tío Juan and Tía Tula said they would trick me and laugh at me – something that most Gitanos I already knew did anyway, including Tío Juan and his wife. So I paid little attention and begun to spend time with Manuela and her children, who lived in Middle Street. They in turn used much energy vilifying Tío Juan and his family: Tío Juan wanted

Figure 3.1 Two 'little hairy ones' (*peluditos*) during a visit to the river near Escalona (Toledo) organized for the Gitanos of Jarana by the social workers.

to take advantage of me, Manuela explained; I should never trust him. By then the daughters-in-law and granddaughters of Tía Tula and Tío Juan had begun to comment on my ungratefulness: I did not care for them, they had opened their houses to me, fed me, taken me selling in the streets of Madrid, and I neglected them. They acted coldly towards me, ignoring my greetings when I passed by, no longer inviting me in for a cup of coffee. The same happened when I met a family from the Lower Street: then it was Manuela and her children who complained of my ungratefulness and inconsistency.

I also soon realized how, although the Gitanos of Jarana spend much of their day in the street, chatting in small groups or taking a stroll, they invariably tend to do so with their kin. In the summer, groups of related men set up folding chairs and tables and play cards under the shade of a tree. On winter evenings, they build open fires by the entrance of their houses and discuss the events of the day. Men do not go to chat with unrelated men: instead, they join their patrilineal relatives and, with less frequency, their mothers' or their wives' kin. Women do the same, finding numerous excuses to pop into the houses of their sisters-in-law, cousins and sisters, to have a coffee together, or spend the siesta hours watching the daily soap opera before the children come back from school.[1]

Because of their role in the organization of political relations among Gitanos, kinship links work as an essential factor giving sociability in Jarana its fragmented character. As I explain at length in the third part of this book, groups of patrilineally related men, with their wives and children – which I call 'patrigroups' for reasons that I lay out in Chapter 7 – work as units or sources of mutual support in situations of conflict among unrelated Gitanos. These conflicts often lead to physical confrontations – injuries and sometimes deaths – and hence to blood feuds, which the Gitanos call *ruinas* or *quimeras*. The Gitanos believe that any quarrel, no matter how small, can easily lead to a feud: then whole patrigroups may have to flee to escape retaliation, leaving their houses and possessions behind. *Quimeras* are events that many of the Gitanos who live in Jarana have experienced and that all dread. Tía Tula, for example, told me how in her one recurring nightmare she dreams that her family is involved in a *quimera* and some of her children and grandchildren are murdered. In fact, only a few years before they were resettled in Jarana, one of her sons killed a Gitano who had insulted him while drunk, and narrowly escaped a lengthy jail sentence. The family of the dead man then retaliated and gravely wounded one of Tía Tula's grandsons, who was a small child at the time. The Gitanos stress that the main way of avoiding feuds is to fraternize only with kin because they are the people who, in the event of a quarrel or a fight, would not want to take revenge.

My friend Clara gave me a clear description of the workings of patrigroups. She explained how, because of the constant threat of *quimeras*, Gitanos want their 'families' (*familias*) – that is their patrigroups – to be 'strong' (*fuertes*) vis-à-vis others, to have at their disposal the fighting force of many men. The stronger a patrigroup is, the less they have to fear from other Gitanos, the more likelihood that they will be able to live undisturbed. In Jarana, it is the Foros who boast the largest number of grown men or *varas* (fighting sticks). This has enabled them to dictate the 'law' (*ley*) that no drugs are to be sold in the neighbourhood. Smaller patrigroups who would like to traffic 'from home' can do little in the face of the Foros' strength: were they to begin selling drugs in Jarana they would most certainly risk starting a full blown feud.

One of the consequences of the need for patrigroups to be 'strong' is the fact that Gitanos prefer young couples to live with the husband's parents after their marriage. Closely related men – particularly brothers, but also cousins, uncles and so on – can then draw on each other's support more easily than if they lived far apart. At the same time, and because networks of kin do extend outside Jarana into the rest of the city and beyond, the Gitanos work at keeping in regular contact with their close patrilineal relatives who, through choice or through Payo resettlements, may live further away. Take for example the patrigroup to which Clara belongs, and that in Jarana is headed by Tío Juan, the Foros: there are Foros in other neighbourhoods of Madrid as well as in Toledo and Avila, two cities in Castile. These Foros are patrilineal cousins and nephews of Tío Juan, and may come to Jarana if there is a wedding, a funeral or a *quimera*, to celebrate or mourn with their kin, or to fight alongside them.

Although the Gitanos put much less stress on matrilineal than on patrilineal links, the former may also be significant in shaping Gitano daily life. Firstly, the Gitanos who live in Jarana have used and continue to use marriages – which are most often arranged by parents – in order to create closely knit groups of people who are related in more than one way. Thus, they display a strong preference for marrying their relatives – both patrilateral and matrilateral – which means that a person's affines are frequently also their consanguines and that matrilineal kin are also patrilineally related. For example, four of Tío Juan and Tía Tula's seven children have married their first or second cousins. Secondly, even if an unrelated man and woman marry, so long as the wife's and the husband's families live close by, matrilateral relatives and more rarely affines may co-operate economically and be emotionally involved in each other's lives. In general, my experience of Jarana tells me that the Gitanos find it easy to point to a clearly defined group of people to whom they feel close and with whom they are at ease in day-to-day interaction: relatives of one type or another with whom they would be unlikely to feud.

Space, Kinship and the Construction of Identity

The Gitanos of Jarana make tangible this kinship-based segregation through their use of space. The neighbourhood consists of four rows of twenty terraced houses along three streets. The social workers in charge of the resettlement in 1989 decided to respect the Gitanos' wishes, and so patrilineally related men, together with their wives and children tend to occupy adjacent houses.[2] In Upper Street Tío Juan and his sons and grandsons with their wives and children – the Juanes, as they are called in the neighbourhood – occupy six contiguous houses. Another of his sons, Manuel, lives in Lower Street surrounded by his sons: one lives in the house adjacent to his, and two have built shacks – one in his father's yard, the other in the yard of his brother. Next to the Juanes in Upper Street live Tío Rufo – Tía Lola's husband – and Tío Ernesto, two brothers who refuse to speak to each other due to a long-standing disagreement but who nevertheless chose to be resettled together, next to their elderly father, who lives alone. Tío Rufo's son Francisco lives with his wife and five children in a shack in his father's yard, and his cousin Pedro, who is also married and has three daughters, lives in another shack in his father's yard. The pattern repeats itself throughout the neighbourhood. The Sebastianes, patrilineal descendants of a nephew of Tío Juan called Tío Sebas, who had died by the time I arrived in Jarana, occupy most of Lower Street: nine houses in a row. The Juanes and the Sebastianes share patrigroup affiliation: they are all Foros. Together they dominate most of Lower Street and a good chunk of Upper Street, leaving the rest of the neighbourhood to other smaller kin groups.

Patrigroups – patrilineally related men with their wives and children – assert their exclusive control over a section of the neighbourhood by demarcating as theirs the space – pavement and open field – immediately in front of their houses. Those Gitanos who earn their living as scrap collectors, for example, place their scrap metal on the pavement outside their houses, rather than inside their yards. Many Gitanos stretch lines for hanging clothes to dry between two trees in the same space. Households take care of, or neglect the trees and ornamental bushes that are planted outside their respective doors. Many have fenced off a section of the pavement: some Gitanos park their cars there; others have planted vegetables and herbs. Every Gitano in the neighbourhood is acutely aware of which area belongs to whom. When going shopping to Villaverde, for example, or to the Evangelical church, the Gitanos avoid walking past the houses of non-kin, even if that means making long detours. Unrelated next-door neighbours taking the sun by their doorsteps on a spring afternoon will not even acknowledge each other. And, similarly, children play with their siblings and cousins, rarely with non-kin, and always in the section of the neighbourhood where their relatives live.

There are also contrasts in observable wealth among different Gitano households, with a greater degree of uniformity to be found among kin. Some houses appear bare, lacking almost all furniture, and their inside walls – originally white – have turned dark grey from the smoke of coal fires. Others display co-ordinated sitting rooms with huge shiny curtains, freshly painted walls, flowery sofas, glass tables and enormous porcelain tigers or dogs. Ways of earning a livelihood play a key role in the generation of these differences and members of the same patrigroup often engage in the same trades and support each other economically. In Jarana, it is usually Gitanos who have official permits for street vending who rank highest in this consumption scale. Their position contrasts quite sharply with those who call for scrap or who sell illegally in the streets and are persecuted by the police who often take away their merchandise.

A combination of differences – to do with kinship or even religious affiliation, and with wealth – is reflected by a broad pattern of spatial distribution. In Upper and Lower Streets live mainly people who state that they belong to *casas buenas o de respeto* ('good or respectable houses'): independently of their economic status they picture themselves as being clean and honest, and as earning their living decently – that is, they state that they do not sell drugs. A large number are Evangelical converts and many are Foros. The majority have quite stable ways of earning their livelihood: they have municipal permits to sell in open markets or street corners and, until 1997, they were allowed to gather scrap from the municipal rubbish dump. On the other hand, fewer of the Gitanos who live in Middle Street are converts. They belong to families who are weaker numerically than those of the other streets and who particularly resent the Foros' strength: they are said to belong to *casas bajas* ('low houses'). Their modes of earning their livelihood are much more precarious overall and they live closer to subsistence levels. These differences within the neighbourhood are clearly visible almost at first sight. Middle Street seems to have been taken out of a textbook slum: the walls are covered in graffiti, the pavement has huge holes because slabs have been removed here and there, and the street lamps have been twisted out of their original shape. Upper and Lower Streets, by contrast, appear to the outside Payo observer to be clean and tidy and, perhaps because they overlook empty stretches of land, almost rural.[3]

The Problem of the Community

> The problem of the community is the limited power of the objectifications through which individuals reproduce their social life (Myers 1986: 260).

By dividing up the neighbourhood in the various ways I have described above and restricting sociability to kin, the inhabitants of Jarana alienate themselves from neighbouring but unrelated Gitanos. They assert their belonging to their kin and deny that cohesiveness with non-kin may be a path to shared identity: not wanting to spend time with unrelated Gitanos, preferring to stick to their own relatives, makes them more, rather than less, Gypsy. The Gitanos, they say, are a people who solve conflicts through feuds. Because a *quimera* may arise out of the most trivial of quarrels, and because its consequences can be so drastic, the Gitanos state that they would rather limit contact to those whom they love, or to Payos, neither of whom would be likely to retaliate. In fact, in Jarana the Gitanos often complain of having been resettled in a neighbourhood of overwhelmingly Gitano population: Payos, they say, make much better neighbours, both because they take better care of the communal spaces, and because they are unlikely to allow conflicts to escalate into feuds.[4]

From a non-Gypsy point of view, Gitano life appears to be ridden with contradictions. On the one hand, the Gitanos view themselves as a people, cut out from the Payos who envelop them. On the other hand, they are obviously preoccupied with enacting, reinforcing and objectifying the fact that they are an internally fragmented group, a group within which interaction is more likely to lead to conflict than to harmony. The Gitanos see themselves as much as Gitanos as they see themselves as, say, Foros or Escopeteros. From a Payo standpoint, it is easy to conceptualize the Gitano shared sense of self, the Gitano shared identity, as being at once a precondition for social life, a given, and something that has to be accomplished or achieved by somehow transcending fragmentation. The Gitanos, however, perceive no contradiction here because for them Gypsyness need not imply communion or cohesiveness.

By distancing themselves from their neighbours, while drawing upon relatives – who may live outside Jarana – for sociable purposes or for support, the Gitanos reject the Payo model of identity where place and sense of self are intertwined. They have ended up living in Jarana, they say, just as they might have ended up in Los Pitufos or El Ruedo – other 'special Gitano neighbourhoods' built by the State. They also reject taxonomies produced by the Administration and the social services – which categorize the Gitanos according to how 'permeable' they are thought to be to the world-views and lifestyle of the dominant majority – in favour of their own classifications. Most importantly, the Gitanos stress kinship affiliation, and the 'enmity' (*contrariedad*) between different kinship groups. The fact that these patrigroups are named, and that they tend towards endogamous marriage, means that it is easy for the Gitanos to conceptualize them as bounded units, distinct from others, which are seen as potential enemies.

An essential condition of a Gitano's claim to Gypsyness is then provided through his or her affiliation to a patrigroup. In this sense, the Gitanos seem not to be very different from other peoples among whom shared identity is transmitted through descent and mediated by a kinship group. However, it is of key importance to remember that it is relatively easy for a Gitano to give up the Gitano way of life and become, if not a Payo, then a *Gitano apayado* – a Payo-like Gitano who has adopted the non-Gypsy lifestyle. By the same token, Payos can earn for themselves a position among the Gitanos if they take up the Gitano way of life – a laborious but not impossible process. Being born a Gitano and a member of a particular patrigroup represents a potentiality for Gypsyness as much as – or more than – a realization of it. As in the description of Oceanic identities put forward by Linnekin and Poyer, among the Gitanos of Jarana 'how you behave (is) at least as important as biological parentage in determining who you are socially . . . people are not simply born into social groups but may – in fact, must – become members through their actions . . . identity is continually demonstrated, a matter of behaviour and per-formance' (1990a: 8). The parallels between this 'Lamarckian' model of identity and the Gitanos' ethnotheories are clear: the Gitanos of Jarana believe that being born a Gitano is not sufficient for the perpetuation of Gypsyness. Instead, Gypsyness needs to be performed in order to be: the inhabitants of Jarana view it above all as a way of life. Such things as 'the Gitanos' or 'the Gitano people' (*el pueblo Gitano)* exist because there are Gitanos who behave and live 'properly' (*como debe ser)* as Gitanos. This includes their behaviour in the face of conflict: feuding represents an objectification of Gypsyness in as much as it is the result of people behaving 'as Gitanos'. In other words, the Gitanos of Jarana root their shared sense of self on their con-ceptualization of the Gitano person as the performer of a morality that they portray as being endorsed by 'the Gitanos' in general – a category that obviously is not restricted to those who live in the neighbourhood.[5]

Thus, within the framework of relations among non-kin, Gypsyness implies adherence to the series of formalized, verbally transmitted moral norms that the Gitanos call *la ley Gitana* or 'the Gitano law'. These norms dictate the form that conflict between unrelated Gitanos should take – through retaliation, mediation by neutral elders and separation in space of the kin groups involved. Feuding makes Gypsyness real to the eyes of the Gitanos: *ruinas* help Gitanos see non-kin as people who, like one self and one's relatives, uphold the 'Gitano law', people who live as Gitanos. Conflicts thus facilitate the creation of an 'imagined community' just as they push Gitanos apart from each other. Moreover, the Gitanos view the *ley Gitana* as being not only prescriptive of how Gitanos should behave but as descriptive of how Gitanos do behave.

Simultaneously, as I describe at length in Chapter 8, the formalized norms that regulate conflict also dictate the behaviour that is expected of men *as Gitano men* across all contexts: they should be courageous but also judicious and discreet, fighting on behalf of their patrigroup but also accepting the mandates of the *hombres de respeto* ('men of respect') or conflict mediators. The *ley Gitana* also prescribes how Gitano women should behave: they should obey their men, be faithful to their husbands and, above all, remain virgins until marriage (I discuss this in detail in Part II). Both men and women should have *conocimiento* (understanding of which is the right attitude to take in each particular occasion) and display the right kind of *respeto* (respect: deference and obedience) towards others – qualities that non-Gypsies lack. It is thus at this level – the level of the person – that uniformity, affinity or correspondence among Gitanos enters into the Gitanos' understandings of themselves.

The Gitano concept of the person – which lies at the core of the Gitanos' views of themselves as a group – draws on two key understandings. Firstly, the Gitanos of Jarana stress links to others as constitutive of who persons are. Identities are interdependent and each person is thought to bear the worth of 'the Gitanos' as a whole: there is a metonymic link between each Gitano and 'the Gitano people'. Secondly, Gitano persons are always gendered: the body is seen to impose an identity that cannot be bypassed and that is rooted in the man/woman (*hombre/mujer*) dichotomy. Having different bodies, however, is not the only thing that makes women different from men: women are thought to be more evil and to have less capacity for 'knowing' (*conocimiento*), as well as deserving less 'respect' (*respeto*) from others than men. Because men and women are different kinds of people, they enact the righteousness of 'the Gitanos' in different ways: I discuss their gender-specific performances throughout Parts II and III of this book. The ideal of the group – a fragmented, conflictive group – is thus premised on the ideal of the person – a gendered person. Lastly, the Payo way of life, particularly the Payo 'styles' of being a man or a woman, are constantly put forward by the Gitanos as the opposite of the righteousness that characterizes the Gitano way of life, as the epitomes of all that is evil and wrong.

Identity Created in the Present and the Question of the Past

If the Gitanos put so much emphasis on creating Gypsyness in the present, what then of their past? As I have explained briefly in Chapter 1, the Gitanos produce only highly schematic and comparatively underdeveloped accounts of their past as a group. They make a clear distinction between 'the Gitanos of before' (*los Gitanos de antes*) and themselves, the Gitanos of 'now' (*ahora*). 'Before' the Gitanos lived in the countryside and were nomadic: they were 'always on the roads' (*siempre por los caminos*). They stole from the Payos and suffered at the hands of the *Guardia Civil*. Lastly, they were poor and had a difficult existence. In Jarana all Gitanos know that this is what life was like 'before' – and they know no more. This is what I was told, by men and women, young and old alike, when they learned that I was interested in 'the history of the Gitanos'. Ministers at the local Evangelical church also made reference to this succinct, stereotyped version of the past when they wanted to emphasize how much more modern and sophisticated the 'Gitanos of now' – particularly themselves – are by comparison with their ancestors.

These descriptions – where 'the Gitanos' appear as an undifferentiated category or a homogenous group of people – contrast with the Gitanos' accounts of their own personal pasts. Firstly, as I explained in Chapter 2, not all Gitanos were nomadic before they moved to the cities: in fact, according to Payo records, the process of sedentarization of the Gitanos begun almost as soon as they appeared in the Peninsula in the fifteenth century (Sánchez Ortega 1986; San Román 1994: 35). This means that, in many cases, personal remembrances are quite different from the Gitanos' portrayal of what the past of 'the Gitanos' as a people was like. Although some of these recollections include themes that also appear in accounts of 'the life of before', this is not necessarily the case.

Secondly, remembrances tend to take the form of personalized anecdotes and to receive some elaboration. Women talk about their weddings, about giving birth or about bringing up their children without their husbands' help; men describe their successes in tricking the *Guardia Civil* or their affairs with Payo women. Even these more detailed narratives remain rare and, above all, brief: throughout my time in Jarana I was constantly struck by how irrelevant their own pasts seemed to the Gitanos. Take the example of Tío Juan, who at the time of my fieldwork was in his late seventies. He had been a famous *tratante* or horse dealer in his youth, and continued earning his living by buying and selling horses well into the late 1960s. From a Payo point of view it is as if his life as *tratante* had never taken place. He keeps no photos of himself with horses, and no mementoes, and he extremely rarely talks about his experiences. All in all, he displays no fondness or nostalgia for a trade that brought him prestige and shaped his way of life for thirty years.

Not only are the Gitanos of Jarana uninterested in looking back into their own lives. They are also extremely reluctant to talk of loved relatives or companions who are now deceased – particularly if they feel themselves to have been *allegados* (emotionally close) to them. They are overcome with sadness and may cry openly when they remember the dead – even those who died decades before – and they seem determined to erase any of their traces from everyday life. After people die, their names are no longer spoken aloud and they are referred to obliquely if at all, through kinship terms. Similarly, the belongings of a deceased Gitano are burned or thrown away, the room where they died locked, and their photographs hidden. This does not mean, however, that dead relatives are forgotten. On the contrary, it is precisely because they are so very vividly remembered that anything that could trigger such overwhelmingly sad recollections has to be carefully curtailed or monitored. When I went to live with Sara and Paco, four years after his mother died, the room where she had passed away was still locked: nobody had entered it since her body had been taken out of the house. Once I moved in, and perhaps because the addition of an extra household member made it necessary, Sara decided to use the room again. Together, and while Paco was away at work, we took the dead woman's bed to the rubbish dump. Then we whitewashed the walls, and Sara brought in new furniture and hung new curtains. Her intention, she said, was to transform the room as much as possible, so that Paco would not feel sad when he passed by it. In fact, I never saw Paco enter the room where his mother had died, or mention her at all – either directly or indirectly. Sara on her part refrained from talking about her mother-in-law in her husband's presence, and only rarely mentioned her when he was not around.

This way of dealing with the dead means that they are indeed remembered, but only by the few who actually knew and loved them.[6] Distant relatives and acquaintances will refrain from alluding to the deceased relatives of somebody else 'out of respect' (*por respeto*).

Grandchildren or great-grandchildren who are born after their grand-parents' death will know next to nothing about their deceased ancestors – their names and little else, sometimes not even that. The genealogical memory of the Gitanos of Jarana is thus extremely shallow, going back no more than three or at most four generations. People know that they are related, but often not the exact nature of the kinship tie that links them. In Jarana, the grandchildren of the deceased Tío Sebas – many of them men and women in their twenties and thirties – are well aware of the fact that he shared patrigroup affiliation with Tío Juan, but do not know what the relationship between the two men was.

Williams has described very similar practices among the Manouches, nomadic French Gypsies who similarly avoid mentioning the dead and dispose of their possessions. He emphasizes that this attitude towards the dead is intimately related to the Manouches' particular way of imagining themselves as a group. Thus, placing the dead among the living in the Gypsies' particular way

> leads to the setting-up of an amnesiac community composed of indiv-iduals endowed with memory. It is necessary to realise that commemora-tion, such as it is organised, leads to the preservation of the more intimate remembrances and does not elicit the creating of a communal memory, a saga-memory, an epic-memory, a memory of the group as group. There is no other support of memory and of the knowledge of self as a group than exchanges with others (1993a: 13).

The Gitano 'life of before' – as a kind of embryonic or abortive com-munal memory – is, as I have explained, clearly separated from the Gitanos' personal pasts and from their recollections of the *difuntos allegados*, the beloved deceased. It refers to an unspecified 'a long time ago', a time separated from the present and, most importantly, *irrele-vant* to it. The 'life of before' is not a developmental period, it does not include events: it is a description of a way of life, permanent and unchanging, rather than of a progression through time. It includes no origin stories, no accounts of how the Gitanos came to be what they are. After the permanence of 'before' comes discontinuity in the form of 'now', a time when the Gitanos live in the cities, are settled and convert to Evangelism. The intervening period between 'before' and 'now' is simply not discussed: it is the realm of the beloved deceased.

In the 'before', fragmentations among Gitanos are obliterated: 'the Gitanos of before' are an undifferentiated unit, neither one kinship group nor another; they are anonymous, belonging to nobody in particular. The very fact that the 'life of before' is very rarely brought to the forefront in everyday life makes it clear that present divisions among Gitanos are not impediments to the production of a Gitano shared sense of self. The Gitanos do not find it necessary to emphasize unity either in the present or in the past. In other words, uniformity in the 'before' does not transcend fragmentation in the 'now'. Simultaneously, by purposefully disconnecting the past from the present, the Gitanos of Jarana make of Gypsyness something that has to be continually brought about or performed in the 'now'.[7] Differences between Gitanos and Payos existed in the 'before' but they offer no legitimating model of the present. The 'life of before' is not a generative period: it provides no blueprint for the 'now'. The 'before' does not necessitate the 'now' and the 'now' does not necessitate the 'before'.

The Gitanos' disregard for the past as a source of shared identity extends itself to their treatment of the physical world around them. Just as they do not locate the roots of their singularity in a generative past, the Gitanos do not encode Gypsyness in any elements of permanent material culture. They have no sculpture, no painting, no architecture of their own, and they make small investment in durable valuables. Objects have short lives among the Gitanos: all through fieldwork I was struck by the facility with which things were broken or lost. Thus, whereas the Payo ethos revolves to a large extent around the production and accumulation of durables, the Gitanos focus on the exchange, fast consumption and rejection of goods that are produced by others. These goods tend to be treated as non-durable and are rapidly discarded. In a similar vein, the Gitanos of Jarana do not use the transmission of property to mark social events: they lack marital or funerary transactions and do not use material compensation in settling disputes. In the absence of any external, material embodiments of shared identity, the gaze of the observer is forced onto the person and its actions.

The Evangelical Church

The model of sociability and of communal identity that I have outlined above competes in Jarana with a new, incipient model that stems from the spread of Evangelism among the Gitanos of the neighbourhood. Alongside the growth of the Gitano Evangelical Church it is easy to identify the development of an alternative way of conceiving 'the Gitanos' as a group, which in turn depends on new institutional supports, new ways of organizing social relations.

The Gitano Evangelical Church – *Iglesia Evangélica de Filadelfia* – is part of a wider Western European Gypsy Evangelical movement. In the early 1960s French Gypsy missionaries – themselves the product of a Evangelical mission campaign carried out by a non-Gypsy in the 1950s – came down to the Peninsula to preach 'the word of God' to the Gitanos (Williams 1991; Jordán Pemán 1990; Cano 1981). The Spanish Gitano Evangelical movement begun to grow, was recognized by the State in 1969, and has experienced its greatest development during the late 1980s and 1990s (Jordán Pemán 1990: 10).[8] Currently there are no data as to the number of Gitano converts – who call themselves *Cristianos* (Christians) or *Aleluyas* – but my experience is that there is a church in practically every area where Gitanos live. In Jarana approximately a quarter of the adult Gitanos consider themselves converted and Evangelism, in one form or another, is part of the daily life of the vast majority of the inhabitants of the neighbourhood.[9]

The *Iglesia Evangélica de Filadelfia*[10] is premised on an ideal of both transformation and continuity with what, in the eyes of the Gitanos, being Gitano means – that is, the 'Gitano way of being' (*la manera de ser Gitana*). Converts stress that not only does one continue being a Gitano once one becomes an *Aleluya:* one becomes a 'better Gitano' (*mejor Gitano*). During services ministers preach the rejection of those aspects of the Gitano lifestyle that do not conform to the Evangelical ideal of love and forgiveness, while simultaneously encouraging converts to act according to the Gitano ideal of 'knowledge' (*conocimiento*) and 'respect' (*respeto*). Central to their reformulation of Gypsyness is a rejection of feuding as a method for solving conflicts. As I explain at length in Chapter 8, *Aleluyas* pride themselves in dealing with confrontations through dialogue and forgiveness, rather than through revenge. They readily provide stories about men forgiving the killers of their fathers, sons or brothers after converting to Evangelism, or about life-long enemies embracing after accidentally meeting at a service.

Once retaliation becomes less of a threat, avoidance of non-kin also becomes less necessary. Or, from a rather different perspective, once avoidance of non-kin is no longer possible – as in Jarana – the threat of retaliation has to diminish: new forms of social relations are needed and the Church provides an institutional framework within which they can develop. Thus, *Aleluyas* come together at services and prayer meetings either at the local church or at each other's houses. They also organize theatre plays and song contests that need the collaboration of non-kin. A few times every year the converts of Jarana join several hundreds of other *Aleluyas* in religious assemblies called *convenciones*. In the course of their daily lives, those converts who are most active within the Church – ministers and their immediate families particularly – often build up close relations with convert non-kin and in the process transcend kinship affiliations. Friendships among such unrelated converts develop regularly, but especially among men – who are more mobile than women because they do not need to take care of the children or the house. They meet up to pray, visit other churches, or socialize and drink coffee together at the church's bar. However, the idiom of relatedness remains fundamental when contesting the construction of interest groups on the basis of religious affiliation. Even within the Church, cliques are most often organized around kinship ties: in Jarana, converts and non-converts alike frequently remark how it is the Escopeteros who dominate the affairs of the local church, because most of the ministers and trainees belong to that patrigroup. During services, converts sit next to their relations. Some patrigroups have larger numbers of convert members than others, and have come to be seen by other Gitanos as 'Christian families' (*familias cristianas*).

As well as developing new types of social relations, Evangelical Gitanos have also constructed a novel version of the past of 'the Gitanos' as a people. They claim that the Gitanos are in fact Jews who got lost during Moses' forty years of wandering through the Sinai desert. As Jews, the Gitanos are a chosen people who now – through their conversion to Evangelism – are about to fulfil God's plan for humanity. The evangelization of non-convert Gitanos is therefore voiced as a primary concern. The separation of Payos and Gitanos is reformulated once the religious difference is emphasized: it becomes a religious divide and not merely a moral divide. Although the Gitanos acknowledge the existence and indeed the importance of Payo Evangelism, they strongly emphasize that Gitano Evangelism is the most faithful to the spirit of the early Church. Gitano missionaries target only Gitano communities, and only Gitanos participate in activities related to the *Iglesia de Filadelfia*. Evangelism thus becomes another way of constructing and thinking about the separation between Payos and Gitanos, and converts continue to portray Payos in essentially negative terms.

The version of the past that converts put forward is not only biblical and prophetic, but also developmental and generative: the Bible, together with a series of accounts of the birth and spread of the Church of Filadelfia, have become the history of the Gitanos. And, in contrast to non-converts, for *Aleluyas* the past does include a blueprint for the present.[11] Thus, fragmentation among Gitanos in the 'now' are downplayed in favour of an ideal of the group as a 'community' – in the sense not only of 'commonness' but also of 'communion'. This does not mean, however, that Gypsyness does not need to be performed or enacted in the 'now': salvation in the eyes of the Gitanos comes firstly through conversion and secondly through a changed way of life. The person thus remains at the centre of the *Aleluyas'* views of the Gitanos as a people. The Gypsyness that Gitano persons have to perform, however, is an Evangelical Gypsyness.

In practice, it is difficult to pin down to what extent this Evangelical view of 'the Gitanos' is displacing or replacing the non-Evangelical perceptions. The picture is certainly a complex one, and results from the uneven spread and short history of Gitano Evangelism in Spain. In Jarana, the Evangelists are first or second generation converts, and *Aleluyas* always have close relatives who have not converted and who demand of them the kind of support that Gitanos usually expect of kin. Moreover, it happens often that converts stop attending services at the local church for a significant period or give up altogether so that their identity as such fluctuates and comes into question. Tío Sebas's family exemplifies these various patterns. He converted to Evangelism a few years before his death in 1990. Of his six sons only the third one, Bastián, had converted before his father's death: he went on to become a well-known minister. On his death bed, Tío Sebas asked the others to promise that they would convert. Only Mancha and Paco were baptized and have remained converts. Pepe and Pija, both drug addicts, have not converted. Pedro attends the local church intermittently.

A similar lack of uniformity is visible in the explanations Gitanos give for their behaviour – explanations that tend to refer to the moral superiority of Gitanos over Payos. At times, Evangelists describe their actions as being proper to *Aleluyas* and specifically set themselves apart from the non-converts; at other times they describe their behaviour as being simply 'Gitano'. Evangelical stereotypes answer, contest or reinforce non-Evangelical ones, and are never completely detached from them. It is therefore clearly not adequate to suggest a dichotomous picture of 'before' and 'after' Evangelism. Evangelism has come into play as yet another medium through which to define personal and communal identities within a framework of rapid social change and of great pressures for acculturation or assimilation. And, because of the intersection of kin-based and religious interests, the 'groups' to which these 'communal' identities refer are not fixed but have a fluid, circumstantial composition.

Conclusions

The pattern that sociable relations take among the Gitanos of Jarana is intimately related to their particular understanding of themselves as a group vis-à-vis the non-Gypsies. Social harmony or cohesiveness are not necessary to the Gitano self-conception. Instead, the Gitanos think of Gypsyness as a community made of people who share the same stance vis-à-vis the surrounding world, who are aware of each other as moral beings – a community in the sense of 'commonness', not of 'communion'. The person lies at the core of these understandings as the performer of the proper Gitano morality and thus the creator of the difference between Gitanos and Payos in the present.[12] The past is downplayed in Gitano world-views: the 'before' is disconnected from and made irrelevant to the present; it provides no blueprint for the 'now'. At the same time, Evangelical Gitanos are beginning to propose an alternative – and as yet incipient – mode of constructing and understanding the group. To them, community should imply communality, cohesiveness and harmony. Correspondingly, they have developed an account of the past that encompasses a plan for the present: in their narratives, the Gitanos appear as God's chosen people. And yet the gendered person, as the performer of the Gitano-Evangelical morality, remains central to their understandings. The rest of this book provides a detailed, layered description of how the Gitanos – converts and non-converts – enact and hence bring Gypsyness into being across different contexts within their daily lives.

Notes

1. Because of the Gitanos' preference for virilocality, married women often turn to their female affines.

2. See Williams (1982: 331) for a description of similar settlement patterns among urban Rom Kalderash in the suburbs of Paris, and Gmelch (1977: 91) for similar practices among Irish Tinkers in Dublin.

3. It is widely acknowledged that significant differences exist within the Gitano population, and that such differences have become more rather than less marked since the Gitanos moved from the rural to the urban areas in the 1950s and 1960s. These differences contribute to the centrifugal forces that I have described in the main text. Thus, authors writing about the Gitanos in the 1990s divide them into four main groups, according to the characteristics of their relationship with the non-Gypsies, their modes of earning a livelihood and their type of housing (de Pablo Velasco 1994: 4–5; García et al. 1996: 78–80; Rincón Atienza 1994: 4–6). These writers identify a first and least numerous group, which they describe as the 'élite within the Gitano minority': young men and women with a high educational level; from families that are 'integrated' socially and/or economically within the dominant population; who often militate in Gitano associations; and who tend to marry non-Gitanos. Secondly, an also small group who 'lives as Gitano' – keeping Gitano traditions and way of life – and who engages in the most profitable of the 'traditional' Gitano occupations: they are mostly flamenco artists or antique dealers. Neither of these two groups is represented among the Gitanos of Jarana or of Villaverde itself, and I have never met any of them. The largest sector of the Gitano population is 'a group in the midst of a strong process of change'. These are Gitanos living in marginal areas, such as Villaverde, in low-quality council housing and often among the non-Gypsies. Because their modes of earning a livelihood have come under very serious threat over the last few years, these Gitanos live 'precariously', and very often draw on State subsidies. On the other hand, their children attend school with growing regularity. Lastly, these authors have identified what they refer to as 'an unstructured and marginal group', second in number to the one above. These Gitanos live in the most deprived areas, often segregated from the rest of the population – in shanty-towns or 'special Gitano neighbourhoods' built by the State. They live 'day by day': they are unlicensed scrap collectors and street vendors, beggars and small-scale drug dealers, with a very strong dependency on State subsidies. They are seen as 'difficult' or 'problematic' by other Gitanos who say that they fail to follow the moral norms dictated by the 'Gitano law'. Their educational levels are very low and their children attend school only rarely. Although they are sedentary, they have no attachments to particular geographical areas and move regularly. The Gitanos who live in Villaverde belong to these last two groups. Most are very poor, living closer to subsistence levels than their Payo neighbours. They engage in marginal occupations: some are licensed vendors or scrap collectors; others sell without licenses, beg, or engage in drug dealing. Some live in a 'special Gitano neighbourhood', Jarana, isolated physically from the rest of the city – these were considered by the social services to be the most reluctant to become 'integrated' with the dominant population. Others live in blocks of flats among the non-Gypsies.

4. Both the GIEMS team in 1976 and San Román in 1990 have noted that Gitanos prefer to live dispersed among the Payos.

5. Linnekin and Poyer emphasize how at the roots of different theories of identity 'are epistemological differences about what constitutes a person' as well as distinctive 'theories of ontogeny', so that '(a)n understanding of community identity must take into account cultural philosophies of person-hood' (1990a: 6). Parts II and III of this book constitute an exploration of Gitano personhood and how it is constructed, layer by layer, across different contexts of everyday life.

6. Bloch and Parry point to the 'relationship between concepts of time and death' (1982: 10). Also, discussing funerary practices they emphasize that the 'social order is a *product* of rituals of the kind we consider rather than their cause' (Bloch and Parry: 6). The purposeful forgetting of the dead can be seen as instrumental in the Gitanos' creation of Gypsyness as a way of life that relies on the present.

7. Discussing the Vezo of Madagascar, Astuti explains how 'Vezo-ness is experienced contextually as an activity, rather than inherently as a state of being: people "are" Vezo when they perform Vezo-ness. Vezo-ness is an identity that binds people to the present . . . The past, by contrast, does not determine what a person "is" at any point in time. The past does not turn into "history" – a chain of events that explains how the present has come to be what it is – for it is constantly shed as people move from one context to the next, from one moment to the next' (1995: 153).

8. The reader will no doubt call to mind the expansion of Pentecostalism among the poor of Catholic countries, particularly in Latin America. Although the parallels with Gitano Pentecostalism are many – particularly regarding ritual and belief – I believe that, to a large extent, the Gitanos are in a category of their own. Latin American Pentecostalism has been described as an 'onslaught on the traditions of popular culture evolved in dialectic with the hegemonic culture of Catholicism' (Lehmann 1996: 192). It grows out of such popular culture and turns against it. Gitano Pentecostalism cannot be reduced to just that: it stands at the cross-roads of popular culture, Catholicism, and Gitano/Payo relations. Gitano Pentecostalism rephrases, not only the boundary between Gitanos and Payos, but the meaning of Gypsyness itself – a category that itself already stands in opposition to the dominant popular culture that, in the Spanish context, is clearly in a dialectic relationship with Catholicism.

9. The practices and beliefs of non-converts do not adhere to any formalized religion. Their relations with the Catholic Church are non-existent or very tenuous.

10. The name *Iglesia de Filadelfia* is borrowed from the Apocalypse (3: 7–13).

11. Although Evangelical Gitanos are creating a new social memory and new patterns of sociability – and hence, arguably, are in the process of develop-ing a new way of constructing sociality – their ways of dealing with the dead have not changed. This is an aspect of Gitano Evangelism that needs further exploration.

12. Discussing the Kalderash of Paris Williams explains how

for those who belong to it ... any community [any localized group of Kalderash] is capable of representing the totality of the Rom universe, culture and society ... [T]hese people 'carry their centre with them'. The authenticity of the Rom is never beyond the community that they form in the here and now, not in space nor in time ... To have the feeling of realizing the plenitude the Rom ... need only show themselves that they are capable of building and maintaining a different life and a different society within the interior of non-Gypsy life and non-Gypsy society (1982: 341).

However, by contrast to the Gitano case, Williams emphasizes the Rom's need to construct unity and uniformity among themselves, for example through communal celebrations (1982: 335–6).

Part II

The Performance of Morality: Dual Moral Standards

The Gitanos of Jarana often talk about how the 'true' (*verdadero*) Gitano life-style is in danger of becoming extinct – and how this is so because of their own failures to adhere to the proper Gitano morality. During my stay in Jarana I often heard Victoria, one of the oldest women in the neighbourhood, complain about the wickedness and lack of chastity of the young girls of the district. On summer evenings, when the Gitanos would take small folding chairs to sit outside in the street and play cards or make small talk, she would tell me which girls were seeing young men without the consent of their parents and which married women had had affairs behind their husbands' backs. And yet, unlike other widows, Victoria always wore colourful dresses instead of plain black. Besides, she never failed to wink her only eye at Tío Juan when she passed by him. So the Gitano men and women of the district described her as the perfect example of the immorality of which she talked to me: to them, she behaved more like a Paya than like a Gitana.

In Jarana, the Gitanos see the 'Gitano way of being' (*la manera de ser Gitana*) as being in constant danger of being swallowed up by the lifestyle of the Payos whom they despise. They believe that, in order to ensure the continuity of 'the Gitanos' or 'the Gitano people' (*el pueblo Gitano*) each individual has to make sure that they conduct every aspect of their daily lives as Gitanos. And what, as an anthropologist, I would call understandings to do with 'gender' occupy a particularly prominent role in their representations. The Gitanos distinguish themselves from the Payos because Gitano women behave modestly, as good, decent women should do, and because Gitano men are generous, righteous, and courageous, as good men should be. The extent to which, among the Gitanos of Jarana, gendered and communal identities and moralities mutually shape each other is well expressed by Devereux's description of Zinacantan where 'gender membership and ethnic membership [are] inextricable' and 'all social signs of gender are ethnically marked' (1987: 99).[1]

Thus, ideas about what men and women are and should be like are central to the Gitanos' picture of themselves and the Payos as two deeply different 'kinds of people' (*clases de gente*). In this context, the awareness of difference is not value-free: the standards are set by the Gitano styles of being a woman and being a man, and the Payos receive very negative appraisals. The following statement by a woman from Jarana exemplifies this point:

> According to the Payo custom women do not marry virgin. What is worse: they are often pregnant when they marry, and nonetheless dress in white for their weddings . . . The only thing Payas want to do is go out with their (male and female) friends, and they leave the children and husbands behind, on their own, lying around, they leave to have fun. The Payo men wash, scrub, iron clothes, they do all the household work themselves! The Payas love to go to discos, and have their bottoms touched by men. A Paya may have up to eight men in a night.

My aim in this second part of the book is to explain how Gitano discourses and practices to do with the management of sexual desire, which occupy a prominent role in Gitano daily life, reflect a key preoccupation with their relationship to the Payos. The boundary between Gypsies and non-Gypsies, as Okely (1983), Sutherland (1977) and Stewart (1997) have underlined for English Travellers and American and Hungarian Rom, is phrased in moral terms. Sexual morality – which permeates the Gitanos' talk on sexual practice and bodily difference – is not only central to personal identity and status, but to the identity and status of the Gitanos as a whole: the two are seen as interdependent. The framework to the practices and discourses which I describe in the three next chapters, as well as in Part III, is provided by the constant engagement of the Gitanos with their identity as such, by their emphasis on marking themselves off from the Payos. Most importantly, the Gitanos' evaluations of persons and of 'the Gitanos' more widely intertwine with a dual moral standard which is based on a perception of men and women as being different kinds of persons. The result is that men and women can be seen to have different 'ranges of efficacy' (Strathern 1988: 93) or ways of affecting the 'imagined community' through their sexual behaviour.

At the centre of Gitano ideas about sexual desire is a preoccupation with female virginity that permeates all aspects of daily life. Similar emphasis on female virginity is found in other areas bordering the Mediterranean, and has often been interpreted by anthropologists as concern with the control of the reproductive power of women (du Boulay 1986; Friedl 1962). In her discussion of urban Naples, Goddard (1987) has put forward the view that, in stratified societies such as those in southern Europe where marriage is central to the construction of hierarchy, women act both as markers and as bearers of the group's deeper identity. Through their reproductive roles women are 'valued most as mothers, carers and guardians' (1987: 185), and are associated with those values, based on generalized reciprocity, through which groups within a single society construct themselves as units. Her argument is consistent with Mary Douglas' (1966) idea that in societies where boundaries are perceived to be important and endangered there is often a special concern with the control of female sexuality: group membership is inherited and it is women's role to maintain its purity – while also having the power to defile it.

Fertility and reproduction are strikingly absent from the Gitanos' talk on sexual difference and sexual intercourse, and what we see instead is a clear stress on the adequate performance of a gendered morality that focuses on the control of sexual desire. In the Gitano case it is the ongoing, continuous enactment of *gitaneidad* or Gypsyness that is perceived to be at stake: a concern with the biological purity of the community is absent from the Gitanos' understandings. Through the enactment of proper Gitano morality Payo individuals can earn for themselves a place among the Gitanos and their origins can come to be downplayed rather than stressed. Thus, after spending a year in Jarana, I was surprised to learn that one of the women who played a most prominent role in the activities of the local Gitano Evangelical church was a Paya who had married a Gitano man in her teens. There was nothing in her physical appearance, manner or way of speaking, or in the way in which the Gitanos treated her, to reveal that she had not been born Gitana. Throughout my fieldwork I met two other Payo women and one Payo man who had married Gitanos and who lived as such. The man had earned the respect of the Gitanos of the district by wearing mourning for his father-in-law like a Gitano would do – black clothes, black scarf around his neck, grown beard. The women behaved modestly, and treated their mothers-in-law with particular deference. All had educated their children as Gitanos and had well-established positions among their affines, so that I seldom heard any reference to their origins except in the form of praise for the enthusiasm with which they had embraced the Gitano way of life. Similarly, the Gitanos viewed me as a liminal person, somebody who displayed the potential for becoming decent and moral. It was often made plain to me that, if I was going to spend time with the Gitanos of the district, I had to behave as a Gitana would do. I was taught to dress, sit, and generally behave 'properly' (*como deber ser*). And when, two years after my fieldwork I returned to the neighbourhood and announced to Tía Tula that I had married in a registry office in England, and that no member of my family had been present, she hugged me, slapped me fondly in the cheek and exclaimed: 'Eloped! Palomi has eloped!' (¡escapaíta! ¡S'a escapao la Palomi!). Although she was perfectly aware that among the Payos there are no elopements as the Gitanos understand them, she chose to give a Gitano meaning to actions that had taken place among Payos thousands of kilometres away.

Lastly, I want to make a point regarding the continuous growth of the Evangelical Church, and its very tangible influence upon the lives of the Gitanos of the neighbourhood. When considering Gitano constructions of personhood and community it is necessary to distinguish not only between Gitano and non-Gitano models of gender, but between convert and non-convert understandings of Gitano masculinity and femininity. Convert Gitanos act as *bricoleurs*, taking up some elements of the non-Evangelical Gitano morality, transforming them and also adding new, Evangelical ones.[2] The relationship between Evangelical and non-Evangelical masculinities and femininities is therefore a matter of competition and mutual constitution. The two models oppose each other only in some areas, and it is often impossible to identify where the convert one ends and the non-convert one starts.

Notes

1. I discuss whether the terms 'ethnic' and 'ethnicity' are useful to describe Gitano theories of identity in the Conclusion.

2. See Stewart (1997: 20) and Okely (1983: 77) for similar descriptions of Gypsies as *bricoleurs*.

Desire, Control and Dual Moral Standards

In December 1993, a few months after I left Jarana, I received a letter from one of my Gitano friends. She asked for my advice regarding a very delicate situation – one that, if mismanaged, could easily lead to a full-blown feud and to the death of several people. My friend was overwhelmed with responsibility, and the letter was dirty where tears had made the ink run:

> My dear and friend Palomi. You will ask yourself why my letter is so early and yours has not arrived yet but I write to you this letter because I have a big problem and there is nobody that I can trust because people could find out and this could reach the ears of my grandfather. Don't tell anybody for the world's sake because otherwise it will be discovered. I am writing to you about my cousin Lola the one who is still single and it is because I have been told that she sees our cousin Pepe the husband of María on her own and I don't know what to do because if I tell her mother she won't believe me and I don't dare telling my other cousin Estrella because she is very impulsive and I think she might spoil everything. Because we have not caught them together yet and we have no proof although I saw them once but I fear that if somebody else doesn't see them I will be left as a liar because Lola told me once before that if somebody caught them they would deny everything. No matter what people asked them they would lie. And I believe they have fallen in love because this is not new and although they tried to break up when I saw them they have not been able to do it and they are seeing each other again. And the person who told me that they are together again has made me promise that I won't tell her name and I don't know what to do because I think of my grandfather how upset he will be and I am going mad: what if I don't say anything and then they elope? I would feel the guilt my whole life. Palomi this is very difficult for me so please help me to find out what to do because if they eloped it might be that there would even be a fight with María's family because she has two children and a Gitano woman cannot be abandoned like that. And

on the other hand perhaps they don't want to elope and they do it only to have fun because they fancy each other because my cousin is very lively. She doesn't care about anything, absolutely anything. I have this doubt. My friend what would you do in my place? Forgive me if some of my words have disturbed you but I have only one close friend and that is you. My cousin Estrella is very clever and if I don't have proof she will say I am a liar and I don't know how my husband would react perhaps he would beat Pepe up and would help me to uncover them.

In Jarana, the Gitanos talk of sexual desire as a central component of male and female personhood, a fact of life that men and women, Payos and Gitanos, have to confront constantly. The extent to which individuals are seen to be successful in controlling their desire is fundamental to the evaluations they receive from other Gitanos. These evaluations become idealized when they are extended to construct portrayals of Payos and Gitanos as two different 'kinds of people'. Thus, central to the Gitanos' perception of themselves as a group vis-à-vis the Payos is the idea that, whereas most Gitanos manage to dominate their sexual drives at least to a minimum degree, Payos – and particularly Payo women – fail *en masse*. By implication, a heavy sexual moral burden is placed on Gitano women: they are given the bulk of responsibility to demonstrate the sexual decency of 'the Gitanos' as a whole.

The extent to which the Gitanos of Jarana are concerned with the regulation of sexual desire within the context of daily life is made clear in the pages that follow. Interactions among kin, the ways Gitanos dress and move, and rules about the management of desire during courtship, all connive to construct sexual intercourse as both desirable and morally ambiguous. This tension is recognized by the Gitanos themselves in speech and action, and is also elaborated upon through physical appearance and manner. In the absence of external media through which to objectify their identity – such as a shared territory, a communal memory or an elaborated material culture – the Gitanos turn to the only thing they really possess: their own persons, that is, their bodies and their behaviour. The management of sexual desire – the idea that the Gitanos are different from the Payos because of their sexual propriety – then becomes a key element in the construction of an imagined community.

However, as my friend's letter reveals, the Gitanos are well aware of the very tangible difficulties implicit in adhering to the standards that Gitano morality sets. Gitano daily life revolves around the ever-present conflict between the way the Gitanos want things to be, and the way things really are. As Stewart describes in relation to the Hungarian Rom, Gypsies not only have to establish a separation between themselves and non-Gypsies but the boundary is a permeable one and 'policing' it is also a central part of the Gypsies' cultural activity (1997: 234). 'Policing' the boundary is important not only because of the need to keep the Gitanos distinct from the Payos, but because it enables the creation of hierarchical relationships within a social context that is strongly egalitarian:[1] if transgressions of the rules become known, they can seriously affect the reputation of the people involved – and hence their ability to influence the course of their own lives and the lives of others. In Jarana this often leads to familial conflicts of the kind my friend above hints at in her letter and, somewhat more rarely, to *quimeras* and deaths. Because so much is at stake, Gitano sociability is made up of layers of knowledge and exclusion from knowledge. Thus, although my friend did tell Estrella about her doubts, and although Pepe's wife and his mother confronted Estrella and Lola accusing them of wanting to spoil Pepe's reputation, the rest of the family – including Lola's father and grandfather – never found out what had happened. Lola was able to marry another man three years later.

In this chapter I provide an ethnographic context for this kind of event. My aim is to lay bare the links between Gitano personhood, Gitano understandings to do with sexual pleasure and desire, and Gitano constructions of a shared Gitano identity. I thus discuss Gitano ideas about femininity and masculinity, about agency and about control.

Personhood, Sex, and Gender

The Gitanos of Jarana think of persons as gendered/sexed: as either *mujeres* (women) or *hombres* (men). In their understandings the distinction between women and men is portrayed as given, fixed and unquestionable, and it is linked to the genital endowment of individuals: *mujeres* are the ones with *chochos* (female genitalia, including vagina, labia and pelvic area), and *hombres* are the ones with *pijas* (penises).[2] This difference, however, is not simply a result of men's and women's bodies: men and women alike stress that 'women are more evil' (*las mujeres son más malas*) and have less capacity for *conocimiento* (knowledge or understanding), and hence deserve less *respeto* (respect; involving deference and obedience) from others than men. These female characteristics make it right that women should be 'below' (*debajo*) men or under their authority. Bodily features combine with non-bodily elements to make up the basis of the Gitano categories *mujer* (woman) and *hombre* (man). These categories are fixed and clear-cut, and provide individuals with a continuity of identity throughout their lifetimes. Simultaneously, what is expected from men and women at different points in their lives – and also within different contexts – varies. To the outside observer Gitano masculinity and femininity seem at once fixed and transient, ascribed and acquired. While the context and performance of gender is continually being adjusted, continuity of identity is provided by the fact that the *mujer–hombre* distinction is perceived as obvious and fixed.

Gitano understandings are different from the North Euro-American ones that serve as the basis for cross-cultural comparison within anthropology. Strathern explains how the 'abstract possibility of a common measure against which comparison proceeds is part of what makes Euro-Americans imagine equality between the sexes' (1995: 48). This possibility of equality is strongly rejected by the Gitanos, who view it as a negative feature of the Payo lifestyle. The Gitano ethos is based on the assumption of 'kinds of people', with 'kind' receiving as much emphasis as 'people'. This makes the discriminations between Payos and Gitanos and between men and women the very basis of their world-view.

From a classic and now rather outdated anthropological standpoint,[3] the Gitano notions 'man' and 'woman', appear to be at once categories of gender and categories of sex: as gender categories they encompass and transcend understandings about bodily difference; as sex categories they are made up of culturally specific ideas about the body that emphasize the genitals and focus on sexual activity and sexual pleasure, and on their appropriate management. The distinction between the two dimensions is, however, purely analytical: the Gitanos do not separate one set of understandings from the other, and the type of genitals individuals have is seen to point to the positions they can and must take throughout their lives. Although they are aware that *la homosexualidad* (homosexuality) exists, the Gitanos view it as something that happens among the Payos, and they pay no attention to the possibility of ambiguities to the man/woman distinction or of non-heterosexual practices.

Childhood and the Sexed Body

The Gitanos of Jarana make good use of modern medical technologies, so that the sex of a child may be determined either before or at birth.

The categories are already hierarchically ranked: men are thought to be 'better' (*mejores*) than women, and to have better lives. Thus, in Jarana boys tend to be much preferred over girls, and the news that a woman is carrying a girl is usually received with disappointment. From the moment of birth, adults emphasize and celebrate the child's genitals, particularly in the case of boys but also in girls. As well as conveying to the children a particular evaluation of the categories 'woman' and 'man' or *niño* (boy) and *niña* (girl), their attitudes encourage them to be proud of their genitals – and to develop a self-identity in which the genitals explicitly occupy a central place.

The words that define the genitals – *pija* (penis) and *chocho* (internal and external female genitalia) – can be defined as 'neutral' in the sense that they do not carry inherently polite or rude connotations. They are used as loving terms of address to children and often become nicknames. They are also made to stand, in a metonymic way, for the male or female children – thus, pregnant women are often asked whether they are carrying a *chocho* or a *pija*. Together with their points of reference these are among the first words to be learned. Affection to children up to the age of five or six is shown by rubbing or grabbing their genitals, or by kissing and biting them there, so that children come to strongly associate displays of affection with their genitals. On one occasion I went with Sara and her children to visit my family – who themselves live in Madrid – and I witnessed as my sister took Sara's son David, who was then two years old, in her arms and praised him saying 'how handsome you are!'. When he heard this, and to my sister's astonishment, he got down from her lap, pulled down his trousers and said 'yes, look', pointing to his penis and expecting further praise.

Although both boys' and girls' genitals are treated with fondness, the boys' are particularly celebrated: mothers love playing with their young sons' penises, photos of naked boys aged two or three are hung in the walls of most Gitano houses, and young boys are very much encouraged to be proud of their penises. The fact that boys are preferred and given preference over girls and the greater – and more joyful – attention that is given to their genitals is essential in the creation of these early masculinities and femininities and coherent with other practices that also contribute to the process. I always saw David's parents and relatives favouring him over his older sister, Nina. During my fieldwork, when he was two and she was six, she was very often made to give him her toys, or to leave her mother's lap when he wished to sit there. Many of the references made to David's masculinity served to advance his privileges as did the mentions of Nina's femininity: because she was a *moza* (young woman) she had to 'give up' so that he, a boy, could have. She fought and resented this, but could not deny the fact that he was a boy and she was a girl. She witnessed the adults around her displaying David's penis and, like them, she often praised it. Nina and David exemplify how the language of the body may 'extinguish discourse . . . in a subjectively experienced consent which is equally an acknowledgement of the rightness of things as they are' (Godelier 1986: 232). Their case illustrates how, through the management of the male and the female body in daily life, the categories *mujer* and *hombre* are phrased as relational and hierarchical, and come to be involved in unequal relations from the very moment of birth. That is, they have clear social and cultural bearings, rather than being restricted to the mere – or 'neutral' – identification of given differences.

Agency, Desire and Fulfilment

To the Gitanos of Jarana, then, men and women are different kinds of people with different positions in life. Their representations of sexual intercourse (*chivar*), on the other hand, point to areas of similarity. The Gitanos view sexual desire as part of the make-up of male and female persons and they portray intercourse as – at least potentially – enjoyable for both, and to be inherently coveted. In the Gitanos' verbal statements it is often the body that appears as the subject that enjoys sexual activity, and both pleasure and desire are frequently located in the body or in parts of it: *que tu cuerpo se la goce* ('may your body enjoy it'), *le pica la almeja* ('her clam [vulva] is itching'), *pierde el culo por él* ('she loses her arse after him') are commonly used expressions. Bodies, individuals and their actions are all intertwined and together make up the Gitano concept of the person.

In Jarana, sexual desire is thought of as very difficult to resist and the wish to have sex is often identified as a motivation for action. Desire is evaluated negatively when, because of it, individuals are thought to have failed to act in acceptable manners, either by excess or by default. The image of the man or the woman who cannot control themselves and hence become dependent on others is a particularly pitiful one. This was the case for Teresa, whose husband Rufo is a drug-addict. His behaviour towards her is considered appalling by other Gitanos in Jarana: he fails to help her support their children, and often beats her up very severely. During fieldwork I saw his family help Teresa with emotional and financial support, but also criticize her heavily: they often said that she should leave Rufo in order to give him a lesson, but that she was unable to do it because she 'loses her arse for him' – that is, because her love/desire for him is too strong.

Simultaneously, desire may be portrayed in a favourable light to justify behaviour that is nonetheless known to be morally wrong: it is when individuals are perceived to display self-assertiveness – an attitude of which the Gitanos highly approve – in pursuing their wish that their yearning is most likely to be positively judged by others. This was made clear to me when, together with three Gitano women from Jarana, I discussed the case of a 17-year-old widow who had eloped with the husband of her dead husband's sister. Although the women agreed that this is one of the worst things a woman can do – partly because of the position in which the abandoned woman is left, with a dishonoured dead brother and without her husband – they surprised me when they said that the young widow had 'done well', because she was 'more beautiful than the other', and added the proverb *el muerto al hoyo y el vivo al bollo* ('send the dead to the grave and let the living eat cake'), meaning that she was right to want to have fun.

Most importantly, individuals see themselves as entitled to sexual pleasure within the framework of a socially sanctioned relationship. The Gitano women of Jarana are ready to make use of modern 'advancements' and to turn to Payo experts in order to achieve what they see as rightfully theirs. In a letter Elena explained to me how

> I too have to tell you many things about Joaquín (her husband) because we went to the psychologist and it was very good for both of us to tell each other our things about love and since then we have advanced a lot because we feel free when making love and he feels much better and even his personality changes.

A few months later, however, Elena was fed up with Joaquín's moodiness and its effect on their sexual life:

> Palomi I talked with Joaquín about us because I was fed up with his bad moods and I was not happy that when he wanted then we could lie together and then to spend a lot of days without even kissing each other, but I didn't tell him I was going to leave him because I wasn't going to do so because I have got three children but I told him that I was going to move rooms and sleep with my daughters but I also told him that if I had to go as far as that it wouldn't be for a few days it would be for life because I am not like other Gitanas who are the slaves of their husbands and only open their legs when their husbands want them to.

Joking is the context in which *chivar* is most often described as pleasurable and also tempting. In sexual joking – between people belonging to the same or different age-gender groups – the Gitanos elaborate on the idea of *chivar* itself, without necessarily referring their personal experiences. For instance, much sexual teasing and playing takes place between sisters- and brothers-in-law, and between first cousins, both married and unmarried. I first came across this kind of behaviour one evening while I was watching TV with Marga, her husband Pedro, Marga's first paternal cousin Luis, his wife Rosa, and some other members of their family. Pedro started playing at fighting with Rosa. As part of the game, he took hold of her breasts and bit one of them. Then Marga went to Luis and squeezed his genitals with her hand so hard that she hurt him. All throughout the sequence the people present laughed and cheered.

Women chatting on their own very often jokingly boast about their pleasure and desire, about those of their husbands, and about the frequency of their sexual relations. On a summer afternoon, I sat with a group of about twelve women of different ages – some married and some unmarried – while they were chatting, jokingly but also seriously, about sexual relations. They teased Pili – a woman in her late teens – about her husband being away on a trip and her missing 'that'. She said: 'now that I feel like it, I can't do it, I want it so much I wake up earlier in the morning'. All the other women laughed. One said: 'with the kind of life we women lead, this is part of the little bit of goodness we have, the only time when we really enjoy ourselves' (*con la vida que llevamos las mujeres, esto es de lo poquito bueno que tenemos, la única vez que nos divertimos de verdad*). In fact, whether women state that they enjoy sex or that they do not, the idea that it *should* be enjoyable is not contested even in more 'realistic' contexts – such as when they discuss particular aspects of their own personal experiences with women friends and relatives.

Morality and the Control of Desire

Despite being grounded on the perceptions of intercourse as enjoyable, and of sexual desire as integral to what men and women are like, Gitano morality puts great stress on control. The result is that, in conversations and in daily life, sexual interest and practice tend to come across as morally ambivalent. Sexual joking conveys this ambiguity: it portrays what sexual activity is thought to be potentially like, while implicitly alluding to the fact that people's actual experiences often do not correspond to that image – and it is seldom clear whether the lack of fit is a result of the individual's ability to control sexual desires or their failure to achieve them. Overall, the ability to exert control over sexual desire is portrayed as one of the key elements that differentiates Gitanos from Payos – who are granted equal sexual desire but whose immorality is unquestioned and constantly under-lined. This emphasis revolves around the idea that women should dominate their wishes much more than men: they should remain virgins until marriage, they should always be faithful to their husbands, and they should not remarry if they are widowed. When Pepe's wife and his mother found out that he had been having an affair with his unmarried cousin Lola they were quick to point out that it was Lola's reputation that would be blemished if the liaison was made public. While Lola's and Pepe's female kin were arguing and insulting each other, Estrella made fun of María, Pepe's wife, for being indifferent to the fact that her husband had successfully cuckolded her. However, Estrella later told me that María was right: should knowledge of the issue transpire outside the limits of the extended family, Lola would never be able to get married – it was only because Lola and Pepe were first cousins that their behaviour was kept secret.

Men, on the other hand, improve their social standing by demon-strating that they are active sexually, although this display should never be indiscriminate – rape, for example, is strongly condemned – and growth in age should be accompanied by increasing self-control. Because of the strict family monitoring of women's sexual behaviour, unmarried men are encouraged to establish sexual relations with Payas, and are expected to have sexual experiences before marriage. Unlike widows, widowers who remarry are not frowned upon and male infidelity is tolerated within limits, so long as it is with Payas and not with Gitanas, and so long as it does not become disruptive to the daily life of the family of the man involved. Adulterous relationships between Gitano men and women do happen but, if they become public, often lead to feuds between the extended families or patrigroups involved. Separations and consequent unions take place, although rarely. The Gitanos of Jarana often stress that it is an essential part of the 'Gitano law' that men or women who enter adulterous relation-ships or abandon their partner should lose access to their children. In fact, I only know of a handful of cases of permanent separation and of remarriage – by contrast, temporary separation, particularly among young couples, is relatively common.

Mocedad

As my discussion on childhood above illustrates, before puberty it is the ascribed – given, unchanging – aspect of masculinity and femininity that the Gitanos underline. With the end of childhood, by contrast, the moral dimension of the sensual character of the male and female bodies is celebrated, and men and women are expected to embrace the dual standard that I have just discussed. The extent to which they are perceived to be successful determines their status within the community. With puberty, therefore, it is the relationship between the ascribed and the acquired facets of masculinity and femininity that becomes the centre of attention.

The Gitanos of Jarana call the span that stretches between childhood and marriage *mocedad*. Girls become *mozas* (unmarried women) around the time when they begin to menstruate.[4] Boys begin to be considered *mozos* (unmarried men) at some stage between twelve and fourteen. For both the transition is gradual. If they have not already done so, upon becoming *mozos* and *mozas*, Gitano children are finally allowed by their parents to leave school[5] and begin to work with other members of their families, either at home – the girls – or outdoors – boys and girls. The contribution of a *mozo* or a *moza* to the household income is often as important as that of a married adult.

Gitanos consider men and women capable of marrying from the very moment they begin to be thought of as *mozos/as*, and *mocedad* is a period marked by the expectation of marriage. In Jarana, men marry from fourteen onwards and women from thirteen to twenty two.[6] Staying single, just like being infertile, is considered a disgrace. Whereas men are expected not to remain virgin until marriage, virginity is the essential prerequisite for female *mocedad*: once a girl loses it she becomes married to the man who deflowered her, if she did not wait to have sexual relations until after the wedding; or else to the man for whom she is deflowered during the wedding ceremony. Thus, although it is possible to elope (*escaparse*)[7] and to marry with a wedding (*casarse con boda* or *bien* – well) among the Gitanos of Jarana the concept of marriage is always linked to the loss of female virginity. The word *moza* is a synonym of *virgen* (virgin), and the opposite of *casada* (married *because* she is a non-virgin). A woman who is publicly known to have lost her virginity by having sex with a man is no longer a *moza* or treated like one – whether the man acknowledges his responsibility and cohabitation follows or not.[8] Thus the word *casarse* (to marry) never refers to cases of remarriage after separation or widowhood – which take place with a certain regularity even if, particularly for women, they are not approved of. The Gitanos then say that a person 'has gone away with' or 'has joined' another (*se ha ido con* or *se ha juntado con*).[9] Whether people abandon their spouses and elope, or 'get together' after being separated for other causes or after widowhood, it is extended cohabitation that is taken as a sign of marriage – and through it that partners get to be referred to as *marido* (husband) and *mujer* (wife).

Thus, both men and women stop being *mozos* only when they become *casados* (married). *Mocedad*, however, is differently experienced by boys and by girls. Sexual prowess and its proof, which are essential to the definition of masculinity through men's lives and until old age, are particularly celebrated during *mocedad:* in Jarana, the Gitanos associate sexual desire with lack of self-control, which is acquired with age and increasing wisdom or knowledge, so that *mozos* as young men are expected to follow rather than dominate their wishes. Since female virginity is so highly valued and closely protected, *mozos* turn to the Payas whose moral value is thought to be null: they are allowed and even encouraged to go out to discos and bars where they meet Payas with whom they engage in relations that are usually short lived.

Sensual Bodies

The definition of male *mocedad* revolves to a great extent around the celebration of the sensual character of male personhood. This sensual character occupies a key place in the construction of the *mozos'* personal identities and is reflected in their physical appearance. Through their dress and bearing *mozos* make themselves appear proud, self-confident and aggressive. Most of them take great care of their looks, wearing expensive-looking clothes and shiny shoes and jewellery, and tying colourful scarves around their necks. They make their mothers or sisters iron their shirts and trousers carefully. *Mozos* often put gel on their hair, which many grow down to their shoulders and only cut after their marriage. The Gitanos of Jarana see strong and curly hair as a sign of beauty and strength in males and females of all ages. In men, long hair is associated with youth and its implications such as impulsiveness or foolishness and with activities such as going out for dancing or drinks in bars and discos. The *mozos'* attitude is usually defiant and even arrogant: their manner exaggerates the proud bearing of the married man, their bodies straight, hands in pockets and chest forward. They are quick to respond to challenges, and few lose an opportunity sexually to provoke a young Paya. Young Gitano men are encouraged to enter the Payo world and establish sexual relations

Figure 4.1 Four *mozos*.

with Payo women: the idea that Gitanos flirt with Payas and take them to bed is used to demonstrate not only the immorality of non-Gitano women, but also that of their men who allow their behaviour and are made ridiculous by it. The Gitano attitude to the boundaries that separate them from the Payos is not therefore just one of protection, but also one of active aggression and even penetration.

Whereas boys see their horizon expand once they become *mozos*, the mobility of girls is restricted. As children, they are allowed to play around the neighbourhood and stay out of the house for hours at a time. They go to school and thus spend a large part of the day away from home. Once they become *mozas* they are expected to remain indoors or else to go out to work with their parents. At most they are allowed to go to the Evangelical church or for a coffee with their older married sisters or with other *mozas*, always within or very near the neighbourhood. A *moza* is praised when 'she does not go further than the door of her home' (*no pasa de la puerta de su casa*). Those who are seen to spend too much time outdoors entertaining themselves are criticized: people say that they *ronean mucho*, that they spend too much time outside the house in worthless pursuits. The word *ronear* in fact means 'to flirt' and the implication is clear in the sentence.

Like boys, girls change their personal appearance once they become *mozas*. During childhood, they are dressed in trousers and miniskirts by their mothers: their sexual morality is not yet significant, so that they can dress like boys or like the Payas. When families organize one-day trips to the river, usually near Escalona, a village in Toledo, *mozas* and married women swim with loose dresses that cover most of their bodies, whereas girls are allowed to wear bathing suits. With the transition to *mocedad*, by contrast, the adequate performance of gender morality becomes significant: from then onwards the way women dress, sit, walk and generally bear themselves becomes both a sign and the very embodiment of their moral worth. Their appearance is expected to be at the same time feminine and Gitano – proper, partly by opposition to the improper morality of non-Gypsy women. Gitanos say that Payas show too much of their bodies – they want to provoke men because they want to have sex – and wear trousers like men. This is an essential component of the reversal of gendered roles that Gitanos identify as a mark of Payo lifestyle.

Gitanas, by contrast, should not wear trousers, bathing-suits or miniskirts. It is ironic that many Payos believe Gitanos to be 'uncivilized' (*incivilizados*) and that one of the ways through which Gitanas are thought to show their backwardness is by wearing trousers under their skirts – something that, according to the Payos, shows that they do not understand that it is 'either/or', and not 'both'. In fact, Gitanas like to wear trousers in winter because they are warmer than skirts, but always wear skirts on top to show their propriety. Similarly, Gitano women are expected to demonstrate their sexual continence through their posture. When they sit – always careful not to show their thighs – most women pull their skirts and tuck them behind the calves even if they are long enough to cover the knees and this procedure is in fact unnecessary. Unless they are alone or with their close family women do not cross their legs but sit upright, crossing their ankles below the seat to keep the thighs together, and resting their hands on their lap. These procedures are important because, among the Gitanos, dress and manner are seen as an objectification of personal inclinations and dispositions. At the river one summer I swam wearing a dress that covered my upper arms and my knees, like the Gitanas did. At one point, one of the women from Jarana approached me and offered to lend me a pair of shorts to wear below my dress. I refused, because I found the dress uncomfortable enough. Other women gathered and insisted that I wore the shorts, to make completely sure that my body was properly covered. One of them argued that 'people see you in church, you always dress properly, you are good, you never give reason for scandal. If they see you now behaving differently, won't they think you were hypocritical then? We tell you this because we care about you.'

Simultaneously, and in some senses paradoxically, Gitano aesthetics tend to stress the sensual character of female bodies, particularly during *mocedad*, but also afterwards. The Gitano ideal of femininity is closer to 1950s Hollywood images of women – plump, curvy, with big breasts and big buttocks – than to the thin and vaporous visions that populate Western women's magazines today. *Mozas* and many young married women make themselves attractive by putting on very tight blouses that emphasize their breasts, and skirts that are long but also very tight and that sometimes have long cuts so that part of the leg is shown. They wear a great deal of make up and large, shiny jewellery, and they curl and/or dye their hair, pinning it high at the top of their heads so as to display its length and abundance. However, if they become too conspicuous they are heavily criticized: they get to be called *revivas* or *roneadoras* – words that are applied only to women. A woman who is *reviva* is a woman who 'knows too much' (*sabe demasiado)*, and her knowledge is not necessarily of the appropriate kind: rather than knowing how to conform to what is adequate according to her gender and age, she knows how to escape the limits that propriety sets. *Roneadoras* are women who want to flirt with men and provoke them sexually.

The way women dress is also one of the fields where power is negotiated, both among kin, and also in other contexts, as among members of the Evangelical Church. Take the following example. Towards the end of my stay in Jarana I helped Sara dye her hair black. She had dyed it blond not so long ago but decided that the ends were damaged and that it would show less if her hair was dark. She knew that her husband would not like the idea, and that if she asked him he would not give her his permission. So we bought the dye and applied it while Paco was at work. When he came back that night he got extremely angry, shouting that Sara had no respect left for him and that all the men in Jarana would laugh at him for the speed with which Sara changed her hairstyle. Sara did not go back to blond, but they did not talk to each other for a couple of days. Thus, married women quarrel with their husbands and *mozas* quarrel with their parents and boyfriends over the definition of what is proper for them to look like. It happens often that a young woman puts on a skirt or a blouse that her parents, boyfriend or husband consider inadequate,

Figure 4.2 Two *mozas* and a girl during a visit to the river near Escalona (Toledo) organised by the social workers.

she is told to take it off and a quarrel follows. As for the Church, all ministers at some time or other forbid young women to sing in the choir as a punishment for being seen wearing mini-skirts or trousers.

Mozas thus enact Gypsyness by physically embodying righteousness. This is visible in the way they dress: the combination of the tendency to look provocative with the restrictions that ideas of decency impose reflects at once the sensual character of the body and the control to which this character is subjected. This mixture of sexiness and restraint can also be seen as a powerful and ubiquitous symbol of the moral superiority of Gitanos over Payos, for the latter are granted the same kind of sexual impulse, but are seen to fail to keep it under control, with the dress of Payo women being one of the indices of this failure.

The Dual Moral Standard During Courtship

Once they become *mozos*, Gitano boys and girls often enter relationships that may grow into courtships. When couples meet in the street and without the explicit consent of their families, these affairs are called *noviazgos de calle* (street courtships). They are distinguished from the *noviazgos formales* (formal courtships) that develop between a couple that has been formally betrothed by their parents. A formal courtship may follow a street one, but this is not always the case.

The Gitanos of Jarana describe the feeling that exists between *novios* (boyfriend and girlfriend) through the term *querer* (to love/be fond of and want somebody), which is close to the English 'infatuation', or through the stronger *amor* which is more rarely used and which suggests a more powerful engagement. *Querer* has implications of sexual desire, fondness, and of wanting to somehow 'have' the other person. Although they are no longer seen as children, *mozos* and *mozas* are expected to show little *conocimiento* (understanding), to behave in an impulsive manner and to do foolish things. *Querer*, which is seen as part of this general disposition, is also thought of as persistent and granted the most serious consideration by adults. It is often enough that a boy loves a girl, if she and her family are acceptable, for the parents to begin negotiations in order to betroth her to him. And vice versa: love is often a factor that a girl's family would take into account when deciding whether to give her to a particular boy. However, although *querer* exists as a concept and a basis for action, the idea that, in order to marry, it is necessary to love a person does not exist among the Gitanos. Other considerations such as personality, reputation, hard work, ability to make money, and the characteristics of the person's family are as significant. If, besides fulfilling these requirements, two young people love each other, so much the better. And, as Grandmother María, who was made to marry a man she did not want, told me: 'at the beginning you do not want him, later with contact *[con el roce]* you become fond of him'. A straightforward opposition between arranged and non-arranged marriages or engage-ments cannot really be sustained, and most cases in fact lie somewhere on a continuum between the two extremes. For example, it often happens that a couple who have not had a street courtship are betrothed by their parents, and then do not wait to have a wedding but have sexual relations and elope together.

In spite of the stress they put on female virginity, Gitanos tolerate the fact that couples who are formally courting have sexual contact 'so long as it is from the waist upwards' (*de la cintura para arriba*), meaning that the girl's genitals must remain in good enough condition to undergo the strict examination that a wedding implies. Although they tend to disapprove, adults are aware that most couples who are street-courting often engage in similar practices. Tío Juan described his early relationship with the woman who has been his wife for more than forty years in very graphic terms. He told me: 'when we were courting we wanted each other a lot, we could not stay apart even for an hour. Before I married her I knew her face and her arse' (*conocía su cara y su culo*), meaning that, although they left the vagina intact, they 'played around' other areas – perhaps practised anal intercourse – and he often saw her completely naked. This kind of sexual relation is seen as something unavoidably tied to *mocedad*. I have even been told that 'these things prepare you for marriage' (*te preparan para el matrimonio*). At the same time, couples who do not limit themselves to the proper degree of intimacy are felt to be wanting in self-control.[10] As Ana, whose 16-year-old son eloped with his 14-year-old formal girlfriend after 'going too far', said: 'the two are dirty pigs' (*son dos cerdos guarros*). Both this perceived lack of restraint and the elopement to which it is thought to lead have very negative undertones.

Conclusions

The Payo world where, according to the Gitanos of Jarana, sexual desire rules women and men, provides the background to the Gitanos' evaluations of each other and of themselves as part of 'the Gitano people' (*el pueblo Gitano*). The Gitanos contrast their own ideals of Gitano propriety with stereotyped images of what they think Payo behaviour to be like. Assessments of particular events are implicitly and even explicitly located at some point on a continuum between these two ideal images: Ana's son and his girlfriend behaved more like Payos than Gitanos; they went 'too far'. The Gitanos often stress that Payos are generally immoral: they neglect and mistreat their children, kill each other in wars and through terrorism, do not pay attention to their elders and do not respect their dead. However, it is their sexual impropriety that receives the greatest elaboration in daily life.

The extent to which the Gitanos value sexual modesty in women and control over sexual desire in both women and men – albeit to different degrees – is revealed most strikingly in the institution that I describe in the following chapter, the wedding ceremony. During Gitano weddings virgin women are deflowered and the proof of their virginity is made into an object of joyful communal celebration. Weddings loom large in the imaginations of the Gitanos of Jarana, as epitomes of Gitano righteousness and as the clearest evidence of Gitano distinctiveness.

Notes

1. By 'strongly egalitarian' I mean that hierarchy is constructed almost solely on the bases of age and gender.

2. The Payos apply the words *macho* (male) and *hembra* (female) to animals and only in some contexts also to humans. These terms explicitly stress the genital nature of gendered differentiation. The Gitanos do not use them. Instead, men and women may be referred to metonymically as *pijas* (penises) and *chochos* (female genitalia), words that do not make reference to pairs of the kind 'human-animal' or 'nature-culture'. The words *pija* and *chocho* do not form part of the Payo repertoire. Instead, Payos use words such as *pene*, *pito*, and *polla* for penis; *pelotas, cojones, bolas* for testicles; and *vagina* or *coño* for female genitals. These words are never used metonymically to stand for male or female persons.

3. Up to the early 1990s, within feminist anthropology

> [o]ne fixed position remained, and that was the distinction between sex and gender. Gender was seen as socially constructed, but underlying that idea was a notion that although gender was not determined by biology, it *was* the social elaboration in specific contexts of the obvious facts of biological sex difference. It did not matter that almost everyone recognized that both biology and culture were historically and culturally variable concepts, as were the relations between them. The problem was that the elaboration of the social determinations and entailments of gender in all their specificity had effectively left the relationship between sex and gender very under-theorized (Moore 1994: 12).

4. First menstruation is not celebrated in any special way.

5. Parents do not think that the skills that children may learn at school are relevant given the kind of life they are going to live as Gitanos. Once children have learned some reading and writing and basic mathematical skills it is considered that they know all that Payos may teach them that might be useful for them in the future. Local authorities, however, insist that Gitano children complete as many years of schooling as possible. This leads to constant confrontations between social workers and Gitano families.

6. Fresno García (1993: 72) states that Gitano men marry between 18 and 22, and women between 16 and 20. My experience of Jarana is different: out of 21 women from the neighbourhood, three had married between 19 and 22, three at 18, three at 17, four at 16, four at 15, three at 14 and one at 13.

7. Eloping (*escaparse*, literally 'to escape') only functions as a form of marriage when the two sides are Gitano. When the woman is Paya and the man Gitano both extended cohabitation and acceptance by the Gitano family are necessary before the union is treated as a marriage. The underlying logic is that Payos do not link marriage to the loss of virginity, hence having sex with a Paya is not enough to make the liaison a marriage.

8. For a married man to deflower a Gitano virgin is consider one of the worst offences. In the handful of cases I have heard of, the couples eloped together for fear of the retaliation of the three families involved – that of the virgin, of the man who deflowers her, and of his wife. Gitanos tend to hold the view that a man will return to his wife, particularly if they have children, and that a woman who has eloped with another woman's husband will later pay the consequences of her act and be abandoned. In practice, however, this is not necessarily the case.

9. To these three forms of marriage – by elopement, with a wedding, or through cohabitation – the Gitanos may add a Payo civil marriage ceremony and/or a wedding at the Evangelical church, although always as a complement, never on their own. Evangelical Gitanos may marry in church only if they also have a Gitano wedding – which may take place before or after the religious ceremony – never when they elope. Marriage *por la ley paya* ('through the Payo law') is undergone by couples who have eloped or who have had a wedding in order to obtain material benefits from the Administration or from charities. Many couples never do it.

10. The same happens with people who abandon their spouses in order to marry and with widows who remarry: the idea that they do it in order to fulfil an uncontrolled and improper sexual drive is always present.

five

The Female Body and Gendered Moralities

Early in my fieldwork in Jarana, Tía Tula told me that she had decided to explain to me 'how the Gitanos get married'. She opened a drawer and took out a small and withered plastic bag. Inside were three white squares of cloth that she carefully spread over her bed. 'Among the Payos', she said, 'there are no decent women. But with us, in order to get married, you have to prove that you are pure. We take the virginity out of women's bodies with the handkerchief. These are the handkerchiefs of my daughters-in-law.' She passed her finger over the handkerchiefs, which were marked with round yellow stains, and added: 'You see, each of these two ones has three roses. In this one there is only one and some blood, the girl was too closed and we stopped. My daughters-in-law are decent, even Rosa who eloped. Rosa was a virgin, a good woman. This is what you have to take to England, let the English know we Gitanos are decent.'

The Gitanos and Spanish Gendered Moralities

At the centre of the Gitanos' descriptions of themselves lies the notion that Gitano women control their sexual drives; evidence of their control is obtained at the wedding ceremony, when a white handkerchief is used to take 'flowers' (*flores*) out of their bodies, as tangible proofs of their decency. By contrast, the Gitanos emphasize to the point of boredom that Payas do not even attempt to curb their sexual drives. The Gitanos find evidence of the Payas' immorality through multiple media – contact with Payos, television and cinema, popular magazines and so on – and they give the character of an axiom to the idea that all non-Gitano women are sexually promiscuous and insatiable. When, during fieldwork, I tried to explain to my Gitano friends that I knew some Payo women who had kept their virginity until marriage, I was met with the strongest scepticism. To the Gitanos it

87

did not matter that, as Paya, I might know more about the Payo way of life than they did: they were secure in their belief that they knew better, and were always ready to provide plenty of examples of the Payas' indecency that they had gleaned through personal experience or through hearsay from other Gitanos.

It is this framework of fundamental and axiomatic difference between the Payo and the Gitano moralities and lifestyles that provides the Gitano wedding ceremony with its strong symbolic and emotional charge. The Gitanos see the ritual of the wedding as that which embodies most clearly the superiority of Gitanos over Payos. Female chastity – expressed through ideals of either shame as among the Hungarian Rom (Stewart 1997) or of purity and pollution as in the cases of the English Gypsies and the Rom who live in California (Okely 1983; Sutherland 1975a) – is a widespread ideal and a marker of communal identity among Gypsies throughout the world. Paradoxically, it was also an ideal endorsed by the dominant Francoist ideology until relatively recently in Spain: Martín Gaite (1987a) has explained how dominant discourses of femininity and masculinity during the 1940s and 1950s and even up to the end of the dictatorship in 1976 clearly endorsed an ideal of gender relations that revolved around female sexual restrain and male pre-marital – or even post-marital – promiscuity. The preservation of female virginity until marriage occupied a key role in these dominant representations: because it was in men's nature to 'attempt to take advantage' (*intentar aprovecharse*) of women, it was women's responsibility to ensure that relations between the genders remained 'chaste and pure' (*castas y puras*).

Historical and literary analyses of gender reveal that a concern with female chastity has existed in Spain at least since the seventeenth century (Ortega López 1988; Matín Gaite 1987b; Perry 1990). These same analyses, however, make it clear that this concern has constituted just one of several available models of gender relations. Morcillo Gómez, discussing the history of feminism in Spain, makes the point that the 1936–9 Civil War 'involved the fight between two different models of womanhood' (1988: 57; see also Martín Gaite 1987a: 26–30). Thus, during the Second Republic that immediately preceded the War, a series of extremely significant legislative steps took place. These included the legalisation of civil – as opposed to religious – matrimony, of women's right to vote and of divorce. In 1936, once the War had started, the Generalitat de Catalunya (Catalonia's local government) legalized abortion. With the establishment of the dictatorship these steps were reversed and a much more conservative gender morality became official. Through the extremely effective influence of the

Sección Femenina de Falange[1] women were encouraged 'not to comment on an order, but only to fulfil it' and 'to obey and, through your example, to teach others to obey ' (Morcillo Gómez 1988: 82). They were told that 'you are no longer in charge of acting, but rather of helping others to act', and that their role was to be 'the wheel of the chariot, rather than the charioteer'. And, whereas the preservation of virginity until marriage came to be portrayed as essential to female morality, 'the man who remained virgin until marriage was looked upon as an *avis rara*, and nobody thought that he would be successful as suitor, husband or father' (Martín Gaite 1987a: 101).

However, it would be wrong to see these differences as merely straightforward reflections of a conflict between 'conservative' and 'liberal' or 'modern' views of gender relations. Not only political orientation but region of origin within Spain as well as social class have in fact been fundamental factors of variation. For example, it was in Catalonia that abortion was made legal at the beginning of the Civil War. Pitt-Rivers, in his ethnography of the Andalusian village of Grazalema, written in the mid-1950s, stresses the idea that

> Anyone acquainted with the social history of Europe will have observed the variation in the customs relating to sex, both from one country to another, but above all from one social class to another within the same country and historical period, while on the contrary certain values are characteristic of a particular class throughout European history. The 'immorality' of the aristocracies is traditional . . . In fact, generally speaking, there is a difference in attitude not only between the sexes but also between the Andalusian *señorito* and the pueblo (*plebs*). It cannot be said to amount to a serious difference in values so much as a difference in the opportunities to implement or defy them (1961: 118).

It seems that, under Franco, defying the dominant ideology was easier for those who inhabited not only the highest but also the lowest social echelons. In the poorer suburbs of the large cities where the Gitanos settled in large numbers from the beginning of the 1950s the double moral standard endorsed by the Francoist regime was not necessarily observed. Martín Gaite explains that

> the periphery of the large cities was a hot subject for the producers of the official morality, because it was there that the foci of postwar rebellion were sustained . . . it was generally acknowledged that (there) young men and women treated each other without any kind of restraint, and that parents remained completely indifferent towards the behaviour of their children (1987a: 94).

She describes how in 1944, the Puente de Vallecas, which was considered by the representatives of the Francoist regime to be the most marginal and problematic of all the suburbs of Madrid and was also widely known as 'Little Russia', came to be declared by local officials a 'zone impassable to healthy ideals' (1987a: 95). That neighbourhood, they said

> is a nest of political resentment, social phobias, hate of religion, and contempt for moral principles. Within it there is a wide area, where at least 89 per cent of the inhabitants live, which can be considered impenetrable, for we have not found any means of instilling healthy ideals or of drawing people to a regenerating atmosphere (La Moralidad Pública y su Evolución, 1944; quoted in Martín Gaite 1987a: 95).

The picture nowadays is even more fragmented and the situation of the Gitanos vis-à-vis the morality of the rest of the Spanish population is more difficult to ascertain. It is clear that, with the transition to democracy, different models of masculinity and femininity compete on a much more equal grounding – hence Thurén's statement that 'there is a strong awareness among most Beniturians [Benituria is a *barrio* in Valencia] that there are many ways to live and think' (1988: 149). Contraceptives were legalized in 1979 – and with them State sanctioning of sex for purposes other than reproduction – and the same happened with divorce in 1981 and with abortion in 1985, steps that were taken among much public debate and controversy. Discussing changing gender relations and ideologies in Valencia, Thurén explains that 'the two main themes the informants see in the changes in the gender system are the disappearance of the old code of sexual morals and the increase of women's participation in social life' (1988: 30).

Placing the Gitanos within this broader social and historical context makes it clear that their emphasis on female chastity is part of a wider Spanish one. At least since the Early Modern period, dominant discourses on gender in Spain have made space for a double standard that divides women according to whether they are 'decent' or 'from the street' – a distinction that has often worked along the lines of class (Perry 1990) and that has been considerably eroded with the establishment of a secular democracy. The Gitanos share, or have adopted, the same differentiation but they have adapted it to their need to differentiate themselves from the Payos: *their* women are 'decent', all others are 'from the street'. It is clear that they have chosen to endorse one of several available models of gender relations. In this sense, in the late twentieth century they have to be seen as a Spanish people with a characteristically Spanish morality – but a morality that is particularly conservative. Lastly, it is extremely significant that the Gitanos themselves deny any continuity between their own understandings and those of the non-Gypsies, and that they have chosen as the focus of their communal identity a bodily feature that is completely absent from the Payos' representations.

Female Virginity

From classical times onwards, throughout Southern Europe the breaking of the hymen has been considered the sign of the loss of female virginity (Sissa 1989).[2] This is certainly a powerful idea among many Spanish people today,[3] although its validity is being challenged by alternative folk-medical models. Among the Gitanos of Jarana, by contrast, virginity depends on a combination of several elements. Gitanos firmly believe that old Gitanas are able to deduce the kind of sexual relationship a young woman has had from the aspect of her genitals. Throughout fieldwork, women – young and old, married and unmarried – often described to me how old Gitanas are able to tell whether a woman is *abierta* (open) as opposed to *entera* (whole), that is, whether full intercourse has taken place, or whether she merely is *rozada* (rubbed or jagged) or *picoteada* (pecked) because the couple have been 'playing around that area' (*jugando por esa zona*) without actual penetration. In young girls the area surrounding the entry to the vagina is believed to be pink and glossy, and to turn dark – brown, grey or black – with the contact of the penis and of other objects such as trousers or tampons. As they become older the genitals of women are thought to turn 'harder' (*duro*), more difficult to be 'opened' by a man. Women who remain unmarried after they turn twenty get to be called *mozas viejas* (old unmarried women), a derogatory expression with no masculine equivalent. Gitanos say that 'those ones have to be opened with a screw-driver, they no longer have it tender' (*a esas hay que abrirlas con destornillador, ya no lo tienen tierno*).

Hence, for a woman to be considered truly untouched she has to have rosy, tight external genitals. However, she is thought to be a *virgen* (virgin) until her *honra* is spoilt or lost: the Gitanos of Jarana believe that inside the body of a virgin woman there is an *uva* (grape), a white or greyish hard grain the size of a small chick-pea which contains her *honra*.[4] This is a yellow fluid which is spilt and hence lost when a woman is penetrated by a man for the first time or when she is deflowered by a professional woman (the *ajuntaora*) at the wedding ceremony. By contrast with the *honra*, the Gitanos pay

Figure 5.1 An elderly Gitano woman.

relatively little attention to the hymen: it is considered together with the entrance to the vagina and the surrounding area, and contributes to making it appear untouched and tight. They thus view it in a way that is closer to that of modern doctors – flesh that makes the entrance to the vagina narrower – than to the popular Southern European belief in a membrane that seals the woman's internal genitals (Sissa 1989). Similarly, and although it is a widespread idea even today among many Spaniards, the Gitanos of Jarana do not treat blood shed during intercourse or in the wedding ritual as the sign of loss of virginity:[5]

blood is said to appear either when the woman is older and therefore 'hard to open', or at the wedding ritual if it is performed by an insufficiently experienced woman. Bleeding is thus evaluated negatively and, in descriptions of wedding ceremonies, is consistently down-played.[6] Answering my questions, Clara wrote to me

> Only rarely they [the *ajuntaoras*] draw blood, only if the girl does not stand still, and some women know how to do it better than others. The *honra* is a yellow stain, we have talked about this before, you were telling me that the yellow liquid could grow again (during fieldwork I suggested that the *honra* could be lubricating fluid) and I told you that it cannot, and that when you have been with a man, even if only two or three times, the old women can tell.

The Gitanos put as much emphasis on the fact of virginity itself – which to them implies decency and virtue – as on the preservation of its proof. As well as using the word *honra* to define the physically tangible proof that a woman has never had full sexual intercourse with a man, they also apply it to the decent behaviour that its existence in the body of a young woman demonstrates – hence the adjective *honrada*, which can be translated as decent or virtuous in a sexually oriented sense. The term situates key attitudes, dispositions and wills inside the female body. A woman's body testifies to her behaviour and becomes the location of her worth: the Gitanos say that 'the woman carries her *honra* (the proof of her decency) inside the body' (*la mujer lleva su honra dentro del cuerpo*). Young women are thus expected to protect their genital virginity, and to take much care not to spoil their bodies through practices – even those other than sexual contact with men – which might mark their genitals: they should not wear trousers, ride bicycles, use tampons or allow medical examinations of their vaginas because all these things 'take a lot from you' (*te quitan mucho*), and Gitanos insist that once a *moza*'s genitals have become dark, it is not possible to know how it happened, so that her reputation suffers even if she claims she did not have sex with a man. The woman who is 'open' cannot undergo a wedding. Although if she is merely 'rubbed' she theoretically can, the mere idea is contemplated with disgust. The Gitanos explain that women who know or suspect that they are 'rubbed' attempt to elope with a man and, if they fail, remain *mozas viejas*.

La Boda Gitana – The Gitano Wedding

The wedding ceremony, the form of marriage that the Gitanos rank highest, is structured around the demonstration and celebration of the virginity of the bride: the groom receives only marginal attention. Its central part is the *ajuntamiento* (from the verb *juntar*, meaning 'to join'): the examination of the *moza* and her defloration by the *ajuntaora*, a professional woman who charges for her services and who is also called to check whether a *moza* is untouched if her family have doubts about her behaviour. Only married women are allowed to enter the room where the defloration takes place. The bride has already washed herself carefully and, although she starts the feast in a standard white bride dress, at this point she may change into an elaborate dressing gown and matching head-dress, made of pink or blue shiny materials. Gitano women state that white stands for virginity, and that 'we marry in white only once, Payas dress in white as many times as they want' *(nosotras nos casamos de blanco sólo una vez en la vida, las Payas se visten de blanco todas las veces que quieren)*. They thus emphasize that whereas Gitanas can only have one wedding in their lives – and then only if they remain virgins – Payas may have many, whether they are virgin or not. In the eyes of the Gitanas the Payas distort the symbolic link between the colour white, virginity and the wedding – a link that to them is both evident and heavily charged emotionally. Changing into a brightly coloured gown for the defloration reinforces the link between virginity and the colour white.

Once in the room where she is going to be deflowered, the *moza* is told to lie down on her back, and a cushion is put under her buttocks, so that she can be easily examined. The *ajuntaora* makes her spread her legs apart and opens the external labia with her fingers so as to examine the colour and tightness of the internal genitals. She confirms that the bride is untouched and states so: 'She is as when her mother brought her to the world' *(Está como su madre la trajo al mundo)*. Other old or experienced women look to verify her statement. The *ajuntaora* then deflowers the bride with a white handkerchief which she herself has bought and adorned with ribbons or lace: she wraps it around her forefinger, pushes it into the vagina, and 'bursts the grape' *(revienta la uva)* taking the *honra* out in the handkerchief. She repeats the procedure – usually two more times – so as to obtain yellow stains which are called 'roses' *(rosas)* or 'flowers' *(flores)*: she ties knots in the handkerchief and when they dry and are undone they do in fact resemble flowers. The *honra* of the woman is said to stay for ever on the handkerchief, even if it is washed or bleached.

The Gitanos make it clear that if the bride happens to have her period at the time of the wedding the *ajuntamiento* cannot be carried out: the blood would make it impossible to see whether *honra* stains had been produced or not. Then the *ajuntaora* limits herself to ascertaining the virginity of the bride from the aspect of her external genitals. Similarly, when the bride starts bleeding as a result of the deflowering procedure itself, the *ajuntaora* stops and the handkerchief is left with only one or two stains on it – something that does not affect the evaluation that the woman receives but is nonetheless considered 'a pity' *(una pena)*.

Although women often describe their weddings as ordeals, they also proudly emphasize the number of *honra* stains they produced. It is the role of the bride's mother-in-law to determine how many *honra* stains will be obtained, and she is the one who keeps the handkerchief after the wedding. The Gitano women of Jarana frequently describe how, at weddings, mothers-in-law ask for more *honra* stains than are necessary in order to prove a *moza's* virginity. The fact that it is the mother-in-law's role to ask for the number of 'flowers' that she wants can indeed be considered a key step in setting up an unequal relationship between the two women: even if only within the ritual context and for a short time, the *suegra* (mother-in-law) has socially sanctioned control over the bride's body. This is so, moreover, at the moment when the latter is proving her righteousness within a context that is heavily charged emotionally and symbolically. Later, a woman may exert physical violence over her daughter-in-law, and has control over her work until the younger couple move into a house of their own – often years after the wedding.

After the *ajuntamiento* the Gitanos celebrate the bride's proper behaviour. The women cry with joy, sing, clap their hands and throw pink and white candied almonds over the bride's belly and legs. The Gitanas are adamant that almonds stand for joy. Then comes what is considered the most moving moment of the wedding, when first the bride's father and later other male relatives and friends take her in their arms – holding her around her thighs, so that the man's face touches her belly – and 'dance her' *(la bailan)* while men and women throw almonds at them and sing traditional songs that praise the bride's behaviour and emphasize how greatly her family is honoured by it (see also Pasqualino 1995). Meanwhile men in twos 'dance' the groom and the rest of the people throw almonds at them. A group of men may take the groom and throw him up in the air again and again. This part of the ritual is followed by the feast itself, when people dance, sing, eat and drink, sometimes for two or three days.

Figure 5.2 A father 'dances' his daughter during her wedding (courtesy of Liria de la Cruz).

Figure 5.3 A father 'dances' his daughter during her wedding while, in the background, two men 'dance' the groom. (Courtesy of Liria de la Cruz).

The *Honra* and Anthropological Interpretations

During my fieldwork in Jarana I approached three Spanish doctors wanting to find out which anatomical feature provided the anchor for the Gitanos' ideas about the female body and female virginity. I was told that there was none, that the *honra* did not exist, and that it was all in the Gitanos' imaginations – or in mine. I began to feel even more uncomfortable with my material than I already was: although I had been given innumerable accounts of 'the wedding', had seen several handkerchiefs, and had been taught to distinguish the genitals of a virgin woman from those of a non-virgin, I had never witnessed a defloration because all the couples who married during my stay in the neighbourhood had eloped. When those doctors, one after another, said that there was no biological explanation for the *honra* my confidence begun to disintegrate. I started to speculate whether the Gitano women who had told me about 'the wedding' and with whom I had discussed both their bodies and my own had lied. After all, I knew well that Gitano sociability is made up of shifting layers of knowledge

Figure 5.4 A male relative 'dances' the bride during a wedding (Courtesy of Liria de la Cruz).

and exclusion from knowledge: because of my age and gender, and because I am a Paya, I have always been an outsider, even in the eyes of my closest Gitano friends.

I considered the *honra* an unsolvable mystery until I met an anatomist who reviewed my material and explained that he believed 'with 90 per cent of certainty' that what the Gitanos call the *honra* corresponds to what doctors trained in the Western tradition call the Bartholin's glands (Peter Abrahams: personal communication 1996). These exist inside the vaginas of all women, in the inner labia. They are a main agent contributing to the lubrication of the vagina during intercourse. When pressed they evacuate their content at the base of the hymen. A standard Spanish manual of anatomy describes them as follows:[7]

> These vulvo-vaginal glands are relatively small in girls, grow rapidly in size during puberty, present their greatest development during adulthood, and wither gradually with the decrease in sexual activity. These formations have therefore a purely genital signification. Their volume varies from being that of a pea to that of a small almond, and it is often different in each side of the vagina. Most often they are grey yellowish in colour . . . Their consistency obviously changes with the amount of secretion they have produced: they are hard and resistant when their cavities are expanded by the liquid that they discharge; on the other hand, once they have evacuated their content they become soft and flaccid (Testut 1931: 1215).

The parallels between this description and the descriptions of my Gitano friends are obvious: both refer to physical, tangible, observable elements; yet it is clear that both consist of what anthropologists call 'cultural constructions'. However, the Bartholin's glands occupy no place in the Western popular – as opposed to scientific – ideas of biological femaleness. As a consequence, they play no role in anthropological models which, as we know, draw heavily on Western folk constructions.

Neither the *honra* nor the Bartholin's glands correspond to what have been described by anthropologists as the 'obvious facts of biological sex difference' (Moore 1994: 12), those attributes of human bodies that 'cannot be ignored and *require* interpretation' (Errington 1990: 17). The assumption that such attributes exist and that they are everywhere and always the same would make an understanding of the Gitanos impossible. In English popular discourse, as in Spain among the Payos, a woman is a woman because she has a vagina, breasts, and certain quantities of the right hormones, not because she has Bartholin's glands. Among the Gitanos, a woman is a woman because she has – or has had – the *honra* inside her body. Just like the anthropological vagina or penis – and unlike the Bartholin's glands – the *honra* is a 'constitutive construction'. This means that, within their own particular cultural contexts, these elements have acquired the 'character of being that "without which" we could not think at all' (Butler 1993: xi). The *honra* is not simply an anatomical feature: it is the centre of a whole series of practices and understandings that constitute Gitano identity and Gitano social life.

The Gitano emphasis on the *honra* as the true proof of female virginity constitutes a particularly sharp statement of cultural distinctiveness. Like many other Spanish people through time, the Gitanos have chosen to emphasize the 'decency' *(decencia)* of their women as the sign of their superiority over those who live around them. In this sense, they are not very different from supporters of the Francoist regime in the 1940s, 1950s and 1960s. However, the object that the Gitanos have chosen as sign of their singularity does not form part of the cultural repertoire of other Spaniards. Until recently, the Gitanos zealously guarded heir knowledge about the *honra* and its place in their conceptions of themselves. Gitano weddings remained 'secret' to all but a few Payos up to the 1980s. In their particular emphasis on female chastity – a variation of a Spanish theme – the Gitanos position themselves simultaneously at the core and outside the parameters of Spanish culture and society. In this sense, the wedding ritual can be seen as an adequate symbol of Gitano life more widely.

Desire and Elopement

In spite of the stress they put on female virginity, the Gitanos of Jarana believe that courting couples will experience sexual desire for each other, and they tolerate their sexual contact so long as it is 'from the waist upwards' *(de la cintura para arriba)* – meaning that the *moza's* genitals must remain in good enough condition to undergo the strict examination that a wedding implies. Couples who exceed this limit are felt to be wanting in self-control. Because the *moza's* body is thought to reveal whether she has had any genital sexual contact, Gitano custom demands that couples who 'play below the waist' elope. As an observer, my experience is that the reasons that may make young Gitanos elope are very varied. Events that affect one individual are thought to concern their close kin, so each elopement is influenced by many different interests, pressures and recommendations. Couples elope not only when they think that the *moza* is no longer in the right condition to face a wedding, but also when their wishes as to whom or when to marry do not coincide with those of the older people of their families.

In April 1993, when I was living in Sara's house, her younger sister Marga eloped with her paternal first cross-cousin Pedro. The couple were in their teens and, although they had not had a 'street courtship', had been formally engaged for four months – their engagement had been arranged by their older relatives. For a few weeks after the elopement everybody in the family seemed to talk only about it, each person ready to put forward their explanations of the event and what they thought the consequences would be. Clara, Marga's and Sara's older sister, told me that the elopement was Pedro's fault. Marga was not very happy with their relationship and had repeatedly threatened to break up. Pedro was very much in love with her, and he knew that the more they waited the greater the chances would be that the engagement would be broken. He put pressure on Marga to elope and convinced her in a moment of weakness. On the other hand, Sara, another of Marga's sisters, explained how at some time during their courtship the couple had some sexual contact without limiting themselves to 'the waist upwards'. Marga was still 'whole' but they ignored the extent of the damage and when Marga asked for Sara's advice, she told her to elope, telling her stories about the terrible fate of women who had been found to be 'rubbed' when they were about to be deflowered. One of these stories was particularly frightening because it involved Pedro's paternal grandmother, Tía Tula, who was likely to have played a prominent role in Marga's wedding: according to Sara, 'everybody' knew that Tía Tula had spat on the genitals of a bride who was 'pecked', greatly shaming her, her family, and the family of the groom. 'Thankfully' – Sara pointed out – Marga did get frightened and the couple eloped. Lastly, I heard yet another version on the day after the elopement, when Marga and I went together for a walk to the market near the house of Pedro's aunts, where they had taken refuge. There we met several female relatives, all of whom were keen to find out what was going on. Marga described to each of them how, when she and Pedro became engaged in November of 1992, Pedro's and her parents had agreed to wait for at least a year before the wedding. They wanted to give their children time to become accustomed to each other – since it was an arranged engagement – and also needed several months to save the money necessary for the wedding feast. However, from then on Pedro's parents changed opinion several times, one day wanting to break off the engagement and the next to marry them as soon as possible, even with a poor feast. Marga's father then proposed to take charge of most of the expenses himself, or to lend his sister and brother-in-law the money they needed for the wedding banquet, but it did not seem as if things were becoming much clearer. Finally Pedro and Marga became afraid that they would have to wait, and that their engagement might be broken by their parents, and decided to elope.

Regardless of the motivations actors and their families may claim, other Gitanos always suspect that the true cause of an elopement is that the couple have gone too far in their sexual contacts. Eloping, however, is judged differently and bears different implications in the cases of the *mozo* and the *moza*: the Gitanos often explain how 'to us a man and a woman is not the same' *(para nosotros el hombre y la mujer no es lo mismo)*. They state that a *mozo* who tries to get as much as he can from his girlfriend is simply behaving according to what men are like: they say that 'it is known that men are like that and do those things' *(ya se sabe que los hombres son así y hacen esas cosas)*, that 'for the Gitanos a man is not able to restrain himself' *(para los Gitanos un hombre no es capaz de aguantarse)*, and that 'according to the Gitano laws a man has right to everything, and women to nothing' *(según las leyes Gitanas el hombre tiene derecho a todo, y la mujer a nada)*. Mozos do not need to keep their affairs secret as *mozas* do, and their families very often know which *moza* – or *mozas* – a *mozo* is courting. Unless they have some grudge against her or her family, or are aware that her family may have a grudge against them, the *mozo's* family does not restrict his activities. Thus, when he learnt that his daughter Marga had eloped with his own nephew, Esteban cried saying that 'had he been an outsider [*forastero*] I would have understood, because it is alright to get as much as you can out of her, if she allows you, but my nephew should have taken my reputation into account' (literally 'looked at my face'; *mirado mi cara*). The emphasis here lies on the kinship link between Esteban – who is shamed by his daughter's elopement – and his nephew, rather than on the righteousness of Pedro – as a man – eloping itself.

Simultaneously, however, the ideal for a man is to marry a woman for whom he is her first boyfriend and a *mozo* should not want to be engaged with a *moza* that has already been engaged with someone else. Hence of the wedding ceremony it is said that the woman is 'deflowered *for* him' *(ajuntada para él)*. Men lose face if they put up with women who have already been to bed with someone else. As Tía Clara graphically put it, when a woman has physical contact with more than one man, 'the last one gets all the dribble of the other ones' (el último se lleva todas las babas de los otros).

In the women's case, it reflects negatively to be engaged more than once, and in discussions of particular elopements, it is usually the women who are regarded most harshly. The Gitanos often say that when couples break up 'the one that is at a disadvantage is the girl' (el prejuicio es para la chica), and parents will do whatever they can to patch things up. So Tía Clara described to me how she and her husband had to force their daughter to marry a mozo who had been her novio de calle (street boyfriend). When his family went to 'ask for the girl' (pidir a la chica), she locked herself up in her room, yelling that she would not marry him. Tía Clara and her husband were aware that everybody in the neighbourhood knew that her daughter had had a boyfriend, and believed that if she lost this chance to marry a second opportunity might not come up. So they forced her to get engaged and eventually marry.

However, it happens relatively often that mozas are engaged for a period – in a few cases even years[8] – for some reason break up, get engaged again with someone else and marry. Yet the Gitanos regard the serial monogamy of the Payos and their long courtships as signs of their immorality – for they cannot believe that a couple will be able to wait for years before having intercourse. When a woman becomes engaged after having been engaged before, or when parents learn that their daughter or future daughter-in-law may have 'played around', a woman's prospective in-laws or her own kin may demand that she be examined by an old woman or by an ajuntaora. In proclaiming their readiness to have the moza 'checked' (mirada) her family make it public that she is still 'whole' and 'not rubbed'. By the same token, a moza who suspects that her genitals may be damaged has no alternative but to try to elope. Thus, when women's behaviour is evaluated, their readiness – and even their eagerness – to engage in sexual relations is condemned and interpreted as a failure to conform to the Gitano laws. Lastly, women's moral burden is increased by a series of images that portray them as being in the stronger position vis-à-vis the men: the Gitanos of Jarana often say that a moza can lie to her boyfriend, making him believe that he is the first man with whom she had sexual relations and so forcing him to elope with her when in fact he is 'covering the hole made by someone else' (tapando el hoyo que hizo otro). Most importantly, the fact that young men lack the knowledge to distinguish a virgin from a non-virgin woman – knowledge that is the privilege of older women – is thought to be the only factor enabling young women to escape the trap of virginity while preserving their status as proper Gitanas.

Elopements as Rites of Passage

Like weddings, elopements follow a typical rite-of-passage sequence. The couple 'escapes' and take refuge in the house of one of the groom's relatives: there they announce that they have got 'married' – that is, that they have had intercourse. The relative then has to convey the message to the groom's family, who then decide how to tell the parents of the bride. The couple remain a few days at the relative's house until the groom's parents decide to 'bring them back home' *(traerlos pa casa)* – residence after marriage is virilocal. Both the couple's perceived lack of restraint and the elopement to which it is thought to lead have very negative overtones. Although eloping is always considered a good alternative to the Payo lifestyle – approximately every second couple marries by elopement[9] – it also ranks much lower than the wedding in the Gitanos' evaluations.

The different ways in which the groom's and the bride's parents are expected to react and do react, to an elopement are consonant with the dual moral standard of which I have been writing throughout this second part of the book. Women more than men show their proper morality at the wedding, and it is they who fail to do so if they elope. The Gitanos of Jarana state that a woman's elopement is an specially strong blow to her father, who is offended by it, for she shames him: Sara told me how 'when you marry with a wedding you are proud not for yourself but for your father who will be able to keep his dignity' and also that 'at the wedding people praise and admire you for the homage you pay to your father'. If a woman elopes, and specially if she and her boyfriend have some kind of sexual contact in her father's house, the Gitanos say that 'it is as if she had cuckolded her father' (literally, 'as if she had put the horns on her father': *como si le hubiera puesto los cuernos a su padre*). By contrast, it is well known that it is convenient when a *mozo* elopes because his family does not have to spend money on a wedding.

Thus, although elopements are *de facto* threats to the authority of both the bride's and the groom's parents, it is the woman's family that is thought to be the most deeply wronged, and to have the right and the obligation to demonstrate it. When Pedro's sister Teresa eloped with her maternal cross-cousin Paco, her parents and brothers spent three days crying, cursing, fainting and generally displaying their anger and disappointment in very graphic ways. Several times Teresa's brothers and father attempted to run out of the house, claiming that they were going to find and kill her, and had to restrain each other. Her mother burned Teresa's clothes as punishment, and then was 'ill' *(mala)* for two days, sitting wrapped up in a blanket, crying, by the fire. Teresa's father did not eat for three days – just as if he had been mourning a death. The whole family was angry with Paco's parents for staying around for a whole day after announcing the elopement. I was told that they should not have done so, because Teresa's family were in great need to let off steam by swearing, complaining and abusing the couple, and they had to control themselves for fear of offending their in-laws and starting a bigger problem. Teresa's mother developed sores in her mouth, and the general explanation was that they appeared because she had had to restrain herself so much. Neighbouring Gitanos regarded this display of anger and sadness with ambiguity: it was seen as necessary as a Gitano reaction in the face of such immorality, but it was also understood to be temporary. People simply nodded their heads and said that Teresa was 'disgusting, a pig' *(asquerosa, una puerca)*, that she had 'so much hunger' *(tanta hambre)* because she was an old maid, and that Teresa's family would get over it in a couple of days.

As a rite of passage, the elopement is completed when the bride's parents 'forgive' *(perdonan)* the couple. They start by refusing to do it, something that has important consequences for the woman's new position, for it means that they withdraw their support vis-à-vis her new in-laws. This is significant because young women are often in difficult situations in their husbands' households: there they are under the authority of their mothers-in-law, to whom they are expected to show obedience and respect by taking on the largest possible share of the housework – a situation that creates much tension and antagonism. In normal circumstances a woman's kin will support her by showing – through their visits and statements – their readiness to intervene in her day-to-day confrontations with her in-laws.

Ten days after eloping with Pedro, Marga's parents had not yet forgiven her. Clara, Marga's eldest sister, told me how she was passing by Marga's new home when she heard people inside criticizing her father. She knew that these criticisms were aimed at hurting Marga, who had been living at her in-laws only a few days. She explained what a difficult position Marga was in at her in-laws', without the support of her family to protect her from the pressures of Pedro's family who, she said, were known to bully in-marrying women. She talked her mother – Estela – into forgiving Marga, telling her that Marga was not allowed to take showers or to keep the money she earned selling and that her in-laws kept coming into her room so that she 'has no peace, doesn't eat and doesn't sleep'. Before Marga's elopement, and in an attempt to put pressure on Marga so that she would behave herself, Estela had taken a very strong oath, swearing on the soul of her one deceased son that, if Marga eloped, she would only agree to see her again once Marga had a grown child of her own. This elicited much family comment for a few days. However, she now agreed to forgive Marga saying that 'if she had some support on that side [meaning her in-laws], I could keep my oath, but the well-being of my daughter is more important'. So she went to her daughter's new household and, in front of her in-laws, embraced Pedro and Marga – who had thrown herself into her arms, crying.

There are no *leyes* (laws) as to how a mother 'forgives' her daughter after her elopement. Fathers, on the other hand are thought – and expected – to be very reluctant, and are meant to do it in a rather structured manner:[10] other members of the father's family put pressure on him, stressing the youth and corresponding foolishness of the couple. Once he has agreed to forgive them, they come to his house with one or two of his closest male adult relatives – usually the same ones who have taken a prominent part in convincing him to forgive the couple. Their role is to make the first encounter smooth, helping to make small talk. The idiom that is used to sanction the forgiveness is not the justification of misplaced desire but an appeal to paternal love and kinship solidarity.

The Sexual Morality of the Evangelical Church

Evangelical Gitanos accept both wedding and elopement as forms of marriage, and rank them in the same way as non-converts do. In its evaluation of wedding and elopement, the Church of Filadelfia builds on the approaches that I have described. Converts regard their being Evangelists as an addition to, and not a detraction from, their being Gitanos, and they continue to consciously uphold some of those values that they identify as specifically Gitano. Female virginity is thus an essential prerequisite for the Evangelical wedding, and the wedding ceremony at the local church is always accompanied by the Gitano ritual. The Evangelical wedding takes place before or after the Gitano wedding, and the couple is married by a minister, whose authority is also recognized by the Spanish State. The ritual follows the Christian pattern, with an exchange of vows and rings.

As for elopement, so long as the couple remain faithful to each other they are not thought to sin, the rationale being that they entered a monogamous union by having sexual intercourse: Evangelists explain that 'the Bible says that each man is to have only one woman in his life and each woman only one man'. Couples who elope, however, cannot have a wedding at the church because marrying by elopement is evaluated as negatively within the Church as it is outside it. Converts who elope are not allowed to attend services until after two or three weeks have gone by. On the other hand, just as they are 'forgiven' by the family of the bride, their fault comes to be overlooked by the Church. Reference to their forgiveness may be explicit, as in Marga's and Pedro's case. They were baptized four months after they got married by elopement. This is in itself revealing, for converts are only allowed to be baptized when they are thought to be spiritually ready: their conversion must be realized in the righteousness of their lives. In this instance, the fact that Marga and Pedro had recently eloped was no impediment to their baptism. However, while they were in the water, waiting to be baptized, Juan – Pedro's maternal and Marga's paternal uncle and a minister – preached justifying their baptism. He said: 'even if they did not dress in white for a wedding God has now dressed them in white' – converts dress in white, just like brides do, at their baptism when their sins are forgiven and their names written in the Book of Life.

This emphasis on female pre-marital virginity is an instance of the affinity between Evangelical and Gitano ideas that I will discuss throughout the following chapters. It also corresponds to the role that the Evangelical Church plays as a mediator in the complex relationship between change and continuity in the construction of group identity. Although it purports to alter many of what it sees as Gitano ideas and relations linked to gender, converts do not want to get rid of an idea that is central to what being Gitano means.

Conclusions[11]

The Gitanos of Jarana stress that it is difficult to live up to the standards of sexual continence that their gender morality demands. It is easy to see why weddings, revolving as they do around the production of a physical proof of chastity, should occupy such a prominent place in the Gitanos' conceptions of themselves. Elopements, on the other hand, although much less revered, play a function that is arguably more important: they enable compromise. Elopements are premised on the virginity of the bride, but this is a virginity that has to remain assumed and can never be ascertained. By accepting elopements as a form of marriage the Gitanos are able to tell themselves that, among them, all women remain virgins until they marry. The question of whether this is indeed the case or not can then be bypassed. It is clear that, while Gitano weddings exist to proclaim the righteousness of the Gitanos as a people, the role of the elopement as an institution within Gitano life is to blur reality. It is by accepting elopements as proper marriages, even more than by celebrating weddings, that Gitanos can convince themselves that they are different from the non-Gypsies around them. Elopements, which exist on the boundary between the Payo and the Gitano way of life, enable Gitanos to state that, among all Spaniards, they alone are truly honourable.

Notes

1. The *Sección Femenina de Falange* was created in 1934. It was the female branch of the Falangist movement founded by José Antonio Primo de Rivera that provided much of the rhetorical drive behind the right-wing regime after the Civil War. Under Franco the *Sección Femenina* was put in charge of all 'women's affairs' and exercised huge influence through the *Servicio Social* (Social Service). This was a six-month course in household management and 'womanly tasks' which all unmarried women had to fulfil in order to be able to apply for passports and driving licenses, obtain university degrees, work as civil servants, and belong to associations relating to the arts and sports (see Martín Gaite 1987a: 55–73).

2. For alternative non-European understandings of virginity see Boddy 1989, Delaney 1987, and Lindisfarne 1994.

3. I draw on my experience as a middle-class Spanish woman from Madrid, and on my fieldwork in a Southern Aragonese village in 1990 and 1991.

4. Although most of the women that I met in Jarana talked of 'the grape' in the singular, a few stated that there are two 'grapes' rather than one.

5. San Román (personal communication 1995, 1996) has described the same practices for Gitanos of Madrid, Barcelona and Andalusia. Pasqualino, who has referred in passing about *le mouchoir ensanglanté* (1995: 179) has also, in another context, remarked the absence of blood on defloration handkerchiefs (personal communication 1997). Gamella, however, talking of Andalusian Gitanos, gives an account that differs markedly both from my own fieldwork data and from San Román's and Pasqualino's observations. He remarks that

> The bride lies down while an expert woman, who is paid for her services, the *picaora*, or *ajuntaora* or *sacaora*, ascertains that the hymen of the girl is intact piercing it with one of her fingers (or some other element in

some cases) wrapped in a handkerchief, before the mother of the bride and the mother of the groom and, sometimes, before other women of the family.

The small hemorrhage stains the handkerchief with blood producing 'roses' that prove the 'purity' or virginity of the bride and the 'honour' of her family. 'Staining the handkerchief' is a key moment in the life of a woman and her kin (Gamella 1996: 121–2).

Unfortunately, it is not clear from Gamella's account whether he is simply reproducing what his informants told him about the wedding or whether he is unintentionally projecting his own preconceptions about what defloration involves onto their descriptions.

6. San Román encountered the same attitude among the Gitanos with whom she worked (personal communication 1995, 1996).

7. This kind of description should itself be considered in relation to the cultural and historical framework within which it was produced. Testut (1931) talks about the Bartholin's glands being the female correspondent of the male Cowper's glands. This indicates an underlying logic in which male and female are analogous: an understanding of the body as primarily human and secondarily female or male that belongs to the realm of medical discourse. The *honra* has no male equivalent: it defines women and it is defined by being found only in women.

8. Engagements, however, tend to be short-lived: the fear that the couple will have sexual relations often pushes their parents into marrying them as soon as they have enough money to put up a feast – often only a couple of months after the engagement.

9. Out of 49 Gitano women from Jarana, aged between 14 and 80 at the time of fieldwork, 24 had married with a wedding and 25 by elopement. These customary marriages are not binding according to Spanish Law.

10. Whereas the Gitanos of Jarana stress and dramatize the role of the bride's father in forgiving the couple, in her 1976 ethnography San Román emphasized that of the bride's mother (1976: 153–4).

11. Some of the Gitano women from Jarana, particularly the oldest ones (in their seventies or eighties), insist that weddings are becoming rarer, with the number of marriages by elopement increasing as a result of the growing 'looseness' and moral corruption of young Gitano women. I regret that I do not have sufficient reliable material to substantiate or dispute their assertions. However, more than twenty years ago, San Román identified a trend that replicates the statements of these older Gitanas of Jarana. She explained:

I want to underline that the marriage by elopement seems to be much more frequent these days. I believe there is one main reason for this. Young Gitanos clearly acknowledge the wish to acquire a greater freedom when choosing a partner for life ... Some young Gitanos understand marriage as something that concerns exclusively those who are about to marry, and parents' opinions are thought to have little to do with the matter. This different conceptualization pushes young people into using the equally traditional method of marrying on the basis of an individual contract, that is, through the elopement (1976: 154).

By contrast, Gamella puts forward an alternative and interesting possibility. He states that

We do not know to what extent this tradition is ancestral or invented (in Hobsbawm and Ranger's sense) . . . Many Gitanos tell us that their parents or grandparents did not practise it, at least in the form that today is considered 'normal'. It could well be that, contrary to what is usually thought, in the past the wedding was a custom restricted to some groups of Gitanos, but so striking and dramatic that it was considered an 'ideal' that has later been asserted as . . . true proof not only of family honor and female purity but of Gypsyness by more ample sectors of the Gitano minority (1996: 123).

The Politics of the Married Couple

The dual standard about which I have written in the last two chapters, which dictates a different morality for women and for men, is not restricted to the management of sexual desire before marriage. Once they get married, Gitano men and women have to go on performing their *gitaneidad* (Gypsyness) in all realms of daily life. After marriage it is the hierarchical relation between husband and wife that the Gitanos of Jarana emphasize most as sign of their difference from the Payos. However, an analysis of women's views of their relations to their husbands and their positions within their own or their husbands' natal households reveals a wealth of opinions and standpoints that are absent from, say, descriptions of wedding ceremonies. Women are aware that, as Gitanas, they owe respect and obedience to their husbands and their parents-in-law. However, they often express unhappiness or dissatisfaction, and evaluate negatively those Gitano 'laws' that state that they should be 'below' (*debajo*) the men. In a letter, Sara explained how she saw her life and her possibilities as a Gitano woman:

> Look I was engaged with Rodolfo the one who is now married to Pili for almost two years and then we broke up when we were about to marry and in three months I married Paco so who would have told me what was to happen because now I am very happy to have married Paco because I have command over my children and the money as I want and he treats me very fondly and at least takes me from time to time for coffee or to the movies or simply for a stroll. And then I see Pili who has to be below her mother-in-law so that she will give her money for her children's snacks or even for her own sanitary towels and on top Rodolfo beats her up whenever he feels like. And you will know that she has had another son imagine what her life is like with three small children and that kind of husband and parents-in-law my heart falls so look what God delivered me from because I could have gone

through the same situation . . . so whenever you have to take a step call upon God you'll see how he helps you.

In this chapter I explore the different ways in which Gitanos – both women and men, but particularly women – portray marital relations. My aim is to emphasize the multiplicity of ways in which Gitanos evaluate their own and other people's lives. This multiplicity is not usually acknowledged by the Gitanos in their evaluations of their relationships with the Payos: within these evaluations, Payos and Gitanos tend to appear as monolithic moral categories. Below I discuss three main models of marital relations: the first one is upheld by women and men; the second is put forward by women when they want to convey their dissatisfaction with 'the Gitano way of being' (*la manera de ser Gitana*); and the third can be described as 'Evangelical' and represents an innovation on the two previous. An analysis of Gitano talk about married life reveals that Gitanos often evaluate positively aspects of the Payo lifestyle. They do so implicitly – for example by 'borrowing' from the Payos, as in the case of the Evangelical Church – and explicitly – for example by expressing envy at the lives of Payo women, as in the case of many Gitanas from Jarana.

The Harshness of Women's Lives

The Gitano men and women of Jarana put much emphasis on the harshness of women's lives, with women being portrayed as a group vis-à-vis the men: they say that 'being a woman is the lowest thing in life' (*ser mujer es lo más arrastrado de la vida – arrastrado* means something that is dragged or jerked about, the lowest condition in life), and that 'it is very ugly to be a woman' (*es muy feo ser mujer*). The corollaries of women's reproductive activities are often underlined: they have periods and give birth, which are both uncomfortable and painful. Women are said to have 'all the bad things' (*todo lo malo*):

> You bring your daughter up to your taste, with all your love, you teach her well, and then she goes and marries a drug-addict who lives in Valencia or France and who does not allow her to see her family, and beats her up everyday.

In this statement a young woman talks about her anxieties over her daughters, while referring to her own experience as a girl and as the wife of a drug addict. She also talks about the virilocal preference which often puts constraints on the contact women can have with their kin and the support they can receive from them. Finally, she depicts women's dependence on the will of men.

When describing women's lives, the Gitanos of Jarana very often talk about how Gitano women both are and should be *sujetas* to the men – 'tied' to them, from the verb *sujetar* which means to hold, fasten, tie something to something else. The word *sujeta* connotes dependence, incapacity to act on the basis of one's own plans or desires because of someone else's plans and desires. Men as well as women explain that what women can and cannot do should be in the hands of men. They refer not only to their activities, but also to their bodies – what women should and should not look like. In particular, men should be able to impose their will upon women with regards to matters that are seen as indicative of women's sexual morality – for example, having their hair cut or dyed, wearing a particular skirt, going to see a movie or talking to an unrelated man. Tío Ricardo, a middle-aged minister of the Evangelical Church, explained to me how, among the Gitanos, 'women are the bosses, they do whatever they want with the money', but that 'when considering dress or going to places, then it is the husband who is in charge and women often deserve to be slapped'. These ideas are as central to the formulation of Gitano femininity as of Gitano masculinity: it is the men's role 'to allow' (*dejar*) or not to allow women to act in particular ways or engage in particular activities, and to punish them if they misbehave.

Moreover, women's attachment to men is what gives them a position among the Gitanos, and Gitanos often describe how widows and women who are separated from their husbands no longer have a rightful basis from which to act, are despised by other Gitanos, and are constantly watched for signs of immorality. Clara made this very clear talking about her own life:

> Very often I tell my husband: 'go on a trip, I am happy without you'. But if he died I would be nothing, because I would not be able to move, because of people: if I breathed, people would ask why, if I drunk water, if I went out to the street … so that I would be absolutely nothing, while with my husband I am respected, well looked-upon, and no one dares to look at me with bad eyes, because people see that the house of the man with whom I am married is a house of respect and shame.

This kind of statement – to do with relations between women and men – intertwines with other representations of women and women's lives. In particular, the Gitanos of Jarana often emphasize that, as Gitanas, women should be able to endure the hardness of work in the street, problems posed by their husbands and, more generally, difficult living conditions. The positive evaluation of women's 'endurance' (*aguante*) came through in a particularly apparent manner in a conversation I had with Asun about one of her sisters-in-law who is a Paya and who has been completely accepted within the family. In her description, Asun evaluated positively women's capacity for 'endurance' and endorsed the view that the lives of Gitanas are hard as a consequence of the appropriateness of gender relations among the Gitanos – while the Payas have easy lives because among the Payos proper gender relations are reversed. Of her Payo sister-in-law she said that 'she does not pretend to be more elegant than she is, she worked hard and lived poorly, during several years she wore wooden slippers, with open heels, and worked like the Gitanas in the street'. Then her husband started using drugs and, although she considered leaving him, she finally decided against it. According to Asun, 'she endured a lot, the *lacorrilla* [young Paya], she could have done like them, who if they do not get along they leave and do well doing so.' This kind of relationship between women and men is perceived as epitomizing the rightness of the Gitano way of life against that of the Payos among whom women's looseness and rejection of their proper roles leads to all sorts of evils – such as divorce, infidelity, and the disintegration of family ties. Payo men do not control their women, and the latter have male 'friends' (*amigos*), wear inappropriate clothing and fail to fulfil the tasks of the house.

The terms in which the Gitanos phrase the husband-wife relationship – *sujeta* (tied), *debajo* (below), *esclava* (slave) and so on – reflect a sense of both antagonism and dependence that resembles anthropological understandings of subjection or subordination.[1] These images are underpinned by a sense that what is Gitano is also adequate and right. In Jarana, the Gitanos often appeal to proper morality through the sentence 'it has always been the case' (*siempre se ha visto*), implying that there is one rightful model of relations between women and men from which the Payos have diverged. My attempts to elicit other kinds of explanations had little result: when I asked Tío Juan and Tía Tula why it was that among the Gitanos 'men are in command' (*los hombres mandan*), I was told because 'men wear trousers' (*los hombres llevan pantalones*) and also because 'women dress from the head down [wear dresses] and men from the feet up' (*las mujeres se visten por la cabeza y los hombres por los pies*). The point here is that women are women, men are men, they are different from each other, and it is well known what their relationship should be like. Little attempt is made to get beyond this kind of circular logic, besides referring to the differences between the Payo and Gitano lifestyles.

Women's Views

When the Gitano women of Jarana talk both about their own particular experiences, and about the more general conditions of living as
Gitanas, this positive evaluation of 'endurance' may be reversed: then
they resent rather than praise the harshness of their lives and portray
men as being responsible for it. Women talk of themselves as 'slaves
of the house' (*esclavas de la casa*), in the sense that they have to take
care of the children and do the domestic tasks, something that puts
limits on the kinds of activities they can pursue. In addition, they
'have less fun' (*nos divertimos menos*) than men do because there are
fewer recreational activities that are considered appropriate for them.
Men, who have the power to redress this situation do not do it: they
'do not allow women' to do many of the things they want – like going
to the Evangelical church, or for coffee at a friend's house – and they
do not take the women with them when they go out. One of the
questions that women asked me most often during fieldwork was:
'Gitano men are chauvinistic [*machistas*], aren't they?' In this kind of
context the word *sujeta*, although still a marker of shared identity,
acquires negative connotations.

Thus, women portray the character of their lives as a consequence
of two main factors: firstly, it rests on their being Gitanas: as proper
women they are slaves of the house, the children, and their work;
and secondly, it is the result of the character of specific relationships
between specific women and men: men contribute to make women's
lives difficult – some more so than others, and sometimes because
women themselves allow them to. This last idea comes through very
graphically in Elena's portrayal of other women of the settlement
whom she defined as 'slaves of the men, who only open their legs
when the men want them to': they make themselves available to men's
whims, while not demanding that the men fulfil their own need for
sexual satisfaction. This attitude is in direct contradiction with the
Gitanos' positive evaluation of individual assertiveness and fortitude
in men and women of all ages.[2]

These negative evaluations that the Gitanas of the district make of
their own lives sometimes lead to a comparison with the situation of
Payo women, who are – within this context – perceived to be privileged. In my conversations with young married women they often
expressed their envy at my way of life, what they called my 'freedom'
(*libertad*) and they explained how, before they got married and had
children – before their status as Gitanas had risen – they often wished

they were Payas. Their positive evaluation of the Payo way of life may at times be even more extreme. In one of the first letters she wrote to me when I had come back from the field, Sara described how she felt the day we 'escaped' from the neighbourhood and went to Madrid University where we had lunch and she met some of my Payo friends: 'for once I felt free, free and freed and at ease with simple people . . . because your world is so simple that it makes you feel joyful because it is a world where fear and gossip do not exist' (*por una vez me sentí libre libre y liberada y a gusto con gente sencilla . . . por que tu mundo es tan sencillo que te hace sentirte feliz porque es un mundo donde el miedo y el qué dirán no existen*) . At the back of the letter Sara made a drawing of ourselves, holding hands, smiling broadly and wearing trousers. The significance of this gesture is clear when the very negative connotations that wearing trousers have for women are taken into account – and in fact, I have never seen Sara wearing anything but skirts. In a later visit to Madrid, while we were selling pyjamas from a market stall, she said: 'Palomi, you don't know how much I envy you, you do whatever you want, you come and go, I know I am very lucky, my husband does not beat me up, and I do not lack anything but I am not free to do my will'. To this I answered saying that no one is totally free, but she said 'it is not the same, there is a huge difference' (*no es lo mismo, hay una diferencia enorme*).

Therefore, although the Gitano women of Jarana are explicit in their positive evaluation of the ties that link women to the wills of their husbands, and to the house and the children, they may also underline their negative implications and openly express their resentment against them. These two ways of evaluating women's lives are not really alternatives, and may even be generated within the same context: women have often told me that, although they would like to have the easy lives of the Payas, this is simply not possible if they are to remain Gitanas.

Marital Relations and the Concept of Respect

Among the Gitanos of Jarana, the word *respeto* – best translated as 'respect' – stands for the behaviour that individuals should adopt in their relationship to individuals of a higher status so as to demonstrate this differential status. It is realized in two main ways: through deference and through obedience. My friend Clara explained to me how *respeto* is something that 'a woman has to have towards her husband: if her husband asks her for water and she does not give it to him, she does not respect him. If he commands her to make coffee for him

Figure 6.1 Sara's drawing of ourselves.

and his friends and she does not make it, she does not respect him'. The same happens when she dresses, sits or behaves in ways which he does not like. Thus she explained how when she insists on wearing a skirt that her husband Lolo does not like or puts on too much make up, he tells her off saying 'you don't respect me'. Lastly, a woman is not respecting her husband 'when he insults her and she answers back'.

This example illustrates some of the ways in which respect works as a factor in husband-wife relations. Firstly, men – because they are men – are perceived inherently to deserve respect from women, and women – because they are women – are inherently obliged to respect men. Hence respect very often seems to have no point of reference beyond representing the status gap between women and men. This is something that Gitanos learn and try to enact from childhood. In my first summer in Jarana I was sitting in the street with Tío Juan, enjoying cool milkshakes from a load that we had brought that day from the rubbish dump, when we saw Loli and Sandra, two of Tío Juan's granddaughters aged ten and eleven, being teased and bullied by Sandra's brothers, Pepe and Tonel, who were thirteen and fourteen at the time. At one point Tonel pushed Loli's chair from behind, so that she had to get up or fall to the ground, and sat on her chair saying 'you two have to learn to have respect for men' (*teneis que aprender a respetar a los hombres*). Pepe then started pushing his sister with the same intention. The two girls did not attempt to recover their seats, but nonetheless mocked them saying 'they think they are men' (*se creen que son hombres*), making fun of their attempts to portray themselves as grown-ups. Tío Juan laughed at his grandchildren and praised them smacking his lips and exclaiming 'they know a lot!' (*no saben nada*: literally, 'they don't know anything').

Secondly, the notion of respect has a prescriptive dimension and a moral charge to it, and is linked to the propriety of Gitano gender relations. For instance, the Gitanos of Jarana view men's involvement in domestic work as both inappropriate and demeaning, and respect appears very often in connection with women's provision of domestic tasks for men: women respect men when they attend to them while they eat, serving them first and often waiting after they have finished before eating themselves or getting up when both are watching television in order to bring them a glass of water. Respect is also brought into play in relation to men's involvement in or control of those aspects of women's behaviour that have a potentially sexual aspect to them, for example those that have to do with such things as dress, manner and looks. Hence, and as Clara herself explains above, women fail to respect men when they refuse to adapt the way in which they manage their bodies to men's commands or desires. This is conceptualized once again by contrast with the Payos: the Gitanos of Jarana insist that Payas do not respect their husbands in any sense of the word, for they wear inadequate clothing, are not faithful to them, and allow them to contribute to the housework.[3]

Both men and women are aware of the fact that respect is one of the factors that 'tie' (*atan*) wives to their husbands. Respect gives relations between them a hierarchical character not only through the enactment of their differential status, but also by putting the right to control several aspects of women's behaviour in the hands of men. Describing her relationship with her husband, Noemi explained to me how her family lived in another neighbourhood in Madrid, San Blas, where the attitudes of Gitano men differed from those of the men in Jarana. She said: 'it has always been the case that women should respect their husbands, but not the slavery [*esclavitud*] that they want here, in San Blas they are much more tractable', and she added that the Bible says that men have to honour (*honrar*) their wives 'although it has always been the case that the man has to be the head'.[4] Thus, when women talk about respect they may also emphasise the threats that their dependence on the will of men pose to them: Noemi describes 'slavery' as the corrupt exaggeration of respect.

It is the moral dimension of respect that makes the performance of any particular person questionable. References to respect crop up repeatedly in conflicts between couples. Rufo, who is a heroin-addict, is one of the men of the district who beats up his wife most often and severely. One afternoon while we were having coffee Teresa showed to me the bruises that he had made on her legs and shoulder blade with a *virola*, a long wooden stick with a lead end used in fights among Gitano men. She explained how she had faced him, shouting at him that she had never seen her father beat up her mother like that. He yelled back that it was 'because your mother respects your father, but you do not respect me'. To this she answered in disgust: 'there is nothing to respect in you'.

The notion of respect thus provides a code of conduct and is used both to evaluate behaviour and to contest such evaluations. Moreover, it plays a central role in the Gitano conceptualization of men and women as two kinds of persons different from each other. The kind of behaviour that each one is expected to adopt within a relationship governed by respect lies at the centre of Gitano ideas of what it means to be a man and a woman. Men and women have differing relations to respect: men deserve respect because they have a higher status than women; women have to give respect to men because they have a lower status than they do. This difference in status is realized or brought into being in daily life every time a woman displays respect towards a man. And, although respect in relations between husbands and wives is conceptualized primarily in terms of ascription, there is also a sense in which not only women have to strive to behave in the right manner, but men as well have earn respect: a man who does not behave as a proper man loses his right to the respect of others – including his wife's. This notion – as Rufo's example illustrates – provides women with some tools for contestation within a framework of relations that they perceive always as unequal and at times as unfair.

Masculinity and the Evangelical Code

The woman whose husband is a convert and nonetheless complains, should be kept on bread and water, and given a blow from time to time. Now, if it is 2am and he has not come back, little sister, you know he is with the brothers, and you are at peace, while before . . . and sisters, we know that in the Gitano life and in the Payo life all the husbands hit their wives and the woman who says she is not beaten up is a liar.

This statement, which is part of an 'advice' (*consejo*) given by a *pastora* (minister's wife) at a women's prayer meeting in Jarana, embodies some of the most recurrent themes in Gitano Evangelical talk on relations between husbands and wives: she makes reference to the Evangelical moral code of behaviour for men and to the consequent benefits that Evangelism brings to women. Both men and women agree that the growth of the Gitano Evangelical Church has greatly improved the lot of Gitanas, and that it has done so by reformulating the rights and obligations of husbands and wives towards each other, and by outlining a code of behaviour for men that happens to benefit women. This kind of evaluation is a recurrent theme outside and within ritual contexts – in sermons during services and in women's prayer meetings – and occupies a central role in the formal teaching on what men's and women's behaviour should be like once they convert to Evangelism.

At the core of the Gitano-Evangelical talk on husband–wife relations lies more general formulation of what convert male behaviour should be like. This reformulation affects areas of daily life as varied as dress, conflict mediation or dealings with Payos, and appears also in other contexts besides married life, as I explain in Chapter 8. It centres on ideas to do with righteousness, decency and peacefulness among others. At another woman's prayer meeting, Melita, one of the local *pastoras*, preached explaining to the other Gitanas present the advantages that having a convert husband had for women: upon becoming Evangelists, she said, 'men stop doing all the evil things [*se quitan de todo lo malo*], drugs, drinking, going around with other women, stealing, killing, and beating up their wives, except a slap here and there because we sometimes deserve it'. She went on to describe how, after converting, husbands and wives have their meals together and are able to chat. Before, 'the women would feed the men first, and eat what was left, and even fan the flies away for them, now it has all changed'. Converts and often also non-converts often describe the advantages of Evangelism in these same terms, not only when talking about husband–wife relations, but also when discussing the spread of drug addiction among the young or when comparing the Gitano and Payo lifestyles. During services preachers also make use of the same 'before' and 'after' stereotype.

Evangelical Gitanos put a special emphasis on separating themselves from 'the world' (*el mundo*). This is realized through a rejection of those activities that are seen to endanger their 'testimony' (*testimonio*) – the example of decency and righteousness that they have to give to other convert and non-convert Gitanos. Convert men are expected, by other converts and by non-converts alike, to abstain from drugs, alcohol and tobacco, and to give up attending 'worldly entertainments' (*diversiones mundanas*) such as gambling or going to the movies or to discos. Some of these activities – like smoking, drinking or going to discos to chat up Payas – have an important place in the Gitano definition of masculinity and are rejected by Evangelists. Others, especially drug-addiction and its corollaries, are portrayed in the same negative terms by converts and non-converts alike. Evangelists put a special emphasis on fulfilling those manly qualities that command *respeto* from other Gitanos – such as self-control and honesty. At a service a man explained what he was like before his conversion:

> Some of the people who are here know me, they know that no one could stop me [*cortarme el camino*], neither my father, nor my mother, my wife or my son, only one person remembered me, the one who is above. My father was having a surgical operation and I left for a party, and I enjoyed it very much. I was about to abandon my wife and children, because I had temptations to go away, and with God's help I am here.

These stereotypes are significant because converts use them explicitly to establish a direct link between men's behaviour and women's quality of life. Men who convert are said to 'give a better life to their wives' (*les dan mejor vida a sus mujeres*): they behave better towards them and are much less likely to get involved in fights and problems with the police, to be reckless in spending money or to come home drunk. And, more importantly, they are not allowed to beat their wives beyond the occasional slap. In Jarana converts only sanction what they see as low levels of violence from men to women, and circumscribe the situations in which it can be exerted. This attitude is best summarized in the recommendation that Luis received from his convert cousins as to how to treat his 'difficult' wife, Rosa: 'teach her, give her a slap if necessary, but nothing else'. Although husbands are the judges of their wives' behaviour and have the right to punish them when the latter 'deserve' it, they should not beat them as severely as is said to happen 'in the world'. Thus, even if converts clearly construct relations between husbands and wives as hierarchical, they do it in a manner which they perceive as being much more benevolent towards women than the non-Evangelical one. Lastly, Evangelists put much emphasis on monogamy and marital fidelity, not only for women but also for men.

Men's new roles lead to a reformulation of duties between husbands and wives. The Gitanos of Jarana identify what they call *machismo* (chauvinism) as a mark of the Gitano way of life: women should be 'below' the men. When talking as converts, on the other hand, they underline the propriety of women's dependence on their husbands' will but, taking up New Testament texts, they also emphasize the husband's obligation to 'honour and respect his wife'. The following verses recur in services and in conversations between converts: 'You husbands, live considerately with your wives, bestowing on the women, as the weaker sex, since you are joint heirs of the grace of life in order that your prayers may not be hindered' (1 Pet. 3: 7).

Femininity and the Evangelical Code

Just as they propose a code of behaviour for men as husbands, converts also put forward a code for women as wives: at their prayer meetings women ask God to make them into 'ideal partners for our partners' (*compañeras idóneas para nuestros compañeros*). The idioms *compañero/a* (male/female companion or partner) which converts use in place of *marido/mujer* (husband/wife) have clearly egalitarian connotations. However, unlike in the case of men, the women's Evangelical code is not underlined as a trigger of the transformation of gender relations that converts insist results from Evangelism. What we see, instead, is a reinforcement of the Gitano moral rules of female behaviour that I have described through this book. The 'testimony' that convert women are expected to give focuses on such things as physical appearance and sexual-moral behaviour. Converts put much emphasis on dress and manners – to be seen wearing trousers or a mini-skirt is a valid reason to be reprimanded and punished by the minister. To this is added the wife's duty to encourage her husband to persevere and improve in the Christian life, not necessarily with words, but through her exemplary behaviour. Converts often draw on St Peter's recommendation that wives 'be *submissive* to your husbands, so that some, though they not obey the word, may be won without a word by the behaviour of their wives, that they see your *reverent* and *chaste* behaviour' (1 Pet. 3: 1–2, my emphasis). The role that ideas about female morality play in the definition of communal identity among the Gitanos of Jarana happens to be reinforced by Biblical concepts that are very similar in content, or at least easily interpreted in those terms and related to by them. The converts of Jarana have constructed a conceptual affinity between 'proper' Gitano and Evangelical understandings of female morality. Biblical precepts are made to fit into the Gitano emphasis on female modesty and gender hierarchy.

Benita, a woman in her early thirties, is the wife of a deacon of the Church and a regular attender at services. I listened as she and Tía Asun, who is one of the oldest converts in the neighbourhood and a very active woman, talked with a few convert men about the church's cafeteria and how to manage it. Later, Benita approached me and criticized Tía Asun's intervention saying: 'she always wants to know more, if there are four men present she should let the men talk, that is what I understand "Gospel" to mean'. In negatively assessing Tía Asun's behaviour – her acting as if she 'knew' in front of the men – Benita made reference to a key Gitano idea about femininity: it is improper for women to display too much 'knowledge' (*conocimiento*) in the face of men. She brought in an Evangelical evaluation, and it was the shared – Gitano and Evangelical – emphasis on female–male deference and gender hierarchy that acted as the meeting point.

Sexual Morality and the Evangelical Church

Ideas to do with sexual practice and with men and women in relation to it constitute a second aspect of the Evangelical ethos that is of central importance to the analysis of the politics of husband-wife relations. The following quotation is taken from a letter that Clara, who is a *pastora* of the Church, sent to me in October 1993:

> About what you ask me if it is a sin to deny yourself to your husband or to your wife Lolo (her husband, a minister of the Church) says that it is a fault because you make your husband or your wife be in danger of being tempted and committing adultery. He says you have to read it in 1 Cor. 7: 4–5. To me he always said that it was a sin when I was angry and would not allow him to make love. Now when I have read these verses I have realised that it is only a fault and not a sin.[5]

A few months earlier, while I was still doing my fieldwork, she had drawn a distinction between what she called 'in Christ' (*en Cristo*) and 'according to the Gitano way of being, in the world' (*gitanalmente, en el mundo*), which included the attitudes of non-converts and the previous ones of people who have converted:

> According to the Gitanos a man cannot restrain himself. *Gitanalmente* [according to the Gitano 'way of being'] it has always been acknowledged that men need to have sexual relations often, and that they cannot control themselves. If you are staying at my house, and I feed you well, one day potatoes, the next day sausages . . . and you are full up you

won't go to find food elsewhere . . . but if you have not had anything for three days, you would even eat a rotten apple if you had it in front of you. The same happens with men: if they are satisfied with their wives, even if they are not very beautiful they will not go to look for *it* elsewhere.

She went on to tell the story of the wife of a drug-addict: she used to refuse to have sexual relations with him, and so he often beat her up, and finally went off with a drug-addict Paya. Although he was at fault, it was she who was blamed by other Gitanos, because 'she did not give him what he needed so he went to find it elsewhere'. She added that '*gitanalmente*, a man has right to everything and women to nothing: a woman has the obligation to keep her husband satisfied, but he can have as many women as he wants. If a man does not have sexual relations with his wife, she suspects that he has somebody else and they kill each other' (they fight). By contrast according to the Church,

> Our bodies are not our own the husband and the wife should not refuse themselves to the other. It is a sin not to do the matrimonial act [*el acto matrimonial*] because then other temptations might appear. It is as wrong in a man as it is in a woman to refuse to have sexual relations with their spouse.

Her explanation, which takes up an important theme in the converts' views of themselves, contrasts the two settings in terms of how unequal relations within married couples can be said to be. As I have explained in Chapter 4, the Gitanos put much emphasis on women's sexual drive and capacity to enjoy sex. However, they also describe how women are often refused the means to fulfil it, or depend on men who in turn do not necessarily depend on them. The general idea is that, by comparison with 'the world', inequality between husbands and wives is levelled in the Church, and sexual activity fits within this wider pattern. Thus men's power both over their wives and over their own activities is curtailed, and women are granted the right to demand of men not only a passive fidelity but the actual fulfilment of their sexual needs.

Women's Strategies

Although in Jarana Gitano men and women often emphasize women's dependence on the will of men, it is difficult to pin down the extent to which men in fact control women or impose their wishes on them. Relations between couples are negotiated and redefined all the time, albeit within a set of parameters that sanctions men's greater scope for action and control over the lives of others. I do not want to portray physical violence as the only index of men's control or dominance of women, because I believe that there are ideas – such as the concept of respect – and situations – such as women's frequent physical distance from their own kin – which have a great bearing on the extent to which husbands manage to impose their wills on their wives. However, I do want to stress that violence from men to women is widespread among the Gitanos of Jarana, and that several men are well known in the neighbourhood for the frequency and severity with which they physically abuse their wives. Even among converts, who in my experience tend to follow the precept that forbids husbands to beat up their wives, I know of men who make use of physical violence at least to threaten the women.

Whether or not their husbands use physical violence on them, women stress the influence that men have over their lives: the quality of a woman's life is described as dependant to a large extent on the characteristics of her husband. And yet, women's accounts of their conjugal problems show a consistent emphasis on their own assertiveness and capacity to get their way in spite of the restrictions imposed by men. Hence Teresa's statement that

> I have become old before my time. At first, Rufo used to do what he wanted with me. For example, he did not allow me to go to see my mother. Now I do exactly the opposite of what he wants on purpose, even though he beats me up almost every day.

Women attempt to show their assertiveness vis-à-vis their husbands in different ways, and the semi-institutionalized practice that they call *escarmiento* (lesson, warning) occupies a central place among them. The Gitanos of Jarana put much emphasis on the idea that women should only put up with a certain amount of men's behaviour when this is thought to be unreasonable. Moreover, it is a wife's duty to 'teach her husband a lesson' (*darle un escarmiento*) when his attitude towards her – and his more general behaviour – is clearly evil or immoral. *Escarmiento* often implies the awareness and approval of other members of the couple's families: some of the instances that I witnessed in Jarana in fact represented attempts by a group of kin at keeping the behaviour of a particular man in check. The various men who were punished in this way had failed not only in their fulfilment of their obligations as husbands, but in their more general behaviour as well: they were men without dignity or self-control, and often drug-addicts – what the Gitanos of Jarana call *risiones*, or men to be laughed at. The following is an extract from my fieldnotes:

> Tía Tula told me about her grandson Marcos: he is a drug-addict, and from time to time beats up his wife Guapa very badly. She often threatens to leave him but never does it. Yesterday night he did it again. His brothers opposed him, almost fighting with him . . . This morning Tío Juan – Marcos's paternal grandfather – and 'el Gitano Emilio' – Marcos's maternal grandmother's husband – talked to him and told him that if he beats her up again 'we will take her to Talavera [where her family lives] to her father, with the children'. He shouted back that 'she can go if she wants but not taking the children'. His mother Carmina then said that she would not take care of the children if Guapa left without them, and that it would have been different if he had been 'a proper man', and Guapa had left him for another man. But, since it is all due to drugs and his fault, she would not do it.

At other times, however, only part of the family knows what has happened or, if the woman has contacts among the Payos, her disengagement may be even more radical. I wrote the following in July 1994 while in Cambridge, more than a year after I finished fieldwork:

> My mother rung me this morning, and told me that Sara was with her at home; she arrived at quarter-to-eight in the morning with her two children. She eloped because Paco beat her up yesterday night, for the very first time in their married life. I talked with Sara on the phone: she told me that she and Paco have been having many problems recently, and finally yesterday he slapped her very badly . . . Part of the problem had to do with Sara's resentment about Paco submission to his eldest brother. Sara got very angry, and told him that he exists only to do his brother's will. She challenged him saying 'you are not a man, people will say that you are not a man'. It was then that he hit her, so strongly that she fell to the floor. Her daughter Nina was present, 'and I pretended to be strong for her, but Nina was crying'. Then, after he hit her, 'you can't imagine what my tongue was like, I insulted him in all ways, I told him people were going to think he was a *risión* (worthless), you know how awful that is for a man, Palomi'. So, she went to bed, but could not sleep, and at six thirty in the morning, while Paco was asleep, took her children and decided to go on the underground to my mother's house. She said: 'I don't know how that came to my mind. I don't want to leave him, this is just to teach him a lesson, but if I stay at your mum's no one will know where I am, he'll get really scared, because my family won't know where I am, and he'll never do it again'.

Sara stayed for three days at my mother's, and I managed to convince her to let her sister Clara know her whereabouts, so that her own kin

– not her husband – would not worry too much about her. After that she moved to her maternal grandmother's, where she stayed for another couple of days before her father convinced her to go back to Paco. To my knowledge he has never hit her again and, from my talks with both of them, it is clear that his admiration towards her increased greatly after she put her foot down so strongly.

The practice of *escarmiento* therefore provides women with a tool to put pressure on men and thus improve their own lives. However, within a framework in which women derive much of their self-esteem and social approval from their role as wives and household managers,[6] this capacity can be a double-edged sword. As Caro, who left her heroin-addict husband for seven months, explained:

> The life of the Gitanas is very hard, it is not like the life of the Payas. If you are alone you are nothing. If you are a widow you know life is over for you, you trouble everybody. If a woman is separated it is also bad: she has to be careful not to disturb, that her child does not disturb her grandparents, that she does not make noise . . . This was so even if my parents always treated my daughter and my little sister with the same love, and even if they treated me very well.

Without going as far as leaving their husbands and formally drawing on the support of their kin and that of their husbands', women deal with the constraints men put on them in other ways. Firstly, they very often act behind their husbands' backs, sometimes actively deceiving them. Secondly, they may refuse to have sex with them. This is easier for converts than for non-converts because, by limiting the amount of violence men can exert over women, the Church also empowers the latter. This is so even if other Evangelical precepts – such as the emphasis on the wife's submission to her husband – put limits on the women's independence. As in the case of Sara's sister, Clara, women married to converts may go as far as actively and openly black-mailing their husbands. The following are three extracts from my fieldnotes:

> 19th April 1993. Clara has been putting pressure on her husband ever since (about a month ago) he did not take her parents' side on the question of who was to pay for him to have his surgery . . . she has been refusing him, not allowing him to touch her or have sex with her, and also not giving him information about her activities, not giving him any money, and not cooking or cleaning for him.

> 22 April 1993. After being really angry . . . Clara has finally decided to make peace. She told me how she has realised in different ways that

what she is doing is not godly [*no es de Dios*]. Today at the women's fast the pastora insisted that women should be converts even in the home: 'even in the way we scold our children we should be converts'; similarly when women have problems with their husbands they should do their best to get a reconciliation. This and similar things – remorse, talks with other converts and the awareness that she had to give good example to me as a potential convert – have made her give in, although starting from the point that neither she nor her parents will contribute any money or effort towards his operation.

26th April 1993. Although Clara is again allowing Lolo to have sex, she told me that 'I am not the same with him, I control myself so as not to enjoy it. I let him be satisfied and that is it'. Thus he complains that it is 'like doing it to a doll'. She told me that she had done this once before, during another conflict, and he even cried. So now they have this kind of sex, and she cooks and cleans for him. That is, she does not play with him as they usually do, and is cold and short with him. He is very unhappy, and even she is finding it very hard partly because during the day she feels bad from having to restrain herself when having sex. According to her he is amazed at her capacity for controlling herself.

By contrast with *escarmiento*, this kind of blackmail presupposes a feeling of confidence on the part of the woman which comes at least partly from the belief that no great physical violence is going to be used – because her husband is a convert. It also assumes the sexual dependence of a man on his wife, something that again only the Church fully sanctions and hence 'guarantees'.

Conclusions to Part II

Throughout Chapters 4, 5 and 6 I have explored three different contexts within which the Gitanos of Jarana construct men and women as different kinds of persons. By upholding a series of gender-specific moral rules, these Gitanos are able to portray themselves as different from, and superior to, the Payos that surround them. Performances carried out within ritual contexts and within the framework of daily life are equally important in this sense: because the Gitanos perceive themselves as being under constant threat of assimilation into the Payo world, they invest the smallest everyday gestures and activities with a heavy symbolic load. In the absence of a sense of overarching and harmonious Gitano 'society' or 'community', it is these performances that provide the link between persons and the identity of the group, between persons and the ideal of 'the Gitanos' as a 'people'.

The Gitanos of Jarana are aware of the fact that the boundary that separates them from the Payos is a permeable one. They know of Gitanos – friends and relatives – who have become *apayados* (Payo-like) and have given up the Gitano 'way of being' (*la manera de ser Gitana*). They insist that remaining Gitano is very much a choice, a decision taken in the face of a tempting if corrupting and degenerate alternative. Simultaneously, they deny that the Gitano 'laws' – the set of rules and understandings through which they organize their lives *as Gitanos* – may be shaped in any way by the Payo way of living and thinking. They do this partly by building an ideal model of Payo life and morality that is the precise inversion of the way of living and thinking that they exalt as uniquely Gitano.

It is clearly possible to challenge the Gitanos' notion that their gender morality is essentially different from the Payo one – a notion that is central to the way the Gitanos see themselves as a group. Firstly, ideas about masculinity and femininity that the Gitanos portray as 'Gitano' are often undermined by the Gitanos themselves, in action as well as in speech and some Payo practices are – implicitly or explicitly – positively evaluated and even appropriated. These processes are illustrated by the criticisms of the Gitano way of living put forward by the women of Jarana and, more graphically, by the institution of the elopement, which allows Gitanos to behave like Payos and nonetheless remain Gitano. Moreover, the Gitano emphasis on female virginity as a marker of group identity finds close parallels in one of the several models of gender that have co-existed in Spain, in changing forms, at least since the Early Modern period.

Secondly, the Gitanos are by no means alone in having placed a particular gender morality at the core of their shared identity. Throughout the twentieth century, Spanish people have worked through and redefined their competing projects of society by redefining their equally competing models of gender. Politics and gender morality have consistently been intimately intertwined. Seen within this wider context, the Gitanos appear as a group of Spaniards doing what Spaniards seem to have been doing for most of the twentieth century – creating imagined communities by contrast to the imagined communities favoured by other Spaniards, and doing so to a large extent by reference to gender rules and behaviour.

By placing gender mores at the centre of their views of themselves as a group vis-à-vis others, and by endorsing a model of gender relations with strong Spanish overtones, the Gitanos of Jarana locate themselves firmly within the framework of Spanish society and culture. Simultaneously, they distance themselves from such framework and are successful in stating their singularity. They do so by endorsing a view of the female body that *is* different from the Payo understandings, and making of it the cornerstone of their common identity. To the observer the *honra* – which is singularly Gitano – appears as the most striking objectification of Gitano difference.

In the next two chapters I carry the main themes of Part I and II into an exploration of yet another context of Gitano life: confrontations between kinship groups and mediation by male elders. My aim is twofold. Firstly, I add an important layer to my analysis of Gitano sociability as it relates to the Gitanos' particular understanding of themselves as a group: I discuss Gitano kinship and political organizations, as well as Gitano beliefs about conception, gestation, and the physical and non-physical make-up of persons. Secondly, I extend my analysis of Gitano gender through a discussion of the role of men in the performance of Gypsyness and in the construction of 'the Gitanos' as a people.

Notes

1. According to the Shorter Oxford English Dictionary, third edition, 'subjection' stands for 'the act of being subject to, or under the domination of, another'; whereas 'subordination' means 'belonging to an inferior rank, grade, class, or order, and hence dependent upon the authority or power of another'.

2. The Gitanos of Jarana evaluate very positively the qualities of assertiveness and fortitude, which men are better empowered to incarnate than women – and women themselves acknowledge this fact. When they speak from this perspective, or underline this aspect of their experiences, Gitanas can be said to describe themselves as being 'dominated' according to Errington's and Gewertz's definition of the term. These authors refer to the fact that definitions of the person are culturally constructed and state that 'dominance . . . is a relationship in which individuals or groups are impeded or prevented from following the strategies necessary for them to meet the cultural standards which define persons as having worth' (1987: 83).

3. In fact, the Gitanos of Jarana often attempted to tease me by telling me that among the Payos it is the men that do *all* the housework.

4. Noemi's use of the word *honrar* – a verb whose root is the Spanish word *honor* – exemplifies how converts borrow Biblical terminology and incorporate it into their daily life. The Gitanos use the word *honra* – which shares the

same root – to refer to female sexual decency in the way I have explained in Chapter 3. The word *honor*, by contrast, does not figure in their vocabulary except within Evangelical contexts.

5. 'The wife hath no power of her body, but her husband; and likewise also the husband hath no power of his body, but the wife. Defraud ye not one the other, except it be with consent for a time, that ye may give yourselves to fasting and prayer; and come together again, that Satan tempt you not for your incontinency' (1 Cor. 7: 4–5; King James Version).

6. I have discussed women's roles as household managers and breadwinners elsewhere (Gay y Blasco 1995).

Part III

The Performance of Morality: Patrilinearity, Conflict and Masculinity

On my first day in Jarana I was taken by one of the local social workers to meet Ernesto Vázquez Fernández, or Tío Juan, as he is known by the Gitanos of Madrid. I wanted to find accommodation with a Gitano family in Jarana and Tío Juan, being the main figure of authority among the Gitanos of the area, would be able to tell us who had the space and the disposition to house a Paya, or who needed the extra money that a paying guest would provide. Tío Juan was – and is – a tall, very dark-skinned man in his seventies, with an imposing belly and a no less imposing greying moustache. Outdoors and indoors, he always wears a hat and carries a walking-stick, the symbols of prestige of a well known 'man of respect' (*hombre de respeto*) or conflict mediator. He decided that I would be best off living in his house, lending a hand with the domestic work to his wife, Tía Tula, a frightening old woman with a quick temper and a mane of black hair down to her waist.

For the rest of my fieldwork, both when I was and when I was not living with them, Tío Juan and Tía Tula's house remained my home among the Gitanos, and the old couple two of my best friends. On winter evenings, I would sit with them around the fire, watching television and laughing with Tío Juan at Tía Tula's idiosyncratic interpretations of Westerns, Kung-Fu films and Venezuelan soap-operas. On summer afternoons, while Tía Tula napped in the cool darkness of their living-room, and always at my request, Tío Juan would tell me anecdotes from his youth: his adventures during the Civil War, when he escaped conscription feigning imbecility, his travels around the Peninsula, and his tricks on the *Guardia Civil* of this or that little village of Castile. A few months after we first met, he began to tell me about his experiences as a mediator among the Gitanos of Madrid. Alone or with Tía Tula, he would explain to me the intricacies of a marital quarrel in which he had been called to arbitrate; the problems of a Gitano who had illegally bought a council flat from another Gitano only to be thrown out by the police; or his difficulties in keeping drug dealing out of his neighbourhood.

Tía Tula had given Tío Juan four sons, all of whom had been prolific fathers of sons. When I was in Jarana, Tío Juan had at his disposal a fighting force of about twenty adult males, all of them his direct descendants. He also had the collaboration of the sons and grandsons of his much-loved but now deceased nephew, Tío Sebas. The control of his patrigroup – the Foros – over the area was almost complete. Together, Tío Juan and Tío Sebas had set up 'a law' (*una ley*) that no drugs were to be sold in the neighbourhood. When, well into my fieldwork, Tío Juan was reluctantly told by one of his youngest grandsons that 'somebody' was selling drugs in the Upper Street, he staged a display of strength. Juanes and Sebastianes, men and women, young and old, paraded through the neighbourhood yelling threats at 'whoever is selling drugs' and at 'whoever knows who is selling drugs but won't tell'. The men were brandishing sticks; the women walked behind, placing death curses on the dealers and their supporters.

As a well-known conflict mediator in his own right, and as the head of a large and powerful patrigroup, Tío Juan was particularly well positioned to exert his influence over the life of other Gitanos within and outside Jarana. He was a righteous man and his righteousness brought him requests for help from Gitanos in trouble from all over the city and beyond.[1] It was the respect of other Gitanos, their acknowledgement that he had led an outstandingly virtuous life according to the 'Gitano laws', that placed him in such a high, but also precarious, position. In a strongly egalitarian context, where prestige among men is acquired rather than ascribed, Tío Juan was always at risk of losing the deference of other Gitanos. Similarly, had a larger patrigroup been resettled in Jarana, the influence of the Foros over the area would have been seriously circumscribed. The collaboration between Tío Juan and the *Consorcio* – that very much wanted to keep Jarana 'clean', and free of drug-dealing – was in fact essential in establishing the Foros as a kind of 'police force' among the Gitanos of the neighbourhood.

In the pages that follow I build on this brief description of Tío Juan's role and of the role of the Foros among the Gitanos of Jarana. I contextualize the rest of the book by providing a picture of what can be described as political relations among the Gitanos of the neighbourhood. I show how, in spite of the strong emphasis that Gitanos put on age and gender as the bases of ascribed hierarchy, the actual performance or realization of that hierarchy is an on-going, negotiated and precarious process. Rules and norms are fundamental in shaping the Gitano view of the world. But, as these rules are played out and put into action, it becomes clear that they are oriented around the constant reconstruction or renegotiation of social relations. Or, to put it in another way, the prominent place that norms occupy among the Gitanos does not prevent, but instead facilitates, the fluidity and instability of Gitano political life.

The best known ethnographies of the Gitanos have talked about conflict as the place where the structural principles governing Gitano society are made visible. This is particularly so in the case of authors, such as San Román (1976, 1990) and Ardevol (1986), who insist that Gitano kinship organization revolves around patrilineal principles. More recently, Gamella has emphasized that 'the Spanish Gypsies, in the same way as other groups of Gypsies such as the Rom, the Sinte or the English Romanichal, have a cognatic system of filiation, which is reflected in their kinship terminology' (1996: 107). In Jarana, the Gitanos combine a cognatic terminology with a strong stress on patrilineal links. In the pages that follow, rather than taking political units as given, I look at the circumstances and idioms through which people come to stress their patrilineal links at the expense of their bilateral ties. Beliefs about the make-up of persons lie at the core of these mechanisms of amalgamation: in Chapter 7 I explain how ideas and practices to do with agency and personhood provide the conceptual framework for political processes in Jarana.

Understandings to do with men and maleness are also central to these processes. As will become clear below, the staging of political relations among the Gitanos of Jarana presupposes the adequate performance of Gitano masculinity – and it is the content of this masculinity, and the ways in which it is enacted and contested, that I describe in Chapter 8. I discuss how ideas about masculinity are implicated within the context of unequal relations not only between men and women but, most importantly, among men and among groups defined through kinship links. The growing spread of Gitano Evangelism frames the discussion. Therefore, throughout this third part of the book, I touch on, and point to the links between ideas and practices to do with personhood, kinship, masculinity, leadership and religious conversion.

Notes

1. 'Men of respect' do not receive any kind of economic payment or compensation for their time and services. Rather, the opposite is closer to the

truth: many times when he had to go to mediate in a conflict among Gitanos who lived far away, Tío Juan would have to take a taxi – which he payed for himself – or else be driven by one of his sons or grandsons. The main benefit that he reaped was to be given a chance to influence the lives of other Gitanos, as well as an increase in his reputation as good mediator which in turn brought him further calls for help.

sevenseven

Personhood and Kinship Links

Theories of Conception

The views on conception that the Gitanos of Jarana put forward include elements of Payo medical knowledge together with others that do not form part of the cultural baggage of the Payo population among whom the Gitanos live – although they may have done so in the past. The content and the elaboration of these views vary from individual to individual with personal history, gender and age being primary determinants. In Jarana, the Gitanos have access to, and constantly call upon, the Spanish national health service.[1] The Gitano women of the district give birth in hospital, and most – although not all – pregnancies are overseen by doctors. Married women in their teens, twenties and thirties are familiar with Payo medical discourses on reproduction and human fertility. Many use the contraceptive pill or the coil, and have learned about ova, impregnation, and infertility through their own attempts at becoming pregnant or at avoiding pregnancy.[2] Most know that HIV and hepatitis can be passed on through sexual intercourse and those whose husbands are or have been drug users willingly undergo medical check-ups.

During my fieldwork in 1992 and 1993, social work policy dictated a very conscious and organized effort to change Gitano attitudes towards family size and gender relations in general. The social workers that I met in Jarana considered these issues fundamental in fighting the Gitanos' idiosyncrasies and maladjustment to 'society' (la sociedad). They wanted to bring down the Gitano birth rate, partly because they perceived it as a factor leading directly to the subordination of Gitano women, and partly because of the housing problems that a growing Gitano population posed. Among other activities, the social workers organized a series of weekly talks in which women were shown slides depicting the human reproductive systems, and were told about fertilization and foetus development in great detail. These talks were compulsory for all women whose families received the regular economic 'Integration' help or IMI. The social policy of the *Consorcio* selected Gitanas rather than Gitanos as its main targets. Men were less intensively exposed to the influence of social workers, and their knowledge of Payo medical notions is narrower. It is women of middle age and younger who have the widest knowledge of the Payo perspective.

The Gitanos of Jarana often say that it is men who 'provide' or 'make' the child *(ponen el niño)*. They state that 'the woman is like the earth and the man puts the seed' *(la mujer es como la tierra y el hombre pone la simiente)*; that 'the father is the one who begets it, the mother carries it for nine months' *(el padre es el que lo enjendra, la madre lo lleva durante nueve meses)*; and that 'the woman puts/contributes with her body' *(la mujer pone su cuerpo)*. The mother's role is to feed the child during and after pregnancy. Many Gitanos believe that, inside their bodies, women have seven *vasos* – 'glasses' or vessels – where the man's seed falls and the child develops. Boys grow in some of these 'glasses' and girls in the others. The same happens with disabled children: they have their own 'glass'. Because women have seven 'glasses' they can give birth to up to seven children at any one time.

I considered this Gitano theory of conception to be a Gitano idiosyncrasy or an autonomous development until I read Jacquart and Thomasset's account of sexuality and medicine in Europe during the Middle Ages (1985). Discussing competing theories of reproduction from the twelfth century onwards they describe the influence of a series of texts that established that the human uterus was divided into seven 'cells'. One example is the *Anatomia Magistri Nicolai Physici*, written sometime during the second half of the twelfth century. This physician

> describes the womb in accordance with tradition . . . 'The womb is divided into seven cells, three on the right, three on the left, and the seventh in the middle'. The author notes the opinion according to which males are begotten in the right hand and females in the left hand, while the central cell is reserved to hermaphrodites.
>
> One can see here the direct influence of a pseudo-Galenic treatise, translated from Greek into Latin and used from the twelfth century onwards: the *De Spermate* . . . This theory evidently belongs to the Pythagorean tradition of numerological speculation; the importance of the number seven was emphasised in Macrobius' commentary to *The Dream of Scipio* (Jacquart and Thomasset 1985: 34–5).

These theories, which were widespread in medieval and Renaissance Europe, were based on the idea that while the outside of the human body resembles that of a monkey, in the inside it is similar to a pig. They also had their roots in classical Greek ideas about the significance of the number seven. Although the theory of the seven-celled uterus came under increasing challenge in the sixteenth century, many midwives still believed in it in the seventeenth (Jones and Stallybrass 1991) and it is likely that in rural or isolated areas some continued to do so until much later. The similarity between these early European beliefs and the ones supported by many of the Gitanos of Jarana is striking, and points to the fact that the Gitanos belong in the wider non-Gitano world that surrounds them as much as in their own. Ideas that could be considered today to be 'intrinsically' Gitano may in fact have their roots in non-Gitano practices and beliefs.

Among the Gitanos of Jarana, because of this intertwining of ideas from different sources, the picture that discourses about conception reveal is not coherent or singular. 'I thought that . . .', 'this is what has always been said . . . ' and 'no one really knows . . .' are sentences that come up repeatedly. There is a constant revision of understandings and many attempts at reconciling competing sets of views – something that demonstrates the permeability of the Gitanos to the Payo world within which they live as well as their own creativity. The Gitanos of Jarana not only deliver moral judgements on the Payos but may also willingly and consciously incorporate Payo views: in the context of beliefs about reproduction, they often stress that it is the Payos who are scientists and doctors, and who tell them about these theories.

This flexibility does not seem to bother the Gitanos. Tía Tula told me that women's seven *vasos* must be inside the uterus because it is there that children develop – and that she had learned the word *útero* from Payo doctors. Other women, such as my friend Clara, deny the existence of these *vasos* and explain that 'those things are what those older, ignorant Gitanos believe, they don't have any knowledge'. On one occasion I was present when four women in their twenties discussed how is it that foetuses 'eat' while in the uterus. Two of them were adamant that the 'child' eats pieces of the mother's own flesh that float around inside her belly. One laughed at them explaining that 'children' eat through the umbilical cord, not with their mouths. The fourth confessed her ignorance on the matter. The chat became very heated and the women called a female social worker who was passing by to settle the matter. Her statement that foetuses are fed through the umbilical cord was met with strong scepticism by the women who were in favour of the 'eating through the mouth' theory.

An Imprecise Patrilinearity

In Jarana, these theories of conception and gestation feed directly into Gitano political organization: beliefs regarding the make-up of persons are linked to norms and rules that dictate the form that relations between kinship groups should take. Within this sphere of Gitano life, just as in the case of Gitano ideas about conception, patrilineal emphases are combined with bilateral stresses but come to take precedence over them. Thus, the Gitanos of Jarana point to the differential contribution of mother and father to the making of a child to explain why individuals belong to their fathers' *razas*. These *razas* are described by the Gitanos as groups of people – men and women – who are linked by patrilineal ties and who share a common name and certain duties towards each other.[3] It is because the father is the one who 'puts in' the child, that he 'lifts (starts) the lineage' *(levanta linaje)* and that children inherit their father's rather than their mother's *raza* affiliation. The Gitano conceptualization of the *raza* therefore stresses the idea of common origin: Tío Juan told me that 'we all Foros come from the same root, we all belong to the same branch' *(los Foros venimos todos de la misma raiz, somos todos de la misma rama)*. However, the Gitanos of Jarana have a genealogical memory that extends back not more than three or at most four generations, and this sense of shared origin is much more vague than precise. Patrilineal connections extend horizontally in the present, and work more as explanations of present-day ties and tensions that as explorations of past relations.

In Jarana, although a particular Gitano man or woman will know that a series of mutual obligations exist between him or herself and others of his or her *raza* affiliation, they may or may not know the nature of the kinship ties that connect them. A good example of this lack of precise knowledge about common ancestry concerns the link between two patrigroups, the Juanes and the Sebastianes, both of which share *raza* affiliation – as Foros. During my fieldwork, I learnt from Tío Juan that Tío Sebas was the son of one Tío Juan's sisters, much older than he was and long deceased. Keeping in mind San Román's (1976) emphasis on patrilinearity as the single most important concept organizing interaction among Gitanos, I assumed that Tío Juan's sister must have married a patrilineal relative – another Foro – and this was the reason that her descendants and the descendants of Tío Juan whom I met in Jarana share *raza* affiliation. On a later visit to the field I tried to find out whether this was indeed the case, and I came up against the same difficulties that I had encountered during my first period of research, and that I had earlier interpreted as a reflection of the Gitanos' mistrust of Payos like myself. Many of the grandchildren of Tío Sebas and Tío Juan, already in their thirties, simply did not know what the kinship link between the two men had been. Sara, for example, told me that Tío Juan and Tío Sebas were very 'close' *(allegados)*, that 'they loved each other a lot, but I don't know if they were cousins, or perhaps uncle and nephew? Well, something like that, but very, very close.' Moreover, the closer people were to Tío Sebas and his parents, the more reluctant they are to talk about them: the Gitanos of Jarana avoid mentioning the dead because, they say, it brings them such painful memories. Thus, I could persuade Tío Juan to tell me very briefly about Tío Sebas, but his eyes would turn to water as soon as he mentioned his sister, whose name he could not bring himself to say aloud. I found it impossible to ask him about the *raza* affiliation of his sister's husband. This active reluctance to discuss the deceased on the part of some Gitanos, and simple ignorance about them on the part of others, is coherent with the Gitanos' general lack of interest in the past and orientation around the present.

The Gitanos' imprecise but nonetheless strong emphasis on patri-linearity, rooted in theories of conception, is formalized through the 'Gitano laws' *(leyes Gitanas)*. By prescribing that, upon birth, indiv-iduals automatically acquire their fathers' *raza* affiliation, these laws locate men and women within the Gitano formal political universe – a universe that is conceptually divided first between Gitanos and Payos and second along patrilineal kinship lines. People who share the same *raza* affiliation also share juridical personality in the sense that they owe allegiance to each other in confrontations between Gitanos, and also that they are liable to be the object of retaliation when a patrilineal relative has offended or injured a member of another *raza* (see San Román 1976). The concept of the *raza* thus works as the key idiom through which groups of Gitanos mobilize and present themselves as units, not only within situations of conflict but within everyday life: as I explained in Chapter 3, fear of feuding makes the Gitanos avoid non-kin in day-to-day contexts. At the same time, the *raza* is a main facilitator of the fluidity and flexibility that characterizes Gitano political organization: *razas* may appear to be fixed and bounded entities but, as I explain below, in fact they are representations used in the creation of malleable groupings.

Love and Kinship Ties

Summarizing one of the few attitudes that I can confidently say is shared by all the Gitanos that I met during my fieldwork, Clara explained to me: 'To us the family is the most fundamental thing, that is your father, your mother, your siblings, your family, your uncles, your everybody, it is the greatest (thing) there is' *(para nosotros la familia es lo más fundamental que hay, osea tu padre, tu madre, tus hermanos, tu familia, tus tíos, tus todos, es lo más grande que hay)*. This statement expresses the certainty that relatives – especially close ones, within the bilateral extended family – are the essential element in the life of any individual, that for which the greatest love or affection *(cariño)* is felt. In other contexts relatedness, which sometimes is phrased through the idea of shared blood, itself becomes an idiom for expressing affection. In the first letter that I received after I had left the field, Tía Tula and Tío Juan told me that 'it is as if you were of our blood, you run through our veins'. In that letter, as in all those they have written since, they address me as 'dear niece' and sign as 'your aunt and uncle'.

At one level, therefore, affection for both maternal and paternal relatives is taken for granted as unavoidable and unproblematic: one loves one's kin. At the same time, the Gitanos underline the idea that closeness and shared experiences generate affection. Time spent together, having lived nearby and especially 'having grown up together' *(haberse criado juntos)* – as part of the same household or in nearby ones – are considered fundamental in shaping the kind of relationship that individuals linked by kin ties will have. Given the preference for, and actual predominance of, virilocal residence, these ideas tend to reinforce the link to paternal rather than maternal kin, and closer rather than more distant kin. They are thus very significant in giving experiential meaning to the obligation that individuals who share *raza* affiliation have to give support to each other in adverse circumstances. Simultaneously, the Gitanos who live in Jarana use marriages in order to strengthen their links with Gitanos to whom they are already related. Thus, they display a strong preference for marrying their relatives – matrilateral and patrilateral – so that a person's consanguines are often also their affines and patrilineal kin are also related through maternal links. Most Gitanos thus find it easy to identify a group of people to whom they feel emotionally close and among whom conflicts would be very unlikely to escalate into fully fledged feuds.

Towards the end of my time in Jarana Tío Juan became very keen that his grandson Pedro, son of his eldest son Esteban, should marry Marga, a granddaughter of his nephew, Tío Sebas. Sebas and Juan belonged to the same *raza*, the Foros, had grown up together, and had eventually settled down in the same area in their old age. Marga and Pedro are Foros, although they belong to two different sub-sections, the Sebastianes and the Juanes. Pedro is the son of a son of Tío Juan and a daughter of Tío Sebas – he is 'a Juan'. Marga is the daughter of a son of Tío Sebas – she is 'a Sebastiana'. Marga and Pedro are thus cross-cousins. Tío Juan, Pedro's immediate kin, and Marga's father were very keen on the marriage. Marga's mother and sisters, by contrast, did not like the idea because of the Juanes' very strong chauvinist reputation. Paco, Marga's father, insisted that the couple be engaged – something that led to several quarrels with his wife and older daughters and a general ill feeling that lasted several weeks. When facing Estela, Clara and Sara he referred to the memory of his father, Tío Sebas. He explained and repeated how much Tío Sebas would have liked to see two of his grandchildren getting married. He also insisted on how much Tío Juan desired the wedding, and on the great love that Tío Juan and Tío Sebas felt for each other, because they had been brought up and travelled through Spain together, and had even been married at the same ceremony. Eventually Tío Juan and Paco got their way and the couple became engaged and later married.

Patrigroups and Neighbourhood Politics

Those rules and norms of conduct that are thought to mark out proper Gitano ways and make Gitanos different from Payos – the *leyes Gitanas* or 'Gitano laws' – emphasize the primary allegiance of individuals to the *raza* to which they are agnatically linked. According to the Gitanos of Jarana, solidarity among people who share *raza* affiliation should be realized above all in the obligation to join together in attack or defence when one of them has either inflicted or received an injury. However, not all the members of a *raza* are usually concentrated in the same geographical area; they may not even know each other.[4] It is small groups sharing *raza* affiliation – that I call 'patrigroups' – that most often work on this basis of solidarity, patrigroups of any one *raza* being liable to collaborate and, more rarely, to enter into conflict with each other. Often, although not always, a man, his grown-up sons and grandsons and their wives and unmarried children form a unit of association. Two or more patrigroups can easily come together and form a larger one.

The patrigroup headed by Tío Juan is made up of ten nuclear families. They moved into Jarana as a strategic manoeuvre, to join another patrigroup from the same *raza*, the one headed by Tío Sebas, Tío Juan's nephew. Tío Juan had married off his eldest son, Esteban, to Tío Sebas's eldest daughter Tocha, an alliance that was reinforced during my fieldwork when their son Pedro – grandson to Tío Juan and to Tío Sebas – married Marga, the daughter of one of Tío Sebas's sons. When the Juanes moved into Jarana in 1989 the Foros outnumbered any other *raza* in the district: Tío Sebas and his seven sons were joined by Tío Juan, his four sons, with their own grown up sons, their wives and unmarried children. This allowed them to impose the 'law' that no drugs were to be sold in the neighbourhood. Unrelated Gitanos knew that, if they attempted to sell drugs, they would have to fight both Juanes and Sebastianes – even to death. Although many dislike the Foros' hold over the area, there is little they can do. Tío Sebas died in 1990 and his sons and grandchildren – eight nuclear families in Jarana and four in flats in Villaverde – have continued to accept the leadership of Tío Juan in order to keep drugs out of Jarana. They acted as mediators when, during my stay in Jarana, one of Tío Juan's grandchildren had a fight with a member from a powerful *raza* from Villaverde. Yet, unlike the Juanes, the Sebastianes are converts, and see themselves as radically different from the former. They say that the Juanes 'are always getting into feuds, and they are chauvinists, you can see the lives their women live . . . we have a little bit more knowledge'. Thus, depending on the circumstances, Juanes and Sebastianes, having the same *raza* affiliation, act as one or two distinct patrigroups.

The constitution of patrigroups as working units does not follow strict rules. Instead, it is tied to such factors as spatial proximity or political events. This is clearly visible in the case of the Foros. Tío Juan has other patrilineal relatives on whom he may call in extreme circumstances – such as for support in a feud, for example – or who may come to the neighbourhood when there is an illness, a funeral or a wedding. However, it is only the descendants of Tío Sebas that have allied with him and his children for day-to-day political co-operation in Jarana. My use of the term 'patrigroup' is an attempt at conveying this contextual versatility. This flexibility can be identified in the Gitanos' use of the word *familia* (family) by which they refer to nuclear families, to patrigroups, and to the wider and bilateral 'distant family' *(familia retirada)*. *Familia* also refers to the concept or formal representation of the *raza* and hence to members of it that do not belong to what at that moment is ego's 'working' patrigroup, but are liable to be mobilized as such.[5]

I view *razas* as the idiom that allows particular patrigroups – as contextual aggregates of kin – to construct themselves as active political units and call on each other's support under variable circumstances. This stands in contrast with San Román's description of *razas* as the total number of individuals who are able to trace their descent from a male ancestor through the male line (1976: 108, 116–17). Her approach can be made the object of Bourdieu's critique when, talking about affinity, he says that

> it is only when one records these relationships as a *fait accompli, post festum*, as the anthropologist does when he draws a genealogy, that one can forget that they are the product of strategies (conscious or unconscious) oriented toward the satisfaction of material and symbolic interests and organised by reference to a determinate set of economic and social conditions (1977: 36).

Viewing *razas* in the terms that Bourdieu calls for, and focusing on the Gitanos' use of the concept, makes it easier to bring into question the circumstances whereby particular people choose to underline their membership of a particular group, in the process creating the group as such.

As an idiom of relatedness, the *raza* obtains its meaning from its role in conflict situations, when the 'Gitano law' can be seen at its most formal and when the jural aspect of an individual personality – its primary belonging and allegiance to a patrigroup – is accentuated over any others. *Razas* can therefore be characterized by Bourdieu's idea of 'official' or 'representational' kinship, 'the group's self-representation and the almost theatrical presentation it gives of itself when acting in accordance with that image' (1977: 35). The ever-present fear of feuding, moreover, means that the idiom of the *raza* is also used to organize everyday relations in the neighbourhood – particularly patterns of avoidance towards non-kin.

Unlike Gypsies elsewhere (see for example Sutherland 1975) the Gitanos do not rank kin groups according to a fixed hierarchy and, as happens in Jarana, it is their numbers that determine the kind of relations that develop among particular patrigroups. Nuclear families may be separated from their kin through such things as resettlement by the Payos, or through choice. However, there is a strong preference for virilocality. Those nuclear families that live in Jarana 'on their own' *(solos)* – those that do not share *raza* affiliation with anybody else in the neighbourhood – feel disadvantaged vis-à-vis others, and keep in close contact with the rest of their bilateral kin, even if the latter live elsewhere.

In Jarana the Gitanos talk about relations between different patrigroups in terms of their numerical strength or support *(respaldo)* –

and often also resent them. It is here that the *raza* comes into play, for it provides a more or less wide field of connections susceptible to being activated. The Juanes and the Sebastianes, allied in the name of their shared ancestry and the love ties between the elders of the two families, were able to impose their will on the rest of the Gitanos of the district who outnumbered them but were divided. It is significant that the Juanes had to leave the neighbourhood where they had been living until 1989 because of the spread of drug dealing, and their own inability to face stronger patrigroups from other *razas* there.

In 1989, shortly after the Gitanos settled in their new homes in Jarana, somebody started selling drugs. The Foros realized this and organized nightly rounds in order to capture the culprit. After a few days, they caught a Payo drug addict from outside the district who had just bought some doses in the Middle Street. They made him tell them from whom he had obtained the drugs, and expelled him from the neighbourhood. They then forced the widow who had sold the drugs to gather all her belongings and they threw her and her very young children out of the neighbourhood. This family had to spend a winter away in very precarious living conditions before the Foros allowed them to come back. Because of their numbers the Foros were able to enforce the 'law' that no drugs were going to be sold. The widow's patrigroup, which had to leave their original home in Galicia because they were involved in a feud there, has very little support in Jarana or in Madrid more generally.

Razas and Conflict

Among the Gitanos, much of the talk to do with *razas* develops in relation to conflicts or discussions about them. In the section above I have explained that *raza* allegiance is particularly significant in the arena of politics between – rather than within – patrigroups, where the group and not the individual becomes the minimal unit of inter-action. This is what Ardevol calls 'the absence of juridical personality characteristic of the Gitano individual' (1986: 75). In fact, there may have been a decrease in the level of conflict among urban Gitanos in general from the early 1970s to the present. San Román explained how she counted approximately fourteen *ruinas* (feuds, also called *quimeras*) in a single year in the Madrid settlement where she did fieldwork in the early 1970s (personal communication 1995). By contrast, people living in Jarana were not directly involved in any single *ruina* during the time I spent there, although some of their relatives were, and twice patrigroups took refuge in the neighbourhood while escaping retaliation. This decrease in violence is noted by the Gitanos themselves. Sara told me:

> Before there used to be *quimeras* all the time. It has changed a lot, before they did not mind whom they attacked, even little children, and the enmity *(contrariedad*; literally 'opposition') was for life. Now they go wherever they want, they stroll wherever they feel like, and nothing happens. Before, the hostility was for life. Believe me when I say that I do not even know who the enemies *(contrarios)* of my family are.

The Spanish Gitanos deal with conflict and its settlement through the institution of *contrariedad* (from *contrario*, meaning enemy), which gives shape to the idea of retaliation (San Román 1976; Ardevol 1986). Retaliation as a response to attack is always expected, and the Gitanos view it in physical terms, irrespective of whether the injury has been physical or verbal. Who gets involved in conflict depends theoretically on the level of the attack: the stronger it is, the more likelihood and expectation that distant relatives sharing *raza* affiliation will be drawn into it. In Jarana, the Gitanos envisage different levels of conflict between people belonging to different patrigroups in terms of their possible consequences, from 'a couple of punches' *(un par de puñetazos)* to 'a death' *(una muerte)*. Confrontations between women are placed at the lowest level on this scale. Although they sometimes fight with each other, and their fights may escalate to include distant female relatives and extend over time, the Gitanos often state that so long as the men do not get involved in conflicts among women, these are not likely to escalate into a *ruina*.

Ruinas or *quimeras* are the events that, in an institutionalized sequence, follow either a serious injury or a murder. According to 'Gitano law', when a Gitano kills another Gitano any members of the offending *raza* are liable to be the object of retaliation (see San Román 1976). They, together with their spouses, leave their homes and take refuge in areas where the victim's family has no kin, often among relatives. They will also do this if a member of the enemy *raza* is so gravely wounded as to be in danger of death, while they await the outcome. People always keep in mind the possibility that minor conflicts will escalate, and when there is a fight, often even if no major injuries have taken place, it usually happens that members of the same *raza* – to whom they are closely or distantly connected – leave the area until the exact implications of the problem are known. Although it is up to each particular family to decide to provide support to members of the *raza* in case of conflict, the enemy *raza* may leave them no option, by marking them out as potential objects of retaliation. The opposite is also possible. Tío Juan explained how:

> Now, one of the Negrillos has killed a man, and then he has shot the man's son who is now really ill in hospital. But since all of them are Christians (Evangelists), and Christianity is what has changed completely the life of the Gitanos, nothing has happened. They have thrown the family[6] that has done the killing out of their houses, and the brother of the one who did it has remained in his own house, because he has not wanted enmity, he has not come out in defence of his brother, he has not gone to fight, he has not done anything. There has been a death, and shooting, but they do not want feuding, because they belong to the Church and have changed completely, they get along with their lives, even if it is his brother he has not got involved. Their *contrarios* have let it be, although if they had had a different mentality they would have gone to the flat and killed them there.

As soon as possible once the conflict has started, and in order to avoid escalation, the male elders or patrigroup heads *(Gitanos viejos)* on both sides should call other neutral elders who act as judges *(jueces)* and whose role is to pre-empt the escalation *(devitar;* see San Román 1976: 241ff.). These elders mediate between both sides in order to arrive at a settlement which is centred around the separation in space of the two parties involved. I saw 'men of respect' at work in Jarana only once, at the very beginning of my fieldwork. Salis, the son of one of Tía Tula's brothers, had killed his sister's husband after the latter had attempted to kill her and wound any members of her close family. Expecting retaliation from the dead man's family, Salis, his parents, and his brothers and their wives and children had fled from their homes and taken refuge in Jarana, leaving all their possessions behind. They lived out of their cars, parked outside Tía Tula's house, for over a month. The 'men of respect' arrived one afternoon while I was sitting with two of Tía Tula's daughters-in-law learning to alter a blouse that I had just bought. As soon as their cars approached, the children starting shouting: 'the old Gitanos! the old Gitanos are coming!' *(¡los Gitanos viejos! ¡qué llegan los Gitanos viejos!)*. The 'men of respect' were four elderly Gitanos, wearing hats and carrying elaborately carved walking-sticks. They sat on a semicircle in the patio of one of Tía Tula's sons, with Salis and his father and brothers standing in front of them, and Tía Tula's own sons and grandsons completing the circle. The women stayed in the periphery, ready to intervene until Tío Juan stood up and shouted: 'let the women not talk!' *(¡las mujeres que no hablen!)*.

I was banished to the kitchen with the children, and listened to the proceedings from a window over the sink. The 'men of respect' listened to Salis' side of the story, presented the demands of the family of the man he had killed, and haggled for an agreement as to which parts of the city each patrigroup would be forbidden to enter. This was not an easy task: one of Salis' brothers had to give up his permit for selling at a weekly market which was located outside the area that was allotted to his family and all of them had to ask to be resettled by the social services. Throughout the discussions men constantly interrupted each other, shouting their innocence and repeating that it was the dead man who had brought the *ruina* upon himself. The 'men of respect' stayed for over two hours before returning to the family of the man who had died. Eventually an agreement was reached: each patrigroup was allocated an area of the city, and accepted the prohibition not to enter the zone that, from that day onwards, 'belonged' to the other. In the process of the *ruina* the members of two *razas* had become *contrarios*, 'just like cats and dogs' *(igual que los gatos y los perros)* who cannot see each other without wishing desperately to fight. Separating them physically was considered the only way of preventing escalation.

Neutral elders are not usually called upon to settle disputes which do not seem likely to have such tragic consequences as *ruinas*. Minor conflicts are mediated by related elders, and other kin – bilateral or affinal – frequently take an active role. Friends may collaborate and, among converts, ministers are also increasingly being called upon to mediate *ruinas*. As will become clear in the following chapter, however, not everybody is considered reliable enough to be listened to.

Conclusions

Beliefs about conception, gestation and the physical make-up of persons relate directly to the way in which Gitanos mobilize themselves into units vis-à-vis others. As such, they are central to the Gitanos' conceptualization of themselves as a highly fragmented group rather than as a unified or coherent community. The 'Gitano laws' that dictate the institutionalization of conflict through feuding provide a pattern not only for dealing with confrontations but for day-to-day sociability among Gitanos: the inhabitants of Jarana avoid interaction with non-kin for fear of feuding and its consequences and, as I explain in Chapter 3, divide the neighbourhood along kinship lines through such things as their use of communal space. However, at the same time as separating non-kin, conflicts help Gitanos view themselves – relatives and non-relatives – as moral beings, part of a moral community. During

conflicts large numbers of Gitanos live up to the Gitano ideals, upholding the 'Gitano law'. Feuds are thus essential in making it possible for
Gitanos to objectify their image of themselves as a 'people' *(pueblo)*
different from the non-Gypsies.

These same 'Gitano laws' exalt the role of men – epitomized in the
figure of the 'man of respect' – in the construction of the Gitanos'
singularity. Whereas women perform and bring about Gypsyness most
graphically and dramatically through their sexual behaviour, men do
the same through their behaviour in relation to confrontations among
Gitanos. In the next chapter I analyse this facet of Gitano masculinity,
focusing in particular on Gitano evaluations of the behaviour of men
in conflict situations. Simultaneously, I point to what these evaluations
show about how hierarchy and inequality are constructed among the
Gitanos of Jarana.

Notes

1. For insights into the relationship between different Gitano groups and
the Spanish national health service see Rodriguez Martín 1995, Gemella, 1996,
Trigueros Guardiola 1995.

2. Rodriguez Martín (1995) describes the increase in the use of contraceptives
among shack-dwelling Gitanos in Montemolín (Saragossa) as being a result of
a) the pressure of social workers; and b) the wishes of the Gitano women
themselves, most often supported by their husbands as well as their mothers
and mothers-in-law. Anta Félez, talking of Gitanos living in a 'special Gitano
neighbourhood' built by the local council in Málaga (Los Asperones) describes
the 'slow but continuously growing use of contraceptives, which are provided
by the social worker and the local doctors' (1994: 65).

3. San Román, talking of Gitanos from Castile and Catalonia, explained
how they used the term *raza* 'to designate a group of people who consider
themselves descendants of a common ancestor, always through the male line.
Individuals belonging to a *raza* can establish with precision the genealogical
links between themselves and the shared ancestor, whose name they know.
The name of each lineage or *raza* is, in general, related to the name of this
ancestor common to the group. These *razas* or Gitano lineages usually have a
depth of four generations. The members of the same lineage cooperate and
have rights and obligations vis-à-vis each other. In general this is only the
case when the fathers of the eldest men in the lineage are at least sons of first
paternal cousins' (1976: 108). Both Gamella (1996) and Anta Félez (1994), who

worked with Andalusian Gitanos, dispute San Román's emphasis on patri-lineages, and describe *razas* as bilateral kinship groups. Ardevol (1986), however, discussing Gitanos from Granada, endorses San Román's model of Gitano kinship relations.

4. According to San Román, '*razas* are dispersed. A lineage can be spread over different points in Spain' (San Román 1976: 110). The 'Gitanos themselves ignore the exact number of people that make up their lineages' (San Román: 116).

5. Gamella (1996: 102) uses the term *raza* and *familia* interchangeably. San Román (1976: 140) explains how 'to the Gitanos of La Charca and San Lucio *familia* is the word that indicates the relationship between members of the same lineage . . . The term is also used to indicate the nuclear family . . . and relatives more generally'.

6. The word 'family' here refers to a patrigroup made up of a man and his wife, their unmarried children, and their married sons with their wives and children.

Men in the Face of Conflict

Pepe and Gabriel are two men in their early twenties. Gabriel belongs to the Sotos patrigroup, which is one of the patrigroups of Jarana with the largest number of convert members. Pepe is a Juan. Although the Juanes are not converts, Pepe is also a grandson of Tío Sebas: he is Foro both through his father and through his mother and has several maternal uncles (Sebastianes) who are well-known converts. However, he has little day-to-day contact with them. Gabriel is married to a maternal first cross-cousin of Pepe who, like the latter, belongs to the Foros. At the church bar, just before the Evangelical service started, Pepe provoked Gabriel by addressing him by his childhood nickname, *Gallina* ('hen', meaning coward). Gabriel challenged Pepe to come out of the church and, outside, punched him on the face. Pepe then hit Gabriel in the stomach. While they were fighting, Pepe's father, his brothers, paternal uncles and cousins (the Juanes), who live next to the church, came running, shouting and ready to fight with Gabriel and his family. Three of Pepe's maternal uncles, Sebastianes and hence also Foros, wanted to fight as well. The Sotos, however, remained quiet. Tío Juan, together with two of Pepe's maternal uncles who are converts and well-respected men, and Gabriel's father-in-law, who is also Pepe's maternal uncle, managed to calm the angry Foros down. The quarrel was settled with Gabriel being told to stay clear of Jarana for a couple of months, and with the local minister punishing him by forbidding him to attend services at that church for the same period.

Knowledge

The significant characters of this story are not only the two youths who fought, but also Pepe's male relatives, and the group of men who acted as mediators. Below I reproduce an extract of a taped conversation with Clara, a maternal cross-cousin of Pepe and a paternal parallel cousin Gabriel's wife, in which she discusses this quarrel. It is especially revealing of how the Gitanos evaluate men's social worth or standing by reference to their behaviour in the face of conflict:

> If we had not been converts perhaps something [a *ruina* or feud] would have happened, there can be a *risión* [laughable man] who goes and spoils it all . . . Did you hear about those dickheads [*gilipollas*] that came? They even brought 'sticks' [knives and firearms] but my father and uncles were firm, said that nothing had happened, that it was just two young men slapping each other, and that was that, and it was fixed. Tío Juan did the same, he is a 'man of respect' [*hombre de respeto*] . . . My uncle Mancha and some others went there wanting to fight, he is a fool, has no knowledge at all, he could never deserve the respect that people have for my uncle Lucas. My other uncles are respectable men, with education, with shame, but Mancha lives only to be a dickhead. Whenever there is a fight there is also a *risión* who has to make it worse, these are the ones who say 'look what a man I am' [*mira qué hombre soy*]. The ones who are more civilized and have more knowledge try to separate everybody.

This account sets up a dichotomy between two kinds of men, the respectable man, best epitomized in the figure of the mediator or 'man of respect' (*hombre de respeto*), and its opposite, the *risión* or 'laughable man'. These figures can be viewed from two different yet interrelated perspectives. On the one hand, it is possible to see them as stereotypes of male behaviour: through them we obtain access to some important aspects of the Gitanos' understanding of masculinity. At a second level, it is also necessary to consider the practical political implications of these representations.

As San Román explains, the behaviour that the Gitanos expect from men is age specific: 'The Gitano is *mozo* from puberty until his marriage; he is a married man until he is forty or fifty; and he is a *tío* from then until he withdraws from active participation in communal familial life and becomes an old man' (San Román 1976: 204). At each stage men are expected to perform different aspects of what 'being a Gitano man' implies. So masculinity can be said to change its meaning through the man's life cycle. Above all, men of all ages should be courageous and determined to protect themselves, their families and their dead. Thus, Tía Tula spoke very admiringly to me of her nephew Salis, a man in his mid-twenties. He was fixing his car when his brother-in-law Alberto came down the street firing a gun, aiming to attack his wife's family for her supposed infidelity. He gravely wounded Salis in one arm. Salis ran to get a rifle, breaking open the seal of the bullets with his teeth. With one hand he shot Alberto, who died from the wounds a couple of weeks later. Tía Tula compared Salis with his older brother Tomás, a quiet and peaceful man. According to Tía Tula, Tomás should be praised for his ability to stay calm once the *ruina* with her sister's affines had started, and for his capacity to think about the long-term good of his family. In fact, the Gitanos stress that with age, courage and self-assertiveness should be tempered by increasing *conocimiento*, which is the ability to distinguish between appropriate and inappropriate behaviour – for example, in the case of conflict, recognizing when a man should or should not control his anger. This quality – which can be translated as 'knowledge', 'wisdom' or 'understanding' – should modify the behaviour that men display as they become older.

Conocimiento is significant because the attitudes that it is perceived to generate are those that command the respect (*respeto*) of Gitanos – and respect implies deference and obedience from others. *Conocimiento* has a temporal dimension. It may – in fact it should – be acquired through time, either by individuals or by groups. Some families are said by others in the neighbourhood to lack *conocimiento*, to be 'people with feathers' (*gente de pluma*)[1] who have not yet reached the modern or 'civilized' stage at which other Gitanos have arrived. Children are thought to have little or no *conocimiento*, and women to have less than men – just as they are thought to be morally inferior to them, to have a 'worse heart' (*peor corazón*), or simply to be 'worse' (*peores*).

Conocimiento is linked to, but separate from, cleverness or wittiness, which is expressed through the verb *saber* (to know) and which is given a more ambiguous evaluation. *Saber* and *conocimiento* are two complementary but also opposite qualities.[2] To be witty and clever (*saber*) can be good: it is always useful to be able to get the upper hand both in relations with other Gitanos and with the Payos. Grown men can never know too much. By contrast, in the case of women and children, being too clever, displaying an attitude that is not thought to belong to their particular age/gender sphere, is negatively evaluated. On the other hand, having *conocimiento*, having the capacity to discern what is morally just and right is always good, both for men and for women. Older people, and particularly men, before they become senile, are the ones who in theory have the highest degree of *conocimiento* – they are also the ones who command the greatest respect among Gitanos.

The 'Man of Respect' and the *Risión*

As figures or representations, 'old Gitanos' or 'men of respect' (*Gitanos viejos, hombres de respeto*) incarnate those virtues that imply great *conocimiento*. They have a deep knowledge of Gitano laws, of the proper Gitano ways of doing things. They have a considerable understanding of what is proper in moral terms, and character, as well as what middle-class, non-Gitano Spaniards would call 'human nature' (*la naturaleza humana*). They are also truthful and consistent and their word can be trusted. They are polite, conscious of shame – that is, they behave morally, especially in issues that have a sexual aspect to them. They are self-controlled, generous, and ready to support other Gitanos in their needs. The combination of these virtues elicits the respect of other Gitanos and, in practice, it is on this respect that the mediator's capacity to act is based.[3] As Clara told me:

> In our race the 'man of respect' is the most respected, this is why people pay attention to him. It is not because of the support of his sons that Tío Juan is respected [because of the numerical strength of his patri-group]: he has to bring peace, he is not going to bring war . . . It is the same in a fight as when a couple split up: even if you don't want to be with your husband, if he [the mediator] says that you have to do it, out of respect for the old Gitano who comes to reunite you then you have to close your mouth. That is what happened with Carmen, who did not want to go back with Antonio, and Tío Juan came and told her 'go with your husband' and she bowed her head and went.

By acquiring respect – that is, deference and hence obedience – from others, men and women enhance their capacity to exert control over their own lives and the lives of those around them. Among the Gitanos righteousness of behaviour constitutes the basis of acquired hierarchy and, hence, to a large extent also of inequality. Whereas women's respectability is linked above all to their sexual behaviour, among men it is grounded in their ability to behave morally both in their day-to-day interactions with others and, more graphically, in situations of conflict.

Respect has a mixed ascribed and acquired component. Men inherently rank higher than women, and older people inherently rank higher than younger ones – that is, they deserve greater respect. Individuals have to behave according to the standards that their age/gender category dictates in order to be granted the respect that it implies. Respect has to be willingly granted, it cannot be forcefully commanded – otherwise, it is not true respect. In the case of men, it is the extent to which their behaviour approaches the ideal of the 'man of respect' that determines the extent to which other people, within and outside their families, willingly submit to their influence.

The image of the mediator embodies an ideal of masculine behaviour

– a standard against which the behaviour of all grown men is evaluated. This is made visible if we compare Clara's description of Tío Juan's virtues above with her account of the behaviour of her uncles during the quarrel between Gabriel and Pepe. Of her uncles she said:

> People do not have the same respect for my uncle Mancha as they have for my uncle Lucas, and they never will. Because the word of Lucas is always true (*va a misa* – literally, 'goes to mass'). Lucas and some of the others are men with respect, with shame, with education, something happens and they are there helping, somebody has an illness or has some problem and they are there, while the other spends his life playing the fool.

Thus the virtues that Clara admired in her uncles were the ones that, in the first quotation above, she identified as the basis of Tío Juan's respectability: self-control, shame – which is understood in sexual-moral terms – education or politeness,[4] solidarity, and truthfulness. The virtue that embodies all these is *formalidad*. This can be translated through the English 'formality' – in the sense of propriety or decorum, reliability, and of being principled. It can also be glossed as 'respectability'. Clara also explained how in the event of a conflict, 'the ones who are more civilized and have more *conocimiento* do not get involved and rather calm both sides down' (*los que son más civilizados y tienen más conocimiento no se enredan, sino que calman a los otros*). The parallels with the role of the mediator are clear. The figure of the mediator, and the occasions when particular mediators arbitrate, make explicit – in its most formal terms – the link between *respeto* and *conocimiento* which permeates all hierarchical relations among the Gitanos.

The opposite of the figure of mediator is that of the *risión*. The adjective/noun *risión* comes from the Spanish verb *reir* (to laugh), and suggests somebody whose behaviour is ridiculous, laughable. For example, Clara described to me how Tía Tula had slapped her son-in-law Raul, a man well into his forties. Tía Tula had had a quarrel with her daughter Sol – Raul's wife – and the latter and her family had been forbidden by Tío Juan – Tía Tula's husband – to come to Jarana. Raul had defied this. As soon as Tía Tula saw him she ran to him wanting to hit him, and slapped him. This represented a tremendous loss of dignity for Raul. Clara nonetheless took sides against him on the following terms:

> If he had been a formal (reliable, principled) man and with respect Tía Tula would not have dared to do what she did to him. But people say 'he is a *risión*, Raul, let's see if Tula kills him, let her kill him'. Because he is not a man with respect, with shame, that is, he is not well looked

upon [*mirado*]. Because of his disposition, of his behaviour he is a *risión*, and that is very fundamental according to our law. He is not a man with shame, with respect, who knows how to behave, he is a waster.

Men who, despite their age, fail to display an adequate level of *conocimiento* also fail in the fulfilment of the masculine ideal. Hence the reversal that this example demonstrates: as Clara underlines, it is understandable that a woman should hit a man who does not command respect. The Gitanos' use of the phrase 'he is a man *with* respect' suggests that it is not only an attitude that other people have to display towards a man. Rather, men have to have the quality of eliciting respect in others. Both the extract just quoted, and the others above, indicate the basic characteristics of men who fail to achieve this. They are thoughtless, foolish, impulsive, arrogant and childish.

It is significant that the men whom Clara called *risiones* in the quote above were drug-addicts. The drug addict[5] is in fact the archetype of the *risión*. Gitanos very often say that drug addicts 'do not respect anybody, they do not know what they are doing'. This summarizes both what they think of drug addiction, and the reason why drug addicts rank lowest in the Gitano moral scale. Drug addiction is considered and treated by the Gitanos of Jarana as an illness, one that dominates the will and deprives men of the capacity to distinguish what is right and wrong. Drug addicts do not display deference and obedience to their elders. They do not hesitate to steal from other Gitanos. As Clara explained, they boast of their courage and manliness – 'look what a man I am' – and are always ready to engage in quarrels and fights, but never consider the consequences. They 'speak' (*hablan*, that is, offend with words) and, 'like women', they put their own self-interest, their wish to protect their reputation, their own anger, above the interests of their families, which are then dragged into *ruinas*. Thus, it is lack of self-control and of *conocimiento* that epitomizes the drug addicts' character. They are men, but the masculinity that they display is the inversion of the ideal image through which the Gitanos represent themselves to themselves.

In their daily lives men behave 'like' 'men of respect' or 'like' *risiones*. It is in so doing, and in managing to have their behaviour acknowledged along these lines, that they place themselves in hierarchical positions vis-à-vis others – and it should be remembered that, in the Gitano context, hierarchy generates inequality, that is, unequal access to the deference and obedience of others. Thus, not all men who reach their fifties become mediators. The Gitanos of Jarana insist that it is a consistent propriety of behaviour throughout his life that makes a man a 'man of respect' in his old age. 'Men of respect' are called to arbitrate both within and outside their patrigroups, because their merits and exemplary life are widely recognized by other Gitanos. They move across *razas*, as one of the most perfect embodiments of the 'Gitano way of being' (*la manera de ser Gitana*). Sixteen men aged fifty and over – nine of them are over sixty – live in Jarana. Just three, Tío Paco, Tío Juan and Tío Carlos, arbitrate together in problems within the neighbourhood. Tío Juan is the only one who is called to help in conflicts that take place outside Jarana – he even conciliates among *Extremeños*, and among Gitanos who live outside Madrid.

By contrast, besides losing the respect of others, drug addicts are also deprived of many of the rights that other Gitano men of their age enjoy. It often happens that when drug addicts get involved in fights or quarrels, their families do not try to retaliate as they would usually do. Instead, they ask the other family to forgive the drug addict's behaviour, on the grounds that he 'does not know what he is doing' (*no sabe lo que hace*), and that 'it would be a pity if all the pot was lost because of a chick-pea like this one' (*sería una pena que toda la olla se perdiera por un garbanzo como éste*). I provided a good example of the treatment given to drug addicts in Chapter 6. There I explained how Marcos, a grandson of Tío Juan, lost his right to his mother's support in his fight with his wife over the custody of their children when she left him. According to the 'Gitano laws' Carmina, Juan's mother, would have been obliged to take care of her grandchildren if their mother left their father. Marcos's wife Guapa was not considered to be behaving disrespectfully with relation to her husband because of his terrible behaviour towards her. Being a drug addict, he failed to provide her and the children with any economic or emotional support. Carmina rejected Marcos' pleas for help on the basis that he was a *risión*, and added that it would have been different if he had been 'a proper man', and Guapa had been the one who was at fault.

The Evangelical Church and the Reformulation of Masculinity

Before, about ten years ago, they said you were mad if you were a Christian [Evangelist], they didn't want you to go to their house, they said that you brought them bad luck . . . That is, they didn't want to have anything to do with us, they would destroy the houses, beat the ministers up. Christians have gone through many things before arriving where they are now. Before it was shameful to say that you were a Christian . . . now it is a prize, a thing of pride . . . Nowadays the people of the world [non-converts] know that the Church is something good, because through the Church many drug-addicts have given up drugs ... the Church is against drugs, against alcohol, against doing dirty things, adultery, *quimeras*, fights. Now we are in peace and get along with each other. Before there used to be *ruinas* all the time. Twenty years ago they used to kill each other, they were not like now, their minds were more closed and everything was different, they did not live with Payos, there were only Gitanos, there, in four shacks and they were with each other, and made each other angry easily. Now life has passed, we young people coming now are very different, our parents have taught us other things, and we too to our children, so that everything evolves. I am twenty-six and in twenty-six years I have never been in a *ruina*. We may have had a fist fight, but we have never had to leave our houses. Now, just because somebody slaps me, I am not going to bring a *ruina* on the whole family, I shut up and that is it. Often they speak (offend somebody), and others want to start a fight, and yet others say 'stop it, look: we have all the family, we have many children to consider, and we don't want to end up in a field somewhere, because now we live happily in our flats, and we don't have any reason to start that mess. They want to have a fist fight? Fair enough, but let us be.' Because now everything has changed a lot.

In this extract from a taped conversation Clara, a first-generation convert, puts forward a basically progressive/evolutionist picture of change among the Gitanos organizing it around a double Gitano/Payo-convert/non-convert axis. She evaluates the change – from worse to better – in terms of the 'respectability' standard that I have described, and places conflict and masculine behaviour at its centre. Although she attributes the transformation to the changed circumstances – 'life has passed' – she also emphasizes the key role of the Evangelical Church. For, together with this positive perception of social change that the Gitanos of Jarana sometimes underline, both converts and non-converts also state that authentic/proper Gitano values and lifestyle are being 'lost' through the spread of drug addiction. Converts very often picture Evangelism as the Gitanos' only hope of reversing this process that would otherwise lead to 'the end of the Gitanos'. As it happens among the French Manouches, conversion to Evangelism 'is lived as fidelity, or even more exactly as restoration, because the integrity of traditional uses is thought to be somewhat at risk in the world' (Williams 1991: 85; emphasis removed).

The Evangelical Gitanos of Jarana have formulated an ideal of manly behaviour that takes up those aspects of the Gitano morality that 'in the world' work to sanction high status and hierarchy, transforming them in the process. As I have already suggested, Gitano Evangelism does not propose a radical break with what is perceived as the 'Gitano way of being' (*la manera de ser Gitana*). Rather, in a manner parallel to the situation described by Williams for the Manouches, what comes through is 'the coexistence of the proclamation of transformation and of permanence' (1991: 83).[6] This mixed emphasis, however, is selective, and in Jarana its dynamics can be identified at two main levels. Firstly, as Gitanos vis-à-vis other Gitanos, converts define themselves as 'formal' and hence 'respectable'. This allows them to portray themselves as the élite of the Gitano community: they disassociate respectability from its age context, emphasizing its acquired rather than its ascribed component. The result is a transformed pattern of hierarchy and leadership. Secondly, as Gitanos vis-à-vis Payos they separate themselves from those stereotypes that put Gitanos at the lowest scale of the Payo socio-moral hierarchy.[7] They attempt to construct a Gitano identity in terms that are to be seen as respectable not only in Gitano but also in Payo eyes. This points to the reformulation and re-evaluation of what makes Gitanos and Payos similar and different, and indicates a transformation in the Gitano views of themselves as a group (see Williams 1991: 87).

At the core of Gitano Evangelism is the idea of *testimonio* (testimony): this is the example of decency and righteousness that converts as individuals and as a group have to give to other convert and non-convert Gitanos and to Payos. The contents of this testimony are gender-specific and reveal the coexistence of continuity and innovation just stressed. Converts propose a model of masculine behaviour that revolves around the concept of *formalidad*, in basically the same terms described in the section above. Much of the convert emphasis on *formalidad* is centred upon around a rejection of drug addiction and I was told many stories about young men giving up drugs after 'meeting the Lord'. The belief that, as Clara underlines in the quotation above, the Church is 'against drugs, and against all that is evil' was shared by most of my informants. Drugs are said to be 'of the Devil' (*del diablo*), and are *reprendidas* (told off or reprimanded) in prayers and services in the same way as he is. Converts make a very strong attempt to convert and redeem drug addicts, both spiritually and socially.[7]

Paco, the husband of my friend Sara in whose house I lived for part of my fieldwork, was a heroin addict for several years before he converted about two years after their marriage. While I was in Jarana, Sara was always fearful that Paco would take up drugs again. She was

Figure 8.1 Young Evangelical ministers pray for newly baptised converts at the river near Escalona (Toledo).

positive that so long as he stayed in the Church he would not do it, and always took care to encourage him to attend services and prayer meetings. When I visited the neighbourhood in August 1993, I found that Sara was very worried about him because he had stopped attending the services almost completely. Sara told me that she had had a dream in which the Devil had appeared to her and told her that he had taken Paco to the edge of a very high abyss and that if she did not have sexual intercourse with the Devil he would push Paco over. She could see Paco clearly at the top of the cliff and so she accepted. She explained: 'I went through terrible hardships while I was with the Devil'. After they had sex the Devil told her: 'you are stupid, now I have you both'. He pushed Paco, and she could see how he was falling. Then she woke up. She was sure that the dream had been sent to her either by God or by the Devil, as a warning of what would happen to Paco if he gave up the Church totally: he would return to heroin and die. She told Paco about the dream in the hope that it would impress him and he would mend his ways. Although he did not say anything, Sara believed that her account would eventually have some beneficial effect. She also told two of Paco's best friends, both converts, about her dream, so that, seeing that the dream had a supernatural source, they would realize the danger to Paco's life and encourage him to 'return to the Church'. Shortly afterwards he begun to attend services again but has since behaved as an 'intermittent convert'.

In their attempts to reform non-respectable men, converts build on non-convert notions about morality and masculinity. They do the same in their constructions of male leadership: there are clear parallels between the roles or figures of the mediator and the minister. Firstly, converts put great emphasis on the exemplary behaviour and morals of the *ministerios* (ministers and trainees). Among the minister's virtues it is more his righteousness or respectability – which is measured in terms of the hegemonic model of masculinity that I have described – rather than his doctrinal knowledge that is considered significant. In order to illustrate how much care converts take to adjust to Gitano moral standards Lolo, Clara's husband, himself a minister, told me two stories about two ministers of the Church. The first was a trainee minister (*candidato*) whose wife had an adulterous relationship with another man. Even though she repented and he accepted her again as his wife, no congregation would receive her as a minister's wife (*pastora*), and so he had to give up his training. In order to become ministers, Gitano men have to be married: they need a wife who will take care of the affairs and problems of the women of the church, since it is not considered proper for a man to speak with a non-related woman except in the presence of other people. The other minister eloped with one of the girls who sung in the choir of his church. His congregation set fire to his house, and he gave up his ministry. Lolo explained that these men could never have positions of responsibility in the Church because the Bible says that 'no sinner will get into the Kingdom'. When I pointed to Jesus' forgiveness of the adulterous woman he acknowledged that the Church's strictness had much to do with the need to keep up an image of respectability in the eyes of non-convert Gitanos.

Secondly, the degree and kind of authority that ministers (*pastores*) have over their congregations are very similar to those of the elder over his family or of the mediator over the people who call him to arbitrate. Ministers make decisions about things like the organization of religious activities, the punishment of wrong-doers, and the management of the church's money. Thus, they are often called to mediate in conflicts that involve converts – sometimes together with some 'men of respect', sometimes on their own: marital problems, quarrels over selling locations, fights and so on. *Pastores* usually direct particular churches for relatively short periods: the church of Jarana had three ministers during the 15 months of my fieldwork. Usually a congregation is enthusiastic about the new minister and his wife for three or four months before they begin to develop grudges and make it clear that they want them to leave. Thus, just as with the 'men of respect', the minister's authority depends on the acquiescence of his congregation. Moreover, ministers are the recipients of deference in much the same way as mediators are, without regard to age.

Converts endorse understandings about *formalidad* that incorporate non-convert elements, but they also take on specifically Evangelical precepts. Central among these is a rejection of physical violence and retaliation, and hence of non-convert ways of dealing with conflict. This emphasis is not totally alien to some aspects of the Gitano ethos, and can be seen as a continuation of the calculated self-control that respectable men are expected to display. However, it is carried much further than in non-Evangelical understandings. In one of her many attempts at convincing me that the Evangelical Church was a good thing for the Gitanos, Sara explained to me how 'nowadays you can even go to a church in which you have *contrarios*. This is because God unites us, takes away all that is evil.' She told me the story of a man who killed another man:

The son of the dead man swore that he would not rest until he killed his father's killer, you understand, no matter how. Well, many years went by, and he looked and looked for him, without finding him, and he kept saying that he would kill him, and they say that once he even tried, I don't know how, but he didn't manage because the other one was a very brave man. In the end he was taken to jail for trying to kill this man. When he got out of jail he entered the Church and was converted, and they saw each other in a service. And instead of going for him, you know, like the Gitanos do, he went to him and they embraced each other. This is a great testimony.

Many similar stories are often told by converts. Moreover, in their speech and actions, converts may explicitly diminish their solidarity with their kin groups to the benefit of their identity as Evangelists. Hence one of the examples that I quoted in Chapter 7, where Tío Juan described how a convert refused to support his non-convert brother in a *ruina*: 'since all of them (the convert brother and his sons) are Christians . . . they do not want feuding, because they belong to the Church and have changed completely.' The exact extent to which, in the practice, religious affiliation prevails over familial ties varies from case to case and is difficult to determine.

As a young Paya, I was very rarely able to witness discussions or negotiations within or between families, or among ministers and trainees, and had access only to people's descriptions of these events. However, I was present at the local church the day Foros and Sotos publicly forgave each other after the quarrel between Pepe and Gabriel. During the days that followed the fight, Pepe's non-convert agnatic relatives – the Juanes – made a point of going to the church to display their numbers and readiness to fight, although accepting Tío Juan's orders that no confrontation should take place. Among the converts of the district, gossiping, mutual accusations and back-biting went on for several days: many people felt involved because they were related to Pepe or to Gabriel, or to both, in one way or another. Reconciliation was ritually enacted during a service when a visiting Portuguese Gypsy minister ordered the congregation to forgive each other's grudges and embrace each other. Although he did not make any direct reference to the fight, it was clear that he knew about it. As a foreigner he was completely neutral, and as a minister he had the necessary authority to command such a gesture. For about half an hour, with the lights off, and while the choir sung 'spiritual' songs, Sotos and Foros cried in each other's arms. However, the day after this service I witnessed converts belonging to both patrigroups accusing the others of only pretending to have true feelings of forgiveness and repentance.

Hierarchy and Evangelism

Out of the different elements that make up Gitano masculinity, it is those that have to do with *respeto* and *conocimiento* that form the bases of status and hierarchy, and that converts appropriate. This comes through clearly in Clara's statement above, where she sets up an opposition between converts and the Gitano past, and between converts and non-converts in the present. She describes non-converts and Gitanos 'of before' as the antithesis of the hegemonic Gitano ideal of adult masculine behaviour. This self-definition allows converts to construct themselves as the 'better' section of the Gitano community – the one that is more moral and hence more authentically Gitano. Although non-convert Gitanos may contest this representation, they tend to do it by drawing attention to the converts' failures to conform to the moral standards that they preach, rather than by attacking the standards themselves. On the other hand, they may also support the converts' self-definition: many times I have heard non-convert mothers pushing their daughters to go to church, stating their hope that they will find 'a decent husband' (*un marido decente*) – that is, an alcohol- and drugs-free man.

The convert appropriation and transformation of the notion of *formalidad* enables a dual organization of authority based on an 'inside/outside the Church' division. This appropriation leads to the reformulation of the bases of leadership among converts, as well as outside the Church in those areas of daily life that are affected by people's allegiances.[8] The starting point is the fact that converts separate formality/respectability from the age-context with which they are associated 'in the world' (outside the Church). Men try to present themselves as formal and respectable independently of their age. Young men attempt to put distance between themselves and those symbols of masculinity that Gitanos link to youth and lack of self-control or recklessness. During my fieldwork those who sung in the choir in Jarana were forbidden by the minister and themselves made a point of not wearing long hair – as most non-converts do – because it is tied to youth and its correlations – sexual potency, realized through going to bars and discos to flirt with Payas and have sex with them; and with courage without *conocimiento*.

In a similar vein, and even more strikingly, very young men are given positions of authority within the Church. Lolo, Clara's husband,

Figure 8.2 A minister (right) prays for his older brother (middle), about to be baptised.

was unmarried and in his late teens when Carlos, then the minister of Jarana, began to pay attention to him. Carlos baptized and began to train him when he was not yet twenty. Lolo's wife Clara thus became a *candidata* (trainee minister's wife) as soon as she was married, at sixteen. They led their first church, in Segovia, only two years later. It is significant that very young men have come to be considered as potentially respectable – something that does not happen in the case of non-converts. If this potential for respectability is asserted or realized – for example when a young man becomes a minister – the context within which younger men can exert influence grows dramatically. Thus, with the spread of Evangelism, much younger men are given leading roles among the Gitanos.

Parallel with this increased valorization of younger men is a devaluation of old age that contrasts with non-Evangelical understandings. After the New Year's Eve service, Luis, Rosa, Lolo, Clara and I went to Clara's and Lolo's house, to drink some coffee. They started commenting about how a section of the local church was no longer happy with Carlos, the local minister. They thought he was too old and hence inefficient. They gave different examples of how his age had a negative influence. Lolo – who at that time was not active as a minister – ended up saying that Carlos would be better off at home, 'warm by the fire'. He insisted that 'he ought to leave his place to younger men who have a lot to give', whereas 'he has already given what he has'. Clara briefly took Carlos' side, saying that despite his shortcomings he was still a *siervo* – 'serf', a word applied to ministers – and deserved the respect of the Church. Overall, however, the three of them supported Lolo's views.

The way in which converts take up ideas about *respeto* and *conocimiento* show up how significant they are in organizing the Gitano world-views. It reveals the combination of continuity and transformation required by a millenarian movement that – despite its claims – does all but separate itself from the outside world. From an instrumentalist perspective, it seems clear that Evangelism provides young men with possibilities of advancement that are closed to them in 'the (Gitano) world'. That is, the Church generates a combination – young and respectable – which cannot be realized outside its parameters. And it does so while providing enough of a continuity with what are key principles in the Gitano organisation of daily life.

At the same time, the Church and its appropriation/transformation of the notion of respect and its connotations reveals a novel attitude towards the Payo world. In such things as dress and manner,[9] references made in cults, or speech forms, the Church promotes not only an image of *formalidad* but of modernity – hence the temporal references and the elaboration of a social memory made explicit in Clara's statements above. Gitanos describe modernity in terms that bring it very closely to the Payo lifestyle – they link it for example to an ethos that stresses truthfulness rather than cunning in dealing with Payos, or to an emphasis on giving women greater 'freedom' (*libertad*). Convert men, for example, take much care to dress elegantly according to the Payo fashion: they wear dark suits, white shirts and ties. Moreover, whereas Gitanos do not usually greet each other but simply acknowledge each other's presence with a nod of the head, male converts shake hands like Payos do. Converts disassociate themselves not only from symbols of low morals that already exist among other Gitanos – such as drug-addiction – but also from 'backwardness' (*atraso*) and 'lack of civilization' (*falta de civilización*) – that the Gitanos as a group, by contrast with the Payos, are perceived to incarnate. This reveals a view of the Payos that still views them as immoral and yet explicitly values some aspects of the Payo ethos and lifestyle. And the fact that conversions increase regularly, and that non-converts are able to evaluate the Evangelical claim in roughly its own terms, reveals how this image of themselves and of the Payos is not restricted to Evangelist Gitanos, but widespread among non-converts as well. The Church both responds and collaborates in the challenge that life in contemporary Spain – housing, social assistance, integration into the formal structures of the State – poses to the Gitanos.

Conclusions

The Gitanos of Jarana objectify Gypsyness by evaluating men's behaviour against a hegemonic ideal of Gitano masculinity. Hierarchy among Gitanos is produced on the bases of gender/age categories and inequality is built upon hierarchy. Inequality relates to the manipulation of human relations. At the centre of the workings of hierarchy and inequality is the mixed ascribed and acquired character of the ideas of *conocimiento* and *respeto*. The ascribed nature of respect sets limits to the possibilities of particular categories of people – women always deserve less respect than men, and younger people than older people – and contributes to the formulation of their difference. At the same time, its acquired aspect provides the grounding for the construction of certain other categories – such as the *risión* and the 'man of respect' – as well as for the, at least verbal, contestation of its ascribed character. Older men, who are granted more *conocimiento* than younger ones, should also demonstrate it or else lose the respect to which they are entitled through their age. The same can be said of relations between men and women. Only by not taking the hierarchy and the categories it organizes as absolute or given – that is, as solely ascribed – is it possible to understand how the Evangelical Church transforms the Gitano age/gender organization by detaching respect from its age context, and so partially erasing its ascribed character while still using this ascribed facet to regulate relations between men and women, as I explained in Chapter 5.

Notes

1. *Gente de pluma* is a common expression among Gitanos that refers to native North Americans. Many Gitanos worked as extras at the time when 'Spaghetti Westerns' were filmed in Spain and the ones who live in Jarana often equate the word *indio* (Indian) with backwardness and ignorance.

2. San Román (1976: 206–7) describes how personal 'prestige is augmented by knowing much (*saber mucho*) . . . [The Gitanos] use the word *saber* to indicate the ability that a person has to mislead another, to earn money, to dance, or any other capacity. It refers particularly to being cunning and alert without falling into trouble and while benefiting one's family.'

3. This acknowledgement of achievement is also made visible in speech. Gitanos address people who are one or more generations older than themselves by the terms of respect *tío* (uncle) or *tía* (aunt), instead of by their names. When they are not present, though, they refer to them as *la/el* (the) followed by their name – for example *la Carmina*. 'Men of respect', on the other hand, are talked about as *Tío* followed by their names, whether they are present or not, by all the Gitanos of younger generations.

4. Tío Juan shows how politeness and shame are combined. In all our chats, whenever a sexual reference was made, he would add the words 'with your forgiveness' (*con perdón tuyo*). He was always careful not to say rude words.

5. All the Gitano drug addicts that I met during my fieldwork were male except for one. Drug addiction is associated with smoking which is a male-only activity.

6. Anta Félez (1994: 87) similarly explains that the adoption of Evangelism implies 'the recreation of a concrete ideology, which takes place on a daily basis and that implies the restructuring of the Gitano culture, recreating a syncretism between the traditional Gitano symbols and the religious idea of the Evangelicals'. His overall evaluation of the Church, however, is clearly negative: he states that Evangelical Gitanos 'realise a continuous destruction of their own identity (as Gitanos) by breaking up the group' (1994: 86).

7. Comaroff's comments in relation to the growth of Evangelism among the Tshidi of South Africa help to illuminate these Gitano processes. She explains how 'the innovations of the mission not only exacerbated internal contradictions within the Tshidi system itself, they also instituted a set of categories through which such tensions could be objectified and acted upon' (Comaroff 1985: 2).

8. Gamella explains: 'one of the results of the expansion of the Evangelical Church to which Gitanos refer most often is its beneficial capacity to draw young men away from drugs' (1996: 367).

9. Gamella points out that 'there can be conflicts between the principles and hierarchy of the Evangelical Church and others rooted in the Gitano world; for example between religious leaders and kin group leaders' (1996: 368).

nine

Conclusion

From the description that I have provided through the chapters above, the Gitanos of Jarana appear to be very different from the Gypsies among whom other anthropologists have worked – for example the Rom in the case of Sutherland (1975a) and Stewart (1997), or the English Travellers in the case of Okely (1983).[1] Those practices that, to non-Gypsy eyes, appear to be most obviously Gypsy, such as upholding pollution taboos, speaking Romany, being nomadic or dealing in horses, have all been absent – perhaps conspicuously so – from this book. This variation is clearly at least in part a result of the fact that each Gypsy group is immersed within different social and cultural contexts and has undergone different historical processes: as I have explained in Chapter 5, the Gitano cultural baggage includes many Spanish and even Mediterranean elements. However, the Gitanos do share with other Gypsies four extremely significant traits: firstly, they prefer to engage in economic activities over which they themselves exert control;[2] secondly, they are peripheral to the non-Gypsy social, economic and moral hierarchies; thirdly, they invest much effort on keeping themselves distinct from the non-Gypsies and they evaluate this difference in moral terms; and fourthly, they lack what can be called 'permanent' media through which to encode their identity. Although the four are linked, it is the last three features that I want to discuss here.

The Gitanos of Jarana, like those described by Kaprow (1991) in Saragossa, seem to be permanently engaged in the 'celebration of impermanence'. In Jarana this means a series of things. Firstly, although they are fully sedentary, these Gitanos are much more mobile than the majority of Payos who live around them: many have been resettled every few years; others have had to abandon their homes as a result of feuding. Most importantly, they do not conceive of land or territory as foundations of shared identity. Secondly, what can be called their material culture is very limited – they have no sculpture, no painting, no architecture of their own – and they make little invest-ment in durable valuables. In fact, the Gitanos make use of the material world around them in a way that differs significantly from that of the Payos. Whereas the non-Gitano ethos revolves around the accumu-lation of durables, the Gitanos focus on the exchange and fast con-sumption of goods that are produced by others. These goods tend to be treated as non-durable and are rapidly discarded. Objects have short lives among the Gitanos: all through my fieldwork I was struck by the facility with which things became broken or lost. Thirdly, the Gitanos of Jarana lack an elaborate social memory and have no myths of origin in which their common identity could find its roots:[3] they are intent on separating the past from the present, and on denying that the 'before' (*antes*) may hold the blue-print for the 'now' (*ahora*).[4]

This combination of features lends Gitano life a definite air of 'impermanence' but does not mean, as Kaprow (1991) suggests, that the Gitanos lack social structures or institutions, or that their daily life develops in a consistently unsystematic manner – the preceding chapters should be a clear testimony to the contrary, as should the work of other ethnographers such as San Román (1976, 1994), Gamella (1996) or Anta Félez (1994). What the Gitanos' attitude to space, to the material world and to the past indicates, instead, is that the identity of the group is not objectified outside the group itself. Throughout this book I have argued that Gypsyness is to be found in the actions of the Gitanos or, in other words, that it is Gitano persons that carry with them the identity of the group and, in so doing, the ideal of group itself – the 'imagined community'. From the Gitanos' point of view, it is their 'way of being' (*manera de ser*) that separates them from, and makes them better than, the Payos. This 'way of being' can best be conceptualized as a stance vis-à-vis a series of moral norms that the Gitanos perceive as evident and given and that they think the Payos patently disregard. Thus, being a Gitano is not so much a question of having inherited a particular essence or substance, as of having learnt how to live life in the most honourable and righteous manner – and putting this knowledge into practice. In this sense, and following Linnekin and Poyer's dichotomy (1990a: 7–9), Gitano communal identity can be described as being more Lamarckian than Mendelian.

These authors – and others like Lieber, Watson and Pomponio in the same volume (Linnekin and Poyer 1990b) – give to Western 'theories of the origins and meaning of human variability' the label of 'ethnic' theories. They use the word 'ethnicity' to refer to the views according to which people are as they are because they were born to be so. Changes in external circumstances can affect but not completely alter identity. Groups of people sharing biological ancestry are readily seen as units, and social units are readily identified as sharing putative ancestry (1990a: 2).

By contrast, Oceanic theories of cultural identity privilege 'environment, behaviour and situational flexibility over descent, innate characteristics, and unchanging boundaries' (ibid.: 6). Thus, whereas Western ethnotheories have a Mendelian flavour, Oceanic ones can be characterized as Lamarckian: each is built on different understandings about how shared identity is created. According to this model, Oceanic peoples have no ethnicity in the Western sense of the word.

A similar argument has been put forward by Stewart, who explains that the Rom do not base their sense of being different from the surrounding non-Gypsies on a 'primordial, unchosen, traditional identity' into which individuals are born: as a consequence, the Rom cannot be said to have an ethnic identity (1997: 28). The Gitanos of Jarana are like the Hungarian Rom in that they premise their shared sense of self on how they live their lives in the present: a child born to Gitano parents is a Gitano child but she will need to provide constant evidence of her Gypsyness throughout her lifetime in order to be considered a 'true Gitana' (*una Gitana de verdad*). Otherwise, she will drift, turning into *una Gitana apayada*, a 'Payo-like Gitana', until she is no longer part of 'the Gitanos' (*los Gitanos*) or the 'Gitano people' (*el pueblo Gitano*). Because Gitano men and women become *apayados* all the time, the Gitanos view their way of life as perpetually in danger of becoming extinct. By the same token, although Payos cannot become Gitanos, they can earn a place among them if they adopt the Gitano lifestyle and the Gitano morality – that is, the Gitano 'way of being' (*la manera de ser Gitana*). This is an arduous task because almost every single aspect of everyday life can be faced in the Gitano *or* the Payo 'styles' and because Gitanos think that it is extremely difficult to un-learn the wrong ways: Payos attempting to be accepted among Gitanos have to jump through an almost endless number of hoops. As in the Lamarckian model that Linnekin and Poyer outline, the Gitanos 'emphasise the role of social relationships in determining an individual's essential characteristics' (1990: 7). This is why it is important that children of mixed parentage should be brought up among Gitanos rather than among Payos: only then can they truly learn how to be decent, proper human beings.

Take the example of one of Sara's and Clara's maternal aunts, Petra, who married a Payo in her youth and who, by the time of my field-work, had a son and a daughter in their early teens. Petra and her husband had lived in a Payo neighbourhood and had had little contact with her parents and siblings, who had been extremely upset when she eloped with a non-Gypsy and begun to become more and more *apayada* (Payo-like). While I was in Jarana Petra's husband left her for another woman, and shortly after that Petra herself found a lover – a Caribbean immigrant – became pregnant once again, and began to pay less and less attention to her children. Estela, Petra's sister, then asked Petra to allow the children to move in with Petra's mother. She and Petra's other siblings were keen to teach their niece and nephew the Gitano ways, and were particularly eager to find a Gitano boyfriend for Petra's daughter and to marry her off as soon as possible. Then the girl's chances of remaining among Gitanos and of having what Estela called a 'decent life' would increase enormously.

The Gitanos' image of themselves as a group is thus remarkably different from other Western ideas about what makes a mass of individuals a 'people'. In particular, the Gitanos of Jarana lack an understanding of 'the Gitanos' as a society, if we understand by 'society', 'the system or mode of life adopted by a body of individuals for the purpose of harmonious co-existence or for mutual benefit'.[5] The inhabitants of Jarana conceive of 'the Gitanos' as an aggregate of persons, of undefined size, origin and location, who uphold the same morality and stand in the same position vis-à-vis the rest of the world. It is persons rather than groups of people that perform Gypsyness: Estela's status as a Gitana, for example, was not in the least diminished by the fact that two of her siblings – Petra and one brother – had become *apayados*. Unity, cohesiveness and social harmony are all irrelevant to the Gitano's understandings of themselves. Instead, when Gitano persons behave properly according to Gitano standards, their relations are patterned by the 'Gitano law' (*ley Gitana*): they co-operate and interact with kin, and feud with and avoid non-kin. These relations – in which the workings of 'knowledge' (*conocimiento*) and 'respect' (*respeto*) are made evident – are one of the ways in which the 'Gitano way of being' is objectified, just as it is objectified when a woman preserves her virginity until marriage or when an elderly man keeps his tempter in a confrontation with strangers. Through feuds Gitanos validate their knowledge of each other as moral beings: during *ruinas* Gitanos see themselves and other, unrelated Gitanos, behaving according to the 'Gitano law' and in so doing making Gypsyness real. Hence, the role of patrigroups is not to mediate the relationship between the person and 'the Gitanos' as a people. Instead, *razas*, just like 'the Gitanos', are created when people enact Gypsyness (*lo Gitano*). Unequal or discordant relations between patrigroups of different sizes or strengths are similarly manifestations of the 'Gitano way of being'.

At the same time, the Gitanos do not make a dichotomy between persons and 'the Gitanos' as a group because it is persons themselves who metonymically embody the ideal of the group: it is only in action, through personal moral performances, that such an ideal is realized. As I have explained throughout the chapters above, the Gitano concept of the person[6] draws on two understandings. Firstly, Gitano personal and communal identities are interdependent in the sense that each person sustains the worth of 'the Gitanos' as a whole. Secondly, the Gitanos do not make a conceptual separation between individuals, their bodies, and their actions. Together, the three make up the Gitano concept of the person, with the body working as a sign indicating the kind of person an individual is – not only a man or a woman, but a more or less morally acceptable man or woman. The consequence is that, in the Gitano case, sex cannot be disentangled from gender and persons are always thought of as gendered/sexed – that is, as belonging to one of two kinds of people. Transformations undergone by the body are treated as indexes of the person's moral evolution. This is best exemplified by the wedding ceremony, but I also experienced it myself: during the time that I spent with the Gitanos I changed my dress and manner. These shifts were interpreted by the Gitanos as improvements in my character or personality: by spending time in the neighbourhood I was learning to become a more adequate or better woman; I was effectively changing who I was. They often expressed worries as to what would happen to me when I left them.

In the absence of external media through which to objectify their identity, the Gitanos turn to themselves – to their bodies and their actions. Such things as the Gitano emphasis on dressing and moving in 'the Gitano manner' (*gitanalmente*) or on the preservation of female virginity until marriage, indicate that Gitanos of Jarana carry their identity on and inside their bodies. And there is a key difference between the way the Gitanos make their bodies into bearers of group identity, and the way other Gypsies have been said to do it. Both Sutherland (1977) and Okely (1983) have argued that among the Californian Rom and the English Gypsies the body provides a metaphor for social organization. These arguments rest upon structuralist descriptions in which the body is portrayed as being good to think with and 'reduced to the status of a sign' (Connerton 1989: 95). My analysis has stressed metonymy at the expense of metaphor because the Gitanos do not pattern onto their bodies a symbolic elucidation of their relationship to the Payos.[7] Instead, it is through their behaviour – including the way they manage their bodies – that Gitanos make real the fact that they are different from the non-Gypsies. In this sense my approach comes close to Stewart's analysis of shame and pollution taboos among the Rom when he explains that 'it is not that "upper" is to Rom as "lower" is to *gazo*, but that what makes people Rom is that they realise to be human, one must divide the body, and what makes others *gazo* is that they do not' (1997: 230).

Because men and women are different kinds of persons, they incarnate Gypsyness in distinct ways – hence the dual moral standards of which I have talked through the chapters above. Whereas women make real the difference between Gitanos and Payos by remaining virgins until marriage, by being faithful to their husbands and by respecting them and their parents-in-law, men enact Gypsyness when they display courage and knowledge, and when their respectable behaviour elicits respect from others. The hierarchical and unequal positions in which men and women stand – modified by the principles of age and kinship – are thus also objectifications of Gypsyness. Simultaneously, within the context of Gitano life, some people are acknowledged to enact Gypsyness better than others, so that the adequate performance of gendered personhood is transformed into respectability, into prestige and into the capacity to exert more or less control over one's own life and the lives of others. It is therefore the acknowledgement of difference – between Payos and Gitanos and between men and women – that gives Gitano everyday life much of its political character: the extent to which Gitanos manage to fulfil their roles as Gitano women or as Gitano men shapes the relations they establish with other Gitanos.

Most importantly, by adhering to the 'Gitano way of being', the Gitanos are able to tell themselves that the social and moral orders that matter are their own, and not those of the non-Gypsies. Thus, although in many Payo eyes the Gitanos stand at the bottom of the heap, even outside the bounds of 'society' and 'civilization', by performing Gypsyness the Gitanos state that poverty, marginality and powerlessness at the hands of Payo authorities do not determine who they are. When they first moved into Jarana, the Gitanos were enraged to find out that Payo social workers had placed a huge placard at the entrance of the neighbourhood that read: 'Colony for Marginal Population' (*Colonia para Población Marginal*). The sign could be read from passing cars on the highway and the Gitanos were quick to tear it down. Tío Juan, genuinely angry at the social workers, explained the Gitanos' reaction to me: 'there are only Gitanos here, nothing else, that marginal thing, we are not that!' (*¡aquí no hay más que Gitanos, eso de marginal, eso nosotros no lo somos!*). His statement was full of meaning. To Gitano eyes, and even though they are constantly reminded of their low status, marginality to the 'Payo way of being' does not define Gypsyness. Rather, as Williams says of the Kalderash, the Gitanos are a people who 'carry their centre with them' (1982: 341).

In Jarana, Gypsyness means producing constant evidence of the fact that, of all Spaniards, the Gitanos alone know how to live their lives as proper human beings. Gypsyness permeates every single aspect of everyday life: all daily activities can be carried out *gitanalmente*. And it is of key importance to remember that performing Gypsyness involves evaluating one's own behaviour and the behaviour of others against the 'Gitano laws' and allocating corresponding levels of respect and status. In their definitions of themselves, the Gitanos of Jarana make ample space for failures to adhere to the 'Gitano way of being'. A good example is provided by the elopement, an institution which allows Gitanos to behave like Payos and yet to remain part of the 'Gitano people'. Similarly, not every Gitano man is a 'man of respect', but every time a man recognizes the respectability of the mediator he can consider himself to be bringing Gypsyness about.

Throughout my fieldwork I felt that, even if many of them are very poor, even if they have been 'dumped' in a ghetto-like neighbourhood, even if they are finding it increasingly difficult to earn their living in the ways that they prefer, the Gitanos who live in Jarana think themselves to be privileged. Petra's siblings, for example, who were so eager to take her children into their homes and bring them up as Gitanos, felt they had something very important to offer their half-Payo nephew and niece. Clara, Sara, Tío Juan, Tía Tula and many others displayed the same attitude towards me: they were keen to teach me how to become a 'proper woman'. Those Gitanos who belonged to the Church of Filadelfia were even more secure in their knowledge of their own excellence.

Lastly, the Gitanos of Jarana produce proof of their superiority over the Payos not only through their own behaviour, but by constructing an ideal model of Payo life and Payo morality that involves the inversion of the norms that they insist rule Gitano life. Whether this Gitano image of what the Payos are like is a faithful representation of Payo life or not is to a large extent irrelevant: the Gitanos of Jarana dismissed every single of my claims that Payo men are not all weaklings, or that not all Payo women are forever thirsty for sex. What matters is that, by depicting the Payos as amoral, corrupt, and above all, ignorant of what is decent and proper, the Gitanos provide an essential foundation to the images through which they portray themselves to themselves. By disregarding with such determination the possibility that the lives of the Payos might not be altogether evil and negative, the Gitanos of Jarana rhetorically deny that their own 'way of being' may not be as perfect or satisfying as they often proclaim. However, there is more to the Gitanos' self-representations than that: the critiques that Gitano women make of their lives as Gitanas, for example, and the envy that they express at the 'freedom' of the Payas, demonstrate that Gitano dominant discourses do not exhaust the ways the Gitanos see and portray themselves.

My aim in this book has been to build up a picture, layer by layer, of how the Gitanos of Jarana attempt, fail and succeed in realizing their ideal of what being Gitano means. In other words, and because Gitano personhood is always gendered, I have outlined how Gitano masculinity and Gitano femininity are produced through different social contexts in Jarana: wedding ceremonies, elopements, feuds, quarrels between husbands and wives and so on. In so doing, I wanted to describe Gypsyness as something that, in order to exist at all, needs to be continually created or performed by Gitano men and women. I have outlined a particular model of shared identity: one in which it is a person's 'way of being' in the present that enables her, and others around her, to imagine 'the Gitanos' as a people.

Notes

1. The literature on Gypsies is vast, and its quality is sometimes questionable. The following are some works on Gypsies generally and on Gitanos in particular that I have found challenging and thought provoking: on the problems of doing research among Gypsies, Gronfors 1982; Kaprow 1982; and Okely 1992; general ethnographies, Gropper 1975; Sutherland 1975a; San Román 1976; Gronfors 1977; Okely 1983, and Stewart 1997; on Gypsies, history and origins, Sánchez Ortega 1986, Leblon 1985; Okely 1983; Mayall 1988, Fraser 1992; and Gómez Alfaro 1992; on Gypsies and the study of ethnicity, Salo 1977 and 1979;

Mulcahy 1988; Kaprow, 1991; and San Román 1986b (ed.); on the urbanization and proletarianization of Gypsies and other itinerant groups, Gmelch 1977; Gmelch 1986, Gropper 1975; GIEMS 1976; M. Salo and S. Salo 1982; Williams 1982; San Román 1986a, Liegeois 1987; and Stewart 1993; on Gitanos and social change more generally, Ardevol 1986; San Román 1990 and 1994; on Gypsies and religion, Jordán Pemán 1990; Williams 1991 and 1993a; and on Gypsies and gender, Okely 1977; Sutherland 1977; and Stewart 1997. See also the special issues of *Urban Anthropology* 1982 vol. 11, no. 3–4, edited by M. Salo and dedicated exclusively to Gypsies and other itinerant groups, and of *Ethnies*, 1993 vol. 8, no. 15, edited by Williams (1993b) and dedicated to Gypsies.

2. Particularly revealing descriptions are found in Stewart (1997; chapters 6, 9 and 11) and Williams 1982.

3. Although the Gitanos display no interest in finding out where their origins lay, the same cannot be said of Payo academics and *aficionados* who are particularly concerned with establishing 'who the Gitanos truly are'. Thus, the Gitanos, like other Gypsies, have been said to come from India, and this hypothesis has been used as an – at least partial – explanation of their current social and cultural organizations (see for example San Román 1986a).

4. Discussing the Hungarian Rom, Stewart explains how they 'do not seem to care where their ancestors came from. In all the time I have spent in Harangos, I have never once heard a spontaneous conversation about the geographical or historical roots of their own people. And even when the Rom engaged the topic in response to my questioning, this was clearly to humor me and did not reflect any interest of their own' (1997: 28).

5. I have taken this definition from the *Oxford Shorter English Dictionary*, third edition. It is revealing that all the dictionary definitions of the word emphasize cohesiveness, unity and harmony. Take the following: 'the aggregate of persons living together in a more or less ordered community'; 'the state or condition of being politically confederated or allied'; 'a.number of persons associated together by some common interest or purpose, united by a common vow, holding the same belief or opinion, following the same trade or profession'; 'a collection of individuals composing a community or living under the same organization or government'.

6. I take up Strathern's use of the words 'person' and 'individual'. She herself follows Dumont (1977), and applies the word 'individual' to the 'subject of speech, thought, and will, the indivisible sample of mankind'. 'Person', on the other hand, is made to stand for the 'culturally constituted moral entity, one defined by its potential autonomy and independence from others like it' (1981: 168)

7. The Gitanos of Jarana do appeal to a series of rules about how dirty things and parts of the body are to be cleaned. They are concerned with keeping food and utensils that go inside the body separated from objects or substances that are in contact with its surface. However, these norms are much less formalized than the ones that Okely (1983) and Sutherland (1977) describe,

and are much more peripheral to the Gitanos' definitions of themselves than to the self-presentation of the English Travellers or the American Rom. In practice, these norms are often overlooked, and their role seems to be above all rhetorical: they are called upon in speech as an ideal standard which the Gitanos compare with an equally stereotypical picture of Payo habits.

References

Anta Félez, J. L. 1994. *Donde la Pobreza es Marginación: un Análisis Entre Gitanos*. Barcelona. Editorial Humanidades.

Ardevol, E. 1986. Vigencias y Cambio en la Cultura de los Gitanos. In T. San Román (ed.), *Entre la Marginación y el Racismo. Reflexiones Sobre la Vida de los Gitanos*. Madrid. Alianza.

Astuti, R. 1995. *People of the Sea: Identity and Descent Among the Vezo of Madagascar*. Cambridge. Cambridge University Press.

Behar, R. 1986. *Santa María del Monte: the Presence of the Past in a Spanish Village*. Princeton. Princeton University Press.

Bloch, M. and J. Parry. 1982. Death and the Regeneration of Life. Introduction to M. Bloch and J. Parry (eds), *Death and the Regeneration of Life*. Cambridge. Cambridge University Press.

Boddy, J. 1989. *Wombs and Alien Spirits*. Madison. Wisconsin University Press.

Bourdieu, P. 1977. *Outline of a Theory of Practice*. Cambridge. Cambridge University Press.

Butler, J. 1993. *Bodies that Matter: on the Discursive Limits of 'Sex'*. London. Routledge.

Calvo Buezas, T. 1990. *¿España Racista? Voces Payas Sobre los Gitanos*. Barcelona. Anthropos.

Cano, L. 1981. *Un Pentecostés en el Siglo XX*. Sabadell. Cano.

Caro Baroja, J. 1970. *El Mito del Carácter Nacional: Meditaciones a Contrapelo*. Madrid. Seminarios y Ediciones.

Cátedra Tomás, M. 1989. *La Vida y el Mundo de los Vaqueiros de Alzada*. Madrid. Centro de Investigaciones Sociológicas.

1991. ¿Qué es ser Vaqueiro de Alzada? In J. Prat et al. (eds), *Antropología de los Pueblos de España*. Madrid. Taurus Universitaria.

Cebrián Abellán, A. 1992. *Marginalidad de la Población Gitana Española*. Murcia. Universidad, Secretariado de Publicaciones.

Comaroff, J. 1985. *Body of Power, Spirit of Resistance: the Culture and History of a South African People*. Chicago. University of Chicago Press.

Connerton, P. 1989. *How Societies Remember*. Cambridge. Cambridge University Press.

Delaney, C. 1987. Seeds of Honor, Fields of Shame. In D. Gilmore (ed.), *Honor and Shame and the Unity of the Mediterranean*. Washington. American Anthropological Association.

de las Heras, J. and J. Villarín. 1974. *La España de los Quinquis*. Barcelona. Planeta.

de Pablo Velasco, M. L. 1994. *El Fenómeno de las Drogas y la Comunidad Gitana: Orientaciones para un Planteamiento Constructivo*. Madrid. Asociación Secretariado Nacional Gitano.

Devereux, L. 1987. Gender Difference and the Relations of Inequality in Zinacantan. In M. Strathern (ed.), *Dealing with Inequality: Analysing Gender Relations in Melanesia and Beyond*. Cambridge. Cambridge University Press.

Devillard, M. J. 1988. Una Categoría Cuestionada y Cuestionable: el Pueblo. In L. Díaz Viana (ed.), *Aproximación Antropológica a Castilla y León*. Barcelona. Anthropos.

Díaz Viana, L. 1988. Identidad y Manipulación de la Cultura Popular: Algunas Anotaciones Sobre el Caso Castellano. In L. Díaz Viana (ed.), *Aproximación Antropológica a Castilla y León*. Barcelona. Anthropos.

Douglas, M. 1966. *Purity and Danger: an Analysis of the Concepts of Pollution and Taboo*. London. Routledge & Kegan Paul.

Douglas, M. 1970. *Natural Symbols: Explorations in Cosmology*. London. Penguin.

du Boulay, J. 1986. Women – Images of their Nature and Destiny in Rural Greece. In J. Dubisch (ed.), *Gender and Power in Rural Greece*. Princeton. Princeton University Press.

Dumont, L. 1977. *From Mandeville to Marx*. Chicago. University of Chicago Press.

EEPG (Equipo de Estudios Presencia Gitana). 1991. *Los Gitanos Ante la Ley y la Adminstración*. Madrid. Presencia Gitana.

Errington, F. and D. Gewertz. 1987. The Remarriage of Yebiwali: a Study of Dominance and False Consciousness in a non-Western Society. In M. Strathern (ed.), *Dealing with Inequality: Analysing Gender Relations in Melanesia and Beyond*. Cambridge. Cambridge University Press.

Errington, S. 1990. Recasting Sex, Gender and Power: a Theoretical and Regional Overview. In J.M. Atkinson and S. Errington (eds.), *Power and Difference: Gender in Island South East Asia*. Stanford. Stanford University Press.

Fraser, A. 1993. *The Gypsies*. Oxford. Blackwell.

Fresno García, J. M. 1993. La Situation Sociale de la Communauté Gitane d'Espagne. *Ethnies*, 8: 70–8.

Friedl, E. 1962. *Vasilika: a Village in Modern Greece*. New York. Holt, Rinehart & Winston.

Gamella, J. F. 1996. *La Población Gitana en Andalucía: un Estudio Exploratorio de sus Condiciones de Vida*. Sevilla. Junta de Andalucía.

García, H., S. Adorver and M. R. Blanco. 1996. *Minorías Etnicas: Gitanos e Inmigrantes*. Madrid. CSS.

Gay y Blasco, P. 1995. *'Sex', 'Gender' and the Gitanos of Madrid*. Ph.D. Thesis. University of Cambridge.

Gibson, T. 1986. *Sacrifice and Sharing in the Philippine Highlands: Religion and Society Among the Buid of Mindoro*. London. Athlone.

GIEMS (Equipo). 1976. *Los Gitanos al Encuentro de la Ciudad: del Chalaneo al Peonaje*. Madrid. Cuadernos Para el Diálogo.

Gmelch, G. 1977. *The Irish Tinkers: the Urbanisation of an Itinerant People*. California. Cummings.

Gmelch, S. 1986. Groups that Don't Want In: Gypsies and Other Artisan, Trader and Entertainer Minorities. *Annual Review of Anthropology*, 15: 307–30.

Goddard, V. 1987. Honor and Shame: the Control of Women's Sexuality and Group Identity in Naples. In P. Caplan (ed.), *The Cultural Construction of Sexuality*. London. Tavistock.

Godelier, M. 1987. *The Making of Great Men: Male Dominance and Power among the New Guinea Baruya*. Cambridge. Cambridge University Press.

Gómez Alfaro, A. 1992. *El Expediente General de Gitanos*. Madrid. Editorial de la Universidad Complutense. Colección Tesis Doctorales.

Gronfors, M. 1977. *Blood Feuding Among Finnish Gypsies*. Helsinki. University of Helsinki Press.

Gronfors, M. 1982. From Scientific Social Science to Responsible Research: the Lesson of the Finnish Gypsies. *Acta Sociologica*, 25: 249–57.

Gropper, R. 1975. *Gypsies in the City*. Princeton. Darwin Press.

Hooper, J. 1995. *The New Spaniards*. London. Penguin.

Howe, Leo. 1990. *Being Unemployed in Northern Ireland: an Ethnography*. Cambridge. Cambridge University Press.

Jacquart, D. and C. Thomasset. 1985. *Sexuality and Medicine in the Middle Ages*. Cambridge. Polity.

Jones, A. and P. Stallybrass. 1991. Fetishising Gender: Constructing the Hermaphrodite in Renaissance Europe. In J. Epstein and K. Straub (eds), *Body Guards: the Cultural Politics of Gender Ambiguity*. London. Routledge.

Jordán Pemán, F. 1990. *Los Aleluyas*. Madrid. Secretariado Nacional Gitano.

Kaprow, M. 1982. Resisting Respectability: Gypsies in Saragossa. *Urban Anthropology*, 11: 399–431.

Kaprow, M. 1991. Celebrating Impermanence: Gypsies in a Spanish City. In P. de Vita (ed.), *The Naked Anthropologist: Tales from Around the World*. Belmont. Wadsworth.

Laub, E. 1991. El Mundo de los Chuetas Mallorquines. In J. Prat et al. (eds), *Antropología de los Pueblos de España*. Madrid. Taurus Universitria.

Leblon, B. 1985. *Los Gitanos de España*. Madrid. Gedisa.

Lehmann, D. 1996. *Struggle for the Spirit: Religious Transformation and Popular Culture in Brazil and Latin America*. Cambridge. Polity.

León-Ignacio. 1976. *Los Quinquis: una Minoría Marginada*. Barcelona. Bruguera.

Lieber, M. 1990. Lamarckian Definitions of Identity on Kapingamarangi and Pohnpei. In J. Linnekin and L. Poyer (eds), *Cultural Inequality and Ethnicity in the Pacific*. Honolulu. University of Hawaii Press.

Lindisfarne, N. 1994. Variant Masculinities, Variant Virginitites: Rethinking Honor and Shame. In A. Cornwall and N. Lindisfarne (eds), *Dislocating Masculinity: Comparative Ethnographies*. London. Routledge.

Linnekin, J. and L. Poyer. 1990a. Introduction to J. Linnekin and L. Poyer (eds), *Cultural Inequality and Ethnicity in the Pacific*. Honolulu. University of Hawaii Press.

Linnekin, J. and L. Poyer. (eds). 1990b. *Cultural Inequality and Ethnicity in the Pacific*. Honolulu. University of Hawaii Press.

López Varas, M. L. and G. Fresnillo Pato. 1995. *Margen y Periferia: Representaciones Ideológicas de los Conflictos Urbanos Entre Payos y Gitanos*. Madrid. Asociación Secretariado Nacional Gitano.

Martín Gaite, C. 1987a. *Usos Amorosos de la Postguerra Española*. Barcelona. Anagrama.

Martín Gaite, C. 1987b. *Usos Amorosos del Dieciocho en España*. Barcelona. Anagrama.

Mayall, D. 1988. *Gypsy-Travellers in Nineteeth-Century Society*. Cambridge. Cambridge University Press.

Montes, J. 1986. Sobre el Realojamiento de los Gitanos. In T. San Román (ed.), *Entre la Marginación y el Racismo: Reflexiones sobre la Vida de los Gitanos*. Madrid. Alianza.

Moore, H. L. 1994. *A Passion for Difference: Essays in Anthropology and Gender*. Cambridge. Polity.

Morcillo Gómez, A. 1988. Feminismo y Lucha Política Durante la Segunda República y la Guerra Civil. In P. Folguera (ed.), *El Femi-*

nismo en España: Dos Siglos de Historia. Madrid. Editorial Pablo Iglesias.

Mulcahy, F. D. 1988. Material and Non-material Resources, or Why the Gypsies Have no Vises. *Technology in Society,* 10: 457–67.

Myers, F. 1986. *Pintupi Country, Pintupi Self: Sentiment, Place and Politics Among Western Desert Aborigines.* Washington. Smithsonian Institution Press.

Okely, J. 1977. Gypsy Women: Models in Conflict. In S. Ardener (ed.), *Perceiving Women.* New York. Halstead.

Okely, J. 1983. *The Traveller-Gypsies.* Cambridge. Cambridge University Press.

Okely, J. 1992. Anthropology and Autobiography: Participatory Experience and Embodied Knowledge. In J. Okely and H. Callaway (eds), *Anthropology and Autobiography.* London. Routledge.

Ortega López, M. 1988. 'La Defensa de las Mujeres' en la Sociedad del Antiguo Régimen: las Aportaciones del Pensamiento Ilustrado. In P. Folguera (ed.), *El Feminismo en España: Dos Siglos de Historia.* Madrid. Editorial Pablo Iglesias.

Pasqualino, C. 1995. *Dire le Chant: Anthropologie Sociale des Gitans de Jerez de la Frontera.* Thesis. Ecole des Hautes Etudes en Sciences Sociales.

Perry, M. E. 1990. *Gender and Disorder in Early Modern Seville.* Princeton. Princeton University Press.

Pitt-Rivers, J. 1961. *The People of the Sierra.* Chicago. Chicago University Press.

Pomponio, A. 1990. Seagulls Don't Fly Into the Bush: Cultural Identity and the Negotiation of Development on Mandok Island, Papua New Guinea. In J. Linnekin and L. Poyer (eds), *Cultural Inequality and Ethnicity in the Pacific.* Honolulu. University of Hawaii Press.

Prat, J., U. Martínez, J. Contreras and Isidoro Moreno (eds). 1991. *Antropología de los Pueblos de España.* Madrid. Taurus Universitaria.

Rincón Atienza, P. 1994. *Rasgos Culturales y Organización Social de la Comunidad Gitana Española (Síntesis Para Educadores).* Madrid. Asociación Secretariado Nacional Gitano.

Rodriguez Martín, M. C. 1995. *La Comunidad Chabolista de Montemolín: Plan de Intervención y Estudio Longitudinal.* Zaragoza. Area de Acción Social y Salud Pública del Ayuntamiento de Zaragoza.

Salo, M. 1977. The Expression of Ethnicity in Rom Oral Tradition. *Western Folklore,* 36: 33–56.

Salo, M. 1979. Gypsy Ethnicity: Implications of Native Categories and Interaction for Ethnic Classification. *Ethnicity,* 6: 73–9.

Salo, M. (ed.) 1982. Special Issue, *Urban Anthropology*, vol. 11, nos. 3–4.

Salo, M. and S. Salo. 1982. Romnichel Economic and Social Organisation in Urban New England, 1850-1930. *Urban Anthropology*, 11: 273–313.

Sánchez Ortega, M. H. 1986. Evolución y Contexto Histórico de los Gitanos Españoles. In T. San Román (ed.), *Entre la Marginación y el Racismo: Reflexiones sobre la Vida de los Gitanos*. Madrid. Alianza.

San Román, T. 1976. *Vecinos Gitanos*. Madrid. Akal.

San Román, T. 1986a. Reflexiones Sobre Marginación y Racismo. In T. San Román (ed.), *Entre la Marginación y el Racismo: Reflexiones Sobre la Vida de los Gitanos*. Madrid. Alianza.

San Román, T. (ed). 1986b. *Entre la Marginación y el Racismo: Reflexiones Sobre la Vida de los Gitanos*. Madrid. Alianza

San Román, T. 1990. *Gitanos de Madrid y Barcelona: Ensayos sobre Aculturación y Etnicidad*. Barcelona. Universidad Autónoma de Barcelona.

San Román, T. 1994. *La Differencia Inquietant: Velles i Noves Estrategies Culturals dels Gitanos*. Barcelona. Alta Fulla.

Sissa, G. 1989. The Seal of Virginity. In M. Faher, R. Nadaff, and N. Tazi (eds), *Fragments for a History of the Human Body*. New York. Zone.

Stewart, M. 1993. Gypsies, the Work Ethic and Hungarian Socialism. In C. Hann (ed.), *Socialism: Ideals, Ideologies and Local Practice*. London. Routledge.

Stewart, M. 1997. *The Time of the Gypsies*. Westview. Boulder, Colorado.

Strathern, M. 1981. Self-Interest and the Social Good: Some Implications of Hagen Gender Imagery. In S. Ortner and H. Whitehead (eds), *Sexual Meanings: the Cultural Construction of Gender and Sexuality*. Cambridge. Cambridge University Press.

Strathern, M. 1988. *The Gender of the Gift: Problems with Women and Problems with Society in Melanesia*. Berkeley. University of California Press.

Strathern, M. 1995. Gender: Division or Comparison? In N. Charles and F. Hughes-Freeland (eds), *Practising Feminism: Identity, Power, Difference*. London. Routledge.

Sutherland, A. 1975a. *Gypsies: the Hidden Americans*. London. Tavistock.

Sutherland, A. 1975b. The American Rom: A Case of Economic Adaptation. In F. Rehfisch (ed.), *Gypsies, Tinkers and Other Travellers*. London. Academic Press.

Sutherland, A. 1977. The Body as a Social Symbol Among the Rom. In

J. Blacking (ed.), *The Anthropology of the Body*. London. Academic Press.

Tax Freeman, S. 1979. *The Pasiegos: Spaniards in No Man's Land*. Chicago. Chicago University Press.

Testut, L. 1931. *Tratado de Anatomía Humana*. Barcelona. Salvat Editores.

Thurén, B.M. 1988. *Left Hand Left Behind: the Changing Gender System of a Barrio in Valencia, Spain*. Stockholm. Stockholm University Press.

Trigueros Guardiola, I. 1995. *Manual de Prácticas de Trabajo Social en el Campo de la Marginación: los Gitanos*. Madrid. Siglo XX.

Velasco, H. 1988. Signos y Sentidos de la Identidad de los Pueblos Castellanos: el Concepto de Pueblo y la Identidad. In L. Díaz Viana (ed.), *Aproximación Antropológica a Castilla y León*. Barcelona. Anthropos.

Watson, J. B. 1990. Other People Do Other Things: Lamarckian Identities in Kainantu Subdistrict, Papua New Guinea. In J. Linnekin and L. Poyer (eds), *Cultural Inequality and Ethnicity in the Pacific*. Honolulu. University of Hawaii Press.

Williams, P. 1982. The Invisibility of the Kalderash of Paris: Some Aspects of the Economic Activity and Settlement Patterns of the Kalderash Rom of the Paris Suburbs. *Urban Anthropology*, 11: 316–44.

Williams, P. 1991. Le Miracle et la Necessité: à Propos du Developpement du Pentecotisme chez les Tsiganes. *Archives de Sciences Sociales des Religions* 73: 81–98.

Williams, P. 1993a. *Nous, on n'en Parle pas: les Vivants et les Morts chez les Manouches*. Paris. Editions de la Maison des Sciences de l'Homme.

Williams, P. (ed.). 1993b. *Terre d'Asile, Terre d'Exile: l'Europe Tsigane*. Special Issue of Ethnies, vol. 8, no. 15.

Index